INDIRA GANDHI
Woman of India's Destiny

INDIRA GANDHI
Woman of India's Destiny

By
Dr. Varalakshmi Janapathy

KALPAZ

ISBN : 978-81-783-5350-0

First Published, 2018

Published by

Kalpaz Publications
C-30, Satyawati Nagar,
Delhi – 110052
Ph.: 011-47034999, 9811692060
www.kalpazpublications.com
E-mail: kalpaz@hotmail.com

Printed at: G. Print Process, Delhi

Dedicated to
My brother
Sri. M. Veerabhadra Rao
Freedom fighter and Journalist
with warm regards

Contents

Nirmala Deshpande
Member of Parliament
(Rajya Sabha)

AB-98, SHAHAJAHAN ROAD,
NEW DELHI-110003
Tel.: 23782683 Telefax: 23782781
E-mail: nirmala_desh@mantraonline.com

10th December, 2004

Foreword

There is a saying in Sanskrit, a free translation of this would read, "as strong as the *vajra*, the strongest weapon; as soft as the most delicate flower—who can understand the personalities of great people?". It is not at all easy to understand fully the personality of Indiraji and it is still more difficult to describe it in words. Her qualities, that are known, are like the tip of the iceberg. Much more is unrevealed. The attempts of depicting Indiraji's multifaceted personality by Dr. J. Varalakshmi is commendable. She deserves to be complimented for her book, which is the result of hard work of years.

As one who had the rare fortune of being associated with Indiraji in her most difficult days and witness her exceptional qualities, I have always felt that though she was loved and revered by millions not only in India but all over the world and severely criticized by a few, she was never fully understood. When she felt the need to take some hard decisions in the interest of India and its people, she would take them and be prepared to face gladly the consequences. She quoted from Bhagwad Gita after the victory of Bangladesh, "it is the wise men who can keep equanimity both in sorrow and happiness; in victory and in defeat". With my association with her, I can say, that was how she lived her life.

I would like to congratulate Dr. Varalakshmi for the book, which is labour of love.

Nirmala Deshpande
(Nirmala Deshpande)

Preface

It was the year 1975 - The International Women's Year. It was also the year in which, Smt. Indira Gandhi, the Prime Minister who was leading the biggest democracy in the world was branded as a dictator and some elements against her, raised a voice denouncing her and the Allahabad High Court announced a judgement disqualifying her from holding any elective office for a period of 6 years.

Indira's style of functioning was criticised much and she was also accused of not having "Principles or human approach".

I have sought to relate the conditions in the country that led to the clamping of the emergency, 1977 elections and the defeat of the Congress party. What is it that is behind all this and what were the factors and forces that were working against her? What were the aims and objectives of the Congress organisation and how far could Indira divert the attention of the public from the broad perspectives? Is Sanjay's story and the talk of the caucus, a myth or a reality? How far is Sri Jayaprakash Narayan responsible for her defeat? How far could Janata rule the country on the right path ? What was the reality behind the vendetta ? The entire subject matter had been dealt with in detail.

I based my book mainly in answering the above myths and some historical facts. As a great admirer of Nehru's tradition and as a student of Political Science and a keen observer of political and other events in the country, I tried to trace the chronology of events, during the years 1967-1980.

I also tried to discuss at length the basic concepts of Indian democracy and Constitution, so as to give the reader a clue to understand the truth behind the anti-Indira propaganda carried out at length, by the Janata rulers.

Indira Gandhi could win a landslide victory during, 1980 general elections at a time when she was caricatured as a dictator and this was acclaimed as a success on account of her "Charisma", both by her opponents and her supporters as well. What was the great nobility in her personality ? How far could she deliver the goods and could take the country on the right path ? I tried to sum up with a touch on the grave problems facing the country and how their solutions lie in hard work.

I am greatly indebted to my brother Mr. Veerabhadra Rao, a freedom fighter and a journalist who could put me on the right track in my life and in writing this book and could guide me in gathering material.

To Satyanarayana Murthy, my typist for their DTP work. To Bharatha Fine Art Printers, Hyderabad and Kalpaz Publications, Delhi, my thanks for bringing out the book in a short time.

Varalakshmi Janapathy

PART-I

1

Indira Gandhi
Her Charisma and Statesmanship

It was the year 1962. Indira Gandhi was known to the world and to the people in India as the daughter of Jawaharlal Nehru only. I was in the early period of my official career, working as an administrative officer in Vijayawada. One fine morning, news spread in the town that Indira Gandhi, President, All India Congress Committee is to come to the town, to address a political conference. Though hot winds started blowing right from the morning hours, as it was the month of May, some of us, gathered in the railway station, to accord a warm welcome to her. We waited and waited very anxiously. At 12.30 P.M. we came to know, that her train was stopped one furlong ahead of the railway station and she had been taken to the guest house already. We did not want to get disappointed. All of us made a dashing visit to the guest house. Officials in waiting and the police discouraged us and advised us to give up the idea of seeing Indiraji. But we didn't lose courage. Dr. Atchamamba, member of Parliament and Kum. Vedakumari, another M.P. from Elore, were going up to see Mrs. Gandhi. I accompanied them and went in and saw Mrs. Gandhi for the 1st time in my life.

Dressed in a spotless, white khadi saree and a full hands kurta and the "Ghunghat" on, she was sipping tea and chatting with local politicians. We requested her to just walk into the Veranda and give darsan to some women waiting downstairs. She suddenly rose from her seat and walked down the stairs in a hurried manner stating "I will go to them". Such was her magnanimity, she talked to the women, patted their children and distributed garlands and spent nearly 10 minutes with them.

Born in the Regal grandeur of Anand Bhavan, Smt. Gandhi has imbibed in herself dignity and nobility as legacies.

Right from her childhood, Indira was a gallant fighter with the necessary vision and abundant commonsense. She had an amazing capacity to share the feelings of the weak and with a large heart, she was able to estimate the sorrows and sufferings of the millions in India and she could emerge as the custodian of their interests.

Mahatma Gandhi told Indira once when she was a child "There are two kinds of people. Those who do the work and those who take the credit - Belong to the 1st category". Really Mrs. Gandhi belongs to the first category. Behind the soft exterior and the disarming suite she had in her indomitable spirit, self-confidence, a womanly instinct which never goes wrong and sobreness of mind and rare-political sagacity. She consulted as many people as possible, but she made up her mind finally.

Indira Priyadarsini, born in Allahabad on November, 19,1917 and brought up in the buzzing political activity at Anand Bhavan, the home of the Nehrus, inherited certain fine qualities as legacy from her ancestors and could add lustre to her charisma by her polish and refinement and largeness of heart. With her parents, Jawaharlal and Kamala Nehru, constantly in and out of jail, she had chequered and unconventional education. She was sent to one school after another - A kindergarten in Delhi, a convent school in Allahabad at the age of 6 the pupil's own school in Poona in 1932-35, from where she passed her Bombay University Matriculation Examination. She was in Shantiniketan in 1934-35, a year at Bex (Switzerland) in 1935-36 and off and on studies in Summerville college at Oxford between 1936-41. While at school at Poona, students organised a mock-Parliament. When the time came to choose a Prime Minister they chose Indira and probably she might have not known at that time that she would one day become real Prime Minister of India.

Her studies at Summerville were interrupted when she accompanied her father to India during 1938-39. In 1941, she returned to India Via the Cape of Good Hope without taking a degree. But the major source of her education was the series of letters Jawaharlal wrote to her from prison, which were later published as two separate volumes: "Letters from a father to his daughter"and "Glimpses of World History" (Italics).

Even greater part of her education was, her 17 years as the hostess of the Prime Minister's house in New Delhi, Jawaharlal worked hard and long and there were endless streams of visitors including very prominent personalities from all over the world. Meetings and public functions were many. This was a tremendous training for her. She shared the innermost ideas of Nehru and thoughts and helped him in the formulation of policies and vital decisions. She was in a way, chiselled and hammered to shoulder major responsibilities.

She faced many a challenging situations even before becoming a Prime Minister. In 1947, soon after Independence, Mahatma Gandhi, called upon her to work in villages and she arranged meetings of leading persons among Muslims and Hindus as well and succeeded in easing tensions between the two communities. She became a member of A.I.C.C. in 1955. Women's wing of the A.I.C.C. and the youth section of the organisation were taken care of by her and in 1959, she was elected President of Indian National Congress. On assuming the top party post, she declared in clear terms "the nation is in a hurry". We cannot afford to lose time.

As Congress president, she was credited with having taken major decisions, quite contrary, to known policies of Nehru. One instance was the Congress decision to secure the dismissal of the first communist Govt. of Kerala. Another was the party's decision to bifurcate the bilingual state of Bombay.

On Sastri's sudden death in January, 1966, the Congress was faced with the task of finding a new Prime Minister. For the first time, there was a contest for the party leadership and Mrs. Gandhi defeated Morarji Desai convincingly by 355 votes against 169. As she seemed to be meek and mild the party bosses expected her to be subservient, but she fought them bitterly on all fronts. They reacted sharply by expelling her from the Congress party. The party thus split, left her in a minority in both Houses of Parliament. Then she decided to go to the poll for a fresh mandate from the people. The response of the people astonished her critics and her party won absolute majority by winning 350 seats out of 515 in Lok Sabha and she came out with fresh laurels, as a chosen leader of the nation.

To put it in a nutshell, Mrs. Gandhi was a bridge between two generations. The one which fought and won freedom and the other which was anxious to make the best of it, with high aspirations. She could also win over the hearts of the people as their conscience keeper and could take the country move softly from traditionalism to modernism.

She could also emerge as an international figure and as a worthy daughter of a worthy father she could win several international awards. Mother's Award of USA (1953) and the Yale University Howard Memorial Prize (1960) a degree of Doctor of Letters (Honoris causa) at Agra University and the Isabella D'Este award of outstanding work in the field of diplomacy to mention a few and, above all, she was honoured with "Bharat Ratna", the greatest honour conferred on any Indian after her tremendous victory in Bangladesh War in 1971. She does not need any flower garlands or bouquets. People's hearts and her image in their hearts, is the real honour to her personality.

By 1972, she evolved herself as the world's most powerful woman. She was also acclaimed as more radical than Nehru and Sastry but clinged to no "ism" but confronted each problem individually. I would like to quote here a few opinions about her, in this context.

The editorial, *Gaurdian,* dt. 21 August, 1969 writes "What is needed is country of purpose and momentum of reform that would keep the opportunities, the sectarians and the reactionaries behind". This is what Indira Gandhi wanted to achieve exactly by her methods".

I will quote another instance of her policy statement "The Congress is a party of people and not of the bosses".

Sunday Times quoted her as "the most powerful woman in the world". Philip Norman, in his 4-page article mentioned that she, had as many enemies as there were friends. She is "Trimurthy", Brahma, as she is the maker of modern India, Vishnu as she is the saviour of democracy and thridly, she is Siva-who has ruined the Pakistan army".

Once when she was questioned by journalists before 1971 elections whether she is expecting that she would become the Prime Minister she said "anything might happen. I hope I would come back definitely and without any doubt".

During her rule for 9 years before emergency she achieved many things. Emergence of Bangladesh, as an independent sovereign State, signing of Simla Pact in July, 1972, abolition of privy purses, nationalisation of banks, atomic explosion of 1974 are some of the memorable achievements. Nehru's ideology was put into practice and could prove to win to stand the test of times. His daughter, more prudent and more practical minded, could become an indispensable figure in moulding the destiny of the Nation.

On an occasion, she remarked "It was the Congress which had brought democracy to India, laid for it a solid foundation, and was determined to widen and deepen the democratic roots in the country. But democracy should not become a license for a few to make false allegations or weaken the confidence of the country and denigrade its achievements. India continued to be a custodian of democracy in a world where many a country were giving democracy the go-by".

After Lal Bahadur Shastri's death, following the Indo-Pakistan war of 1965, Mrs. Indira was elected as Prime Minister. But the great syndicate leaders like Kamaraj, Morarji and Nijalingappa wanted to keep her as their prisoner and rule the country in her name to preserve status quo. During 1967 general elections, she saw the disaster, the Congress had to face when majority of the states disowned her party and elected opposition parties. She was quick to realise that the country was turning against because there was wide gap between what was preached and what was practised. Following the disaster, during the AICC session, 10 point prgoramme to bring about social change was preached. But in the Faridabad Congress session in April, 1969, the then president of AICC, Sri Nijalingappa mounted attack on public sector and her other progressive policies. Mrs. Gandhi, lost all patience and during the Congress session at Bangalore in July, 1969, she presented her economic note, which contained her "few stray thoughts" to confront the right wing leadership. The syndicate, as a tactical measure, stooped to accept it; but decided to put Sanjeeva Reddy as Congress nominee for Presidentship, after the death of Jakir Hussain.

Mrs. Indira was quick to see through the conspiracy. She knew that the syndicate decided to overthrow her and she had no option but to fight to safeguard secularism and socialism. The guts she showed in challenging the right reaction in the country and the superb craftsmanship of her strategy in beating them hollow, will remain an unparrelled chapter in the annals of Parliamentary democracy of India.

The mid-term poll to Parliament in 1971, gave her a sweeping mandate to introduce social change by Parliamentary methods, broke the backbone of conservative forces. No sooner had she won this remarkable victory. There has Pakistani military crackdown on Bangladesh, which sent 10 million refugees in India. This demographic aggression had upset her plans for *Garibi Hatao* to a great extent.

Her trip to western countries was a remarkable feat of diplomacy. By her performance, she had given a new sense of dignity and strength to India. Nehru had to invent Kamraj Plan to throw unwanted bosses, out of power, but, Indira with one blow, succeeded in driving the undesirables not only out of power but out of Congress also. With her immense understanding of men and matters, she managed successfully, to fight many a political battles. The world was surprised at her landslide win in 1971. "We were prepared for the wind", one diplomatic source said "but we did not expect the storm that is sweeping her back to power". There was, of course, considerable satisfaction that having won the battle in her own right, Mrs. Gandhi may, no longer have to rely on the support, of the more pronounced leftist parties in India for her survival.

1971 Indian elections coincided with renewed uncertainty in Pakistan and so there had been comparison between the two countries in the subcontinent even by the most biased observers. To an impartial eye, India seemed to have emerged as a country showing better image. A triumphant Mrs. Gandhi brimming with self-assurance, described her partys' victory not only as a vote for her leadership but a vote for her party's programmes and policies.

What exactly contributed to the grand sweep by Congress(R) may remain a subject of study among political scientists and sociologists, but the basic factor behind it seems to be that Mrs. Gandhi, could succeed in her theme that she stood by the poor and was determined to work for their betterment. This was her main strong ground. The four-party alliance was faced with a phenomenon, rather than as a political force.

People, by and large, voted on issues also. In some places like Delhi, Congress(R) could make a clean sweep because the middle classes, which voted for Jan Sangh in the last election, 'opted' to vote a party which could provide a strong and stable government at the centre at the difficult juncture in the country's history.

On the whole, 1971 election had been a shattering experience for the opposition parties, whether rightist or leftist. It seemed rather tragic that all the Congress(O) leaders, including Sri Sanjeeva Reddi, whose nomination for the presidential election triggered off to the Congress split, lost the Lok Sabha seat and got further isolated from country's public life.

Everyone realised that her ruthlessness, combined with her mass appeal and charisma, was a devastating phenomenon in Indian politics.

While tackling phenomenon in Indian politics. She consult as many as possible, but she makes her own decision. In the words of Sri. G.K. Reddy "her cold in difference".

Washington Evening Star

After her victory in the elections in 1971, foreign, as well as Indian press congratulated her and acclaimed her as a leader of calibre and vision.

Washington Evening Star wrote:

"While Mrs. Gandhi's style of leadership and the wisdom of her attacks on banks, insurance industry and industrial conglomerates are open to criticism, there is no visible alternative within either Congress party or the other parties to her national leadership".

Under the circumstances, then Mrs. Gandhi's failure to achieve victory in the March Election almost certainly would be a defeat for all of India".

Sunday Times Magazine in a feature writes, "She is stronger than Nehru was. Nehru could not have signed the Indo-Soviet treaty nor set upon Pakistan with single minded Force".

Gaurdian (British) says

"She fought with her own individualism. Her attempt proved to be a success. Parties like Jan Sangh are completely out".

Times (British) while writing an editorial says' "Indira Gandhi fought a political battle and could establish herself as a mighty force. This may inculcate some more enthusiasm in the minds of the people, who were desperate".

N.M. Regov, ambassodar in India in his "memorable days" spells about Mrs. Gandhi and admires her as "a true leader, practical minded, statesman and not only, she is herself a great personality. She is endowed with great mental power. Though seemingly, she is an innocent person, she can work with steadfastness, and an impression, that one gets, after seeing her, I am recording here".

2

How Far Indiraji in the Footsteps of Nehru ?

What was Nehru's concept of democracy ? It was only a means for the fuller development of the individual through a democratic structure by which equal opportunities could be ensured to all individuals, in all spheres - social, economic, cultural and religious. He wanted to eliminate the evils of poverty, hunger, unemployment and inequality. He stressed the need for land reforms, community development projects for the improvement of rural economy, while the pace of industrial development could be accelerated by nationalising the key industries and by encouraging small scale industries.

Democracy demands active and politically conscious citizens. In this age of conflicting ideologies and principles, one must be able to choose and for that he must understand important political and socio-economic issues. Right type of information, discussions, debates and deliberations are the very basis of democracy.

Nehru was a democrat both in theory and practice. His greatest contribution to democracy lies in his new interpretation of democratic ideals and values and their application to a country like India, which has many contrasting characteristics from those existing in the western democracies, viz., undemocratic social institutions, and under-developed economy and widespread illiteracy.

The experiment of democracy in India is crucial and has international significance. If India fails, it will be a great blow to democracy everywhere in the world.

Nehru was no believer in partyless democracy. And for success of democracy, organised and responsible parties were essential, he held. For a massive democracy like that of India, ideological commitments provided through political parties, are still more important for the efficient running of the government.

Against Groupism in the Party:

Nehru always welcomed differences of opinion within the party but he neither encouraged nor aligned himself to any such formations. Though he differed fundamentally, on various issues, with Congress leaders like Gandhi, Patel and others, "his differences of opinion never resulted in groupism".[1]

But, no leader can take the country on the path of success and progress, unless he had the solid popular backing, he felt.

He faced vast audiences with the feeling of a friend. He went straight to them, trusted them to the maximum extent in spite of their backwardness and indisciplined behaviour. He talked to the crowd. He inspired them and himself got stimulated.

In fact, the presence of all the basic prerequisites of a democratic political set-up is not an insurance of democracy in itself. India, with a totally different social and economic background from that existing in the western liberal democracies, started off with full-fledged political democracy and faced many problems from the beginning. Nehru himself witnessed the emergence of certain forces on the Indian scene which emanated from different sources and posed great threat to her democratic character, stability and national unity. It is not feasible to deal with all of them. Nehru had his own reservations on judiciary system also.

Judiciary

He felt judiciary in India was a relic of the colonial era. Due to the multi-lingual, multi-religious and multi-cultural character of the Indian society, and an under-developed economy, there are many challanges to the functioning of democracy, Nehru felt.

Unfavourable Conditons

Agitational approach and growth of violence in public life will not take the country on the right path, he thought. But democracy provides full scope for the expression of dissent, protest and differences of opinion. But, when people frequently resort to violent agitations, demonstrations, fasts, threats of immolation and the like, the very basis of democracy will be seriously threatend. The structure of a democratic society would crack up with the adoption and frequent use of undemocratic means to achieve political ends. There might be genuine grievances of people against the government, but that does not entitle everyone, who feels sore, to take law into his own hands. Extra-Parliamentary pressures have a place in a democratic set up but their frequent use and the attempt to secure policy changes through non-action, is the surest way of undermining political democracy.

Democracy and violence are incompatable and the attempt to settle problems by violent methods is not democracy, but something which is the very reverse of democracy"[2].

Violence means a complete denial of any idea of ordered progress.

Nehru, was a product of the Indian Renaissance and the Indian National movement. A life so varied and so deeply involved in the great freedom struggle and a mind receptive to the main thought currents of India, can hardly be assessed in a few lines. But his untiring efforts in reshaping India are unparalleled. But the comments on his life and work by political thinkers, scholars, commentators, theoreticians, diplomats, world dignitaries are many and varied. He lived up to the high ideals of democracy, though he was branded as a "Popular dictator" and less of a democrat.

To him, Gandhian doctrines appeared to be idealistic and far from realities prevailing in India. But both understood the spirit of India and talked in consonance with the "Conscience of India". He believed in the dignity of the individual and had faith in democracy as a way of life and as a basis of social structure. He gave a broader definition to democracy when he remarked "Democracy is not only political, not only economic, but something of the mind–it involves equality of opportunity to all".

A country most inexperienced in self-government and a people untrained in the processes of the functioning of democracy really need certain special defenses against danger of disruption and disintegration, he felt.

Adult Franchise

Addressing a seminar on parliamentary democracy, Nehru observed "Parliamentary Government is a democratic conception. It means the gradual widening of the franchise till it becomes adult franchise. Democracy implies the active participation of the citizen in the political life of the country and that can be ensured by granting every man and woman the right to vote".[3]

Welfare State

The Indian Constitution contains many provisions which make it a welfare state. The preamble of the Indian Constitution declares :

"We, the people of India — to secure to all its citizens, Justice, Social, Economic and Political liberty of thought, expression, belief, faith and Worship, Equality of status and of opportunity Fraternity assuring the dignity of the individual and the unity of the nation-do hereby adopt, enact and give to ourselves this Constitution".

The Directive Principles of State Policy clearly speak of the basic objectives of a welfare state for India. Article 38 reads: "The state shall strive to promote the welfare of the people by securing and protecting as effectively as it may, a social order in which justice, social, economic and political, shall inform all the institutions of the national life". (Nehru J.L. Independence and after Jan. 22,1947, p. 355).

Nehru did not mention anything about the socialistic pattern of society. No jarganism of any sort was quoted.

Free and Fair Elections

Without free and fair elections public faith in the verdict of the ballot box necessarily suffers and to that extent, there is a failure of democracy".[4]

Nehru was no believer in partyless democracy and for the success of democracy, organised and responsible parties, were essential he held. For a massive democracy like that of India, ideological commitments provided through political parties are still more important for the efficient running of the government.

The Indian Constitution and Nehru's Socialism

The socio-religious and economic democracy can find true expression through institutions of political democracy. The Constitution of free India provides for the basic institutions of democracy–Adult franchise, general elections and civil liberties. In this political frame-work, political parties play their significant role. Nehru regarded all these institutions as essential ingredients of a democratic political set up.

Regarding the basic objectives of the Indian Constitution Nehru stated in 1963 "on Jan. 26th 1950, this new republic came into existence and all our efforts were directed towards realising the objectives laid down-political democracy and economic justice. We called the objective "Socialistic" without adhering to any doctrinaire definition of the word. The system, we evolved was consciously directed towards the welfare of the common man, rather than the enrichment of a few. It is democratic because, its processes are ultimately controlled by public discussion and by Parliament, elected on the basis of universal adult franchise and not by the secret purposes of a privileged minority".

(Nehru's Speeches - Vol. IV - Foreign Affairs Changing India - published in New York, April 1963, p. 405).

Secular State

Keeping in mind, the cultural and religious variety of the country, Nehru was particularly concerned with making India, a secular state by which, he meant "A State in which every group, every individual, has the full freedom to function, according to his own ways, either culturally or in matters of religion." *The Hindustan Times,* June 3, 1950.

Fundamental Rights

For Nehru, individual was always an end and never a means. His idea of structure of the Indian polity was, that it must be based upon the respect for individual freedom and dignity. He emphasized the value of freedom "Every community, and indeed every individual has a right to protection and opportunities for self-development. A free India must gaurantee these human rights to everybody".[5]

Political Parties and Indian Democracy

One of the most unsatisfactory features of Indian politics is the structure and functioning of political parties. They are neither democratic nor federal. The present dependence of political parties on individual leadership is dangerous for Indian democracy. This should be taken note of, by all, concerned with the welfare of the nation.

Our Need–Parties or Fronts ?

Our people, by and large, have demonstrated a capacity for political wisdom, which is remarkable. In spite of limitations, imposed by widespread illiteracy and other noncommitants of socio-economic backwardness, the Indian electorate have behaved with an admirable poise and displayed powers of shrewd judgement. New perspectives would develop as the future unfolds itself. What is needed is a creative effort towards a revolution by consent. Can it be achieved without the pooling of all decent, democratic forces ?

Actually we do stand today at the cross-roads of history. We have to take courage in taking new decisions, and be ready to merge, on a principled basis, in fronts, which, as in the German democratic republic, have reshaped the society.

Indiraji was paving the way, for realising the cherished goals, in the footsteps of Nehru. At Awadi Session of AICC, Nehru opted for the word "Socialistic Pattern of Society". Mrs. Gandhi too was Thinking on the same lines. What the Congress stands pledged to implement was, in essence, a welfare state in which, all the people will be assured of their minimum needs.

Mrs. Gandhi's Views were also the Same

India, does not want the kind of textbook socialism of Western Thinkers and aims at evolving a pattern of its own suited to its needs. Mrs. Gandhi's point of view deserves, indeed wholehearted response from all sections of people.

One of the greatest achievements of Mrs. Gandhi had been, not only to revive the country's faith in itself but also make the world recognise and respect its importance.

There is no magic solution for all the problems of India. Only self-reliance and concerted effort can take her on the right path. Through patient effort, Mrs. Gandhi tried to persuade the people to get themselves involved in the giant task of eradicating poverty, which is number one arch enemy of the Indian Nation. No time should be lost in responding promptly to the clarion call given by the leader.

Success lies in sensing the challanges. 'Winds of change' are flowing. Scientific attitude and socialistic ideology of Indira Gandhi are having a natural appeal for the masses. For as Dom Moraes says immediatly. "She is the only politician in India with a thoroughly modern mind". She, indeed, was a person of more courage, tenacity and will power ! Election Manifesto adopted at the Bangalore meeting of all India Congress Committee in July 1951, speaks of its ideals and goals. Annexure-Election Manifesto (of 1951) of AICC- please refer to the last page.

References

1. Chowdary. R.N.–Nehru in hs own words, p. 64.

2. Nehru's Speeches–Vol. III–speech in Loksabha Feb. 23, 1956, p. 188.
3. Nehru's Speeches Vol. IV 21 Dec. 6, 1957, p. 70.
4. Elec. Commmisson Report on Ist General Elections in India 1951-52, Vol. I, p. 208.
5. Bright J.S. (Ed) Selected Writings of Jawaharlal Nehru, p. 218.

3

The Experiment of Democracy in India Very Crucial

"The future beckons to us. Whither do we go and what shall be our endeavour ? To bring freedom and opportunity to the common man, to the peasants and workers of India, to fight and end poverty and ignorance and disease, to build up a prosperous, democratic and progressive nation and to create social, economic and political institutions which will ensure justice and fullness of life to every man and woman".

Jawaharlal Nehru, the first Prime Minister of Independent India and an architect of modern India, is one of the outstanding personalities of the 20th century. The role played by him during the period of struggle for the freedom of India, and later on also, is highly distinguished and has received appreciation and acclaim from historians, social scientists and intelligentsia, all the world over, not only as a creator of a new ideology but also as a great statesman and a man of letters.

He laid down strong foundations for a strong non-alligned movement, the results of which we are able to see in New India, as a force in the Third World.

During 17 years of his administration he worked hard to industrialise the country, laid down basis for river valley projects like Nagarjuna Sagar, Bhakra Nangal, Damodar Valley Projects, which he called as "modern temples".

He felt the dominating urge to produce more wealth in the country and to wipe out inequalities and to provide social justice. He was the creator of the Planning Commission with a broad vision.

In a sense, economically spreading passage of India from Feudalism to democracy and mediavalism to modernism and the marvellous gains of science and technology have all been the results of certain progressive ideas of Pandit Nehru.

Foundations laid down by Nehru are strong enough to bear the burden path he lighted for us is visible and clear and miraculous mansions can be built on this basis.

"He breathed life into India" said Chester Bowls, paying compliments to Nehru he said "Although he spent 13 years" buried within British Prison walls, sitting alone, watching the seasons follow each other into oblivion, he instilled courage and confidence into the fragile structure of new born nation, during its first difficult days and presented it to the world that here is a wonder that is India.

In his own words, Nehru said "India was in my blood and these was much in her that intrically thrilled me".

He once said "Gandhiji had put an ideal before us, that we should wipe out every tear from every eye". Nehru tried his best to develop India. In his last years, he wrote on his writing a few lines from a poem by Robert Frost.

"The woods are lovely dark and deep.
But I have promises to keep
and miles to go before I sleep
and rules to go before I sleep".

He saw the millions of problems facing India as challenges and tried to usher in, a new era of prosperity and a better deal for his people. The world listened to him as the Voice of India.

The Emperor of Ethiopia once said "We support India not because it is our friend, but because India is in the right. Milton Obote the dynamic leader of Uganda said, We support you (in the conflict with China) and we are willing to say so from any platform". These are so many of the words spoken in support of Nehru's foreign policy.

Democracy demands active and politically conscious citizens. In this age of conflicting ideologies and principles, one must be able to choose and for that he must understand important political and socio-economic issues. Right type of information, discussion, debates and deliberations are the very basis of democracy.

Nehru was a democrat both in theory and practice. His greatest contribution to democracy lies in his new interpretation of democratic ideals and values and their application to a country like India, which has many contrasting characteristics from those existing in the western democracies viz., undemocratic social institutions, an under-developed economy and widespread illiteracy among the masses.

So, the experiment of democracy in India was crucial and had international significance. If India failed, it would be a great blow to democracy everywhere in the world.

Indiraji wanted to bring about change by democratic method. Keeping in view of the true spirit of Nehruism she took several progressive steps to remove poverty and to bring about social justice.

Democracy and the Changing World

Land had been the symbol of status and economic prosperity in the village society. Land was owned by high castes, though they were not really land tillers. The land, with all its rights, became hereditary property of the owners. Though they were less in number they controlled village economy and exploited to poor and down-trodden.

'Garibi - Hatao' was the slogan, by which, she wanted to speed up the social change.

During the British rule, land records were prepared by the Government Agency defining the rights of the land owners. The state was only over all owner of all lands and was entitled to a share of the produce, in the form of land revenue.

But, after attaining independence, certain land reforms were brought about and the political will of the numerically large weaker sections like scheduled castes, scheaduled tribes, landless agricultural labourers, village artisans, became dominant. Democracy, in other words, meant, a wholesale reshaping of the village economy and society. During the course of the implementation of the amended provisions of Law, some problems cropped up and the village societies had to face thorough reshuffling which created problems. So, a strong political will was needed to get things done speedily and efficiently.

So, maximum thrust was laid down on the 20 point economic programme. Assistance from various agencies like corporative societies, lead banks, voluntary organisation was needed. All democratic institutions had to be geared up to meet the new situation.

Nehru was no believer in partyless democracy and for the success of democracy, organised and responsible parties were essential, he held. For a massive democracy like that of India, ideological commitments provided through political parties, are still more important for the efficient running of the government.

Abolition of Privy Purses

An order was issued by the President of India on 6th Sept. 1970, derecognising the rulers.

A batch of eight writ petitions were filed by some ex-rulers and the judgements declared that the petitions were entitled to all their pre-existing rights and privileges including the right to privy purse, as if the order had not been made.

A Special Bench of the Supreme Court, by a majority of nine to two, held that the Presidential Order was ultravires of the Constitution and hence illegal and inoperative. The Special Bench delivered five separate judgements - Three declaring the impugned Presidential order ultravires and two disenting judgements dismissing the writ petitions.

The majority judgement was given by Mr. Justice Shah, with whom Mr. Justice Sikri, Mr. Justice Shelat, Mr. Justice Bhargava, Mr. Justice Vaidyalingam, Mr. Justice Grover and Mr. Justice Dua agreed. The Chief Justice Mr. Justice Hidayatullah and Mr. Justice Hegde delivered separate judgements holding the importance of Presidential Order unconstitutional.

Mr. S.K. Patil, Congress (O) leader, commenting on the Supreme Court's judgement said "the decision was not altogether un-expected, thank god this country has firm faith in the rule of law. This is one more lesson to government, if only it cares to listen what was thoughtlessly and indecently done in sheer desperation has boomeranged. If only a portion of the energy government has been wasting in pursuit of its pseudoradicalism was diverted to fruitful activities, our masses would bless them".

The Kerala Chief Minister, Mr. Achutha Menon, emphasising the urgency of bringing about changes in the country's Constitution said "Abolition of privy purses is a policy subscribed by an overhelming majority of people. If even such a policy cannot be pushed through because of the provisions of the Constitution that Constitution needs, indeed, a thorough over-haul".

The Kashmir Chief Minister, Mr. G.M. Sadiq, said "new ways consistent with the democratic set-up would have to be devised to implement peoples will".

The Marxist leader, Mr. A.K. Gopalan said "Any legislation or reform will be scrapped by the courts as long as the present Constitution rehelps". The Bharatiya Kranti Dal Chairman, Mr. Charan

Singh, speaking in Lucknow, demanded immediate resignation of the Prime Minister.

The rightist opposition groups vociferously demanded resignation of the prime minister and asked the government to respect the Supreme Court's judgement. Some leaders like Dr. Ram Subhag Singh, (leader of the opposition in the Lok Sabha), and Mr. N.G. Ranga, Swatantra Leader, challenged Mrs. Gandhi to seek a fresh mandate from the people.

These were noisy debates in both the houses. Mrs. Indira declared in the Lok Sabha amidst cheers that Government"remains comitted to its policy of abolition of privy purse and privileges by appropriate Constitutional means". Arguing that careful study would be made before the next step is taken, Mrs. Gandhi, supported the order passed.

Of course, the former rulers were willing for a negotiated settlement of the issue. The argument of the princes, in the words of Dr. Karan Singh was "we are as such Indians as the commoners". (Reports UNI and PTI).

The recipients of privy purses numbered 278 and the total payment came to Rs.4.9 crores. Two of them the Nizam of Hyderabad and the Maharaja of Mysore, received more than 20 lakhs a year. At the bottom of the list is the Raja of Katodia, whose purse amounts to Rs.192 a year (UNI).

Garibi Hatao

Mrs. Gandhi must be congratulated on the tenor and timing of her decision to inroduce the slogan of "Garibi Hatao". A shrewd politician with her ear glued to be ground, she has an instinctive ability to assess what is popular and has the courage to go ahead- and do it in the teeth and stiff opposition. The system of Parliamentary democracy adopted in our country after independence is like a hot house plant, which needs much care and attention. It also needs tending before it can take roots. In the process, it would acquire certain characteristics of the soil also. From 1947, for nearly two decades, Sri Jawaharlal Nehru, her father, was guiding the destiny of the motherland. For a true democrat live him, it was a challenge and also an opportunity and the system evolved by place. But our Constitution, which seems to be the most indicate in the world, has certain limitations of its own. No doubt the framers of the Constitution could visualise all possible contingenous yet, every year passing, new situation arise and new politics are to be framed. Any leader has to perform the unenviable task of making the fast-changing system, work successfully, without allowing it to collapse. This can be achieved only by two methods. Either by achieving results in quick succession by drastic steps or by acceptable process of economic development, in a normal way, but with the required dynamism and sincere effort. Our economy is still sluggish. Millions and millions of people are living below the poverty live. Under such circumstances, a leader, who wants to run on the right path, has to lay down a fairly sound infrastructure. In a vast continent like ours, problems are many and also varied. Mrs.Gandhi, being a shrewd woman has paved the pay, for eradicating poverty and for making the country proper.

"Garibi Hatao" one of her slogans, could reach the masses in no time. Being a national leader with the necessary sagacity and image, she could put for her programme of"Garibi Hatao"with the necessary zeal.

Even her sharpest critics like Sri Madhu Limaye of the SSP. (Samyukta Socialist Party) concede that she is a leader on the Indian scene.

People want a change but are not clear in what direction to move and how. Taking into consideration, the basic issue and malady confronting Indian society viz. poverty.

Her two assets were her integrity and her un-canny sense of timing, which kept every one guessing. She did not even care to disown a person, who did not fit in her scheme of things.

Her trip to western countries was a remarkable fear of diplomacy. By her performance, she had given a new sense of dignity and strength to India. Nehru had to invent Kamraj Plan to throw unwanted bosses, out of power, but, Indira with one blow, succeeded in driving the un-desirables not only out of power but out of Congress also. With her immense understanding of men and matters, she managed successfully, to fight many a political battles. US was surprised at her landslide win in 1971."We were prepared for the wind", one diplomatics source said" but we did not expect the storm that is sweeping faction that having won the battle in her own right, Mrs. Gandhi may, no longer have to rely on the support, of the more pronounced leftist parties in India for her survival.

1971 Indian elections coincided with renewed uncertainty in Pakistan and so there had been comparison between the two countries the subcontinent even by the most biased observers. To an impartial eye, India seemed to have emerged as a country showing better image. A trumphant Mrs. Gandhi brimming with self-confidence, described her party's victory not only a vote for the leadership but a vote for her party's programmes and policies.

What exactly contributed to the grand sweep by Congress (R) may remain a subject of study among political scientists and sociologists, but the basic factor behind it seems to be that Mrs. Gandhi, could succeed in her theme that she stood by the poor and was determined to work for their betterment. This was her main strong ground. The four-party alliance was faced with a phenomenon, rather than as a political force.

People, by and large, noted on issued but not for a leader, in some places like Delhi Congress (R) could make a clean sweep because the middle classes, which voted for Jan Sangh in the last election, to vote a party which could provide a strong and stable government at the centre at the difficult juncture in the country's history.

Indo-Soviet Defence Treaty

This Indo-Soviet treaty is a remarkable historic event and it is a tie between the peoples of the two countries. This paved the way for better understanding of each other, exchange of cultural values and alround progress in the political and economic fields. This treaty provided if either country is attacked or threatened with an attack, the two countries would "enter into mutual consultations to take "appropriate effective measures" to ensure peace and security. The treaty signed on 10th August, 1971, would be valid for a period of 20 years.

"Reactionary forces not only in our country but elsewhere too have always been making desperate efforts to obstruct the progress of any country towards socialism and egalitarian society".

The Prime Minister called for massive public support in defeating the conspiracy of anti-socialist forces. She also stressed that acute economic disparities between the high and the low-income groups would have to be eliminated speedily for the country's progress towards socialism and in the larger interests of the downtrodden millions.

Revolutions, Mrs. Gandhi said "were of two kinds–violent and non-violent. A bloody revolution did not solve problems because, it destroyed faster than it would rebuild. For this, there is no other path than the path of peace and reason, non-violence chalked out by Mahatma Gandhi and it is not an easy path. Very true. The path of transformation of society by non-violent methods, had been acclaimed as the best, by the world over especially by all Afro-Asian nations. The very achievement of independence to India, is a standing example that there is no place for the cult of the Bomb and the stick in our hearts. India of Indians, the land of Buddha, has shown violence and taken to the path of tolerance.

A new society free from inequality and exploitation can be ushered in only when there is massive support to the policies adopted by government, from time to time. Mrs. Gandhi who could feel the pulse of the nation, is the only force, who can steer the wheel of peaceful change to progress and modernity and this had been amply proved innumerable times, especially, in critical hours of danger to the nation during her stewardship.

She also raised her voice against the feudal outlook of some officials who ought to contribute to the implementation of certain policies of government.

In an interview for *Socialist India*, weekly of the All India Congress Committee (R) (May 30, 1975) committee, she said that introduction of a new spirit was more important than its root and branch "reform of the administrative procedure". Asked to indicate her conception of the method for socialism, Mrs. Gandhi said "socialism may be a dream for some. But, it is a vital necessity for the vast bulk of our people". The masses had participated in the national struggle in huge numbers and with enthusiasm because they knew that freedom would lead to emoncipation from poverty.

She added "only that society is truly socialist in which the feeling of being exploited has given place to a willing and cheerful participation in national tasks and persons and social objectives are not in conflict".

Mrs. Gandhi further emphasised that the measures taken by her government, such as nationalisation of banks and the take over of general insurance, were intended primarily as important advances in the war against poverty and economic disparity.

She said the government had placed special emphasis on the programme of accelerated land reforms, rural works, support for small farmers and farmers of dry areas. These, along with the increased allocations under the developmental plans and programmes, should all be viewed as part of the "Garibi Hatao" strategy. Deprecating the tendency to multiply rules and apply rigid criteria for different functions, she said "there must be room for experimentation, initiative and innovation" at all stages.

Talking to a few journalists, she said the country's economy had improved considerably and "is poised for rapid advance". Tomorrow's India will be what we make it by today's labours, she added.

Political System and Law

"Law must become a tool of social change"said Mrs.Gandhi, Prime Minister, on another occasion. Similarly she said "Constitution cannot be a closed book and it must be a living document serving a growing and energetic society". Laying the foundation stone for the extension to the Supreme Court building on April 15th, 1975 Mrs. Gandhi noted that our people looked to "the Judicial system for the realisation of their aspirations and for the social, economic, and political justice, which are enshrined in our Constitution.

A political system survives"not by its abstract virtues, but its capacity to fulfill the just aspirations of the people. Especially in a country like ours, gropping relentlessly with problems old and new, the political system should effectively diffuse economic power and opportunities". In this context, Mrs. Gandhi urged that the Judicial arm of the government must ensure, expeditions, in expensive and sympathetic justice".

The ultimate responsibility of Parliament and of the courts Mrs. Gandhi, said "is to pursue the nation and to avert calamities which might weaken its foundations". Differences of opinion, over and tensions "will arise, but sagacity lies in the avoidance of distinctive collisions" she said "we considered Law to be the bed-rock of civilisation holding societies grow, and change, concepts of what is just and right also changes".

"A well adjusted society", she pointed out "achieves balance between the legislature, which makes laws, the executive, which implements laws and judiciary which interprets laws", and said "there is no inherent confrontation between the legislation and the judiciary nor confusion between the legislative and judicial functions".

Mrs. Gandhi noted that the various schemes of legal aid to the poor which were being mooted are "timely and welcome" and expressed the hope that "the fine intricacies of law are not used merely, to help out those who have the power of the purse". Law must give protection to the unlettered and under privileged as well" she added.

In the early times, "Law was a device for the defence of the rights of the few" she further pointed out.

Constitutional Changes

Giving out her opinion on Constitutional changes, she declared that those changes give "purposive meaning to democracy, Intervening in the AICC debate on Constitutional reforms, Mrs. Gandhi said" the proposed Constitutional changes sought to achieve "true justice and true equality" for the common people and give deeper and purposive meaning to democracy. These were completely in line with the direction of the country policies since Independence and even before, she expressed India's determination to continue the march towards progress on her independent path fighting "entrenched privilege" at all levels.

The prime minister pointed out that in 1971 elections, people had given a massive two-thirds majority to the programme of her party, which clearly envisaged changing some parts of the Constitution which was coming in the way of fuller democracy and fuller life for the people.

As a matter of fact, it was not the Constitution, which was coming in the way, but interpretation of it by some. This was what had to be changed.

Mrs. Gandhi castigated critics abroad who criticised developments in India, particularly after the emergency. She observed "they have not shown greater understanding of this country even earlier".

Mrs. Gandhi, said further, that "in considering the question of Constitutional changes" we have to think about some basic matters. What we are fighting against and what for we are fighting for independence.

Raising her voice, Mrs. Gandhi declared "our basic fight is entrenched privilege of a few, whether in the economic field or in the social field or in international affairs. We are fighting for the rights of the common man in India and the common good all over the world. We are fighting for the removal of fear". The fear of speaking up and voicing their difficulties.

This is how she could reach the masses and the common man in the street, even a rickshaw puller, could repose confidence in her as custodian of their rights. It is how she endeared herself to the common people in India. There might be many in India, who had no occasion to see her bodily, but the image of her was enough to create a soothing solace in their hearts that here is a woman, who is their mother and guardian and who will spare no effort to bring them recognition and to remove their suffering. Resolute advance to the proclaimed goal of a just social order could be achieved.

Speaking of the opposition from vested interests and political enemies, and of the far-reaching consequences of the social and economic reforms contemplated by her government. She mentioned about a new deal for the impoverished millions of India.

Thus, Indira Gandhi's political ideas were also based on Nehru's philosophy. Defining her concept of democracy and socialism, Smt. Indira said "by socialism, we do not mean any text book definition of socialism or any pre-conceived theory, but that we should evolve a direction suited to the needs of Indian people".

A country most ineaxperienced in self-government and a people untrained in the processes of the functioning of democracy really need certain special defenses against dangers of disruption and disintegration.

Some trends opposed democratic functioning in India and they reached sharply to such trends that Congress could not control.

20 Point Socio-Economic Programme

The declaration of the 20-point economic programme by the Prime Minister, generated new hopes amongst the countrymen and imparted a new sense of dynamism. The programme, that aimed at economic prosperity, with social justice, caught the imagination of the people and focussed the attention of the public on the areas that needed immediate action.

So, as to bring down prices, government took steps to stimulate production, step up procurement, and to streamline the distribution of essential commodities. A price surveillance committee presided over by the Prime Minister reviewed the price and availability situation from time to time.

Substantial progress had been made in the implementation of land reforms measures. All states excepting Nagaland and Meghalaya where there is community ownership of land, have enacted laws with a view to implement ceiling on land holdings. House sites were allotted for the landless and weaker sections and state Governments have launched an energetic drive to give them assistance to construct dwelling.

All Scheduled banks were instructed to provide finance for social housing schemes. Bonded labour was abolished and labourers thus released were rehabilitated on schemes pertaining to agriculture, animal husbandry, village industries, etc.

Rural indebtedness was liquidated, in respect of marginal farmers, agricultural labourers and rural artisans whose annual income did not exceed Rs. 2,400/- guidelines for issue of consumption loans by cooperatives were issued by Reserve Bank of India.

Agricultural wages were reviewed in all states and the enforcing machinery, consisting of the Revenue, Agriculture, Panchayat Raj Departments was strengthened.

Project-wise financial outlays and physical achievements were estimated in terms of irrigation potential for each state and the outlay was stepped up by Rs.75/- crores during 1976-77 for all major projects. Efforts have also been made to accelerate the minor irrigation programme.

The handloom sector occupied a unique place in India and is next to agriculture and so, a comprehensive programme for deveopment of the handloom industry was formulation and production of controlled cloth of improved quality had been stepped up.

The drive launched by the Income-tax Department for countering tax-evasion is pursued with unabated vigour. Law for confiscation of smuggler's properties, liberalisation of investment procedures income-tax relief to middle class, supply of books and stationery at controlled prices, apprenticeship scheme were the other items of the national programme, that aimed at the over-all development of the people, especially the weaker sections.

Introducing this 20-point programme, Mrs. Gandhi said "the programme deals with the nerve centres of economic and social life of the people". Prime Minister's message to the Nation broadcast on 11th November, 1975, emphasised the importance of hard work, iron will and strictest discipline in the task of reconstructing our economy. The problems of poverty and unemployment in India are colossal and Smt. Gandhi was quite conversant with its magnitude and the urgency that their solution need.

4

Indira's Win as Prime Minister (Her View on Democracy and Welfare State)

On 3rd January 1966, Sastri went to Tashkent and passed away suddenly out of heart failure.

Who is next the Prime Minister of India was a million dollar question in India at that time. Gulzarilal Nanda, the acting Prime Minister asked Indiraji to support him in case she was not contesting.

Many leaders came to her and wanted to find out what was in her mind. She expressed her willingness, if Kamaraj asked her to contest.

After the funeral rites of Sastri were completed, the matter came for discussion. Not only Nanda even Vijayalakshmi Pandit wanted to contest. She came to Delhi cancelling her trip to America. She was Nehru's sister and president of UNO, embassador twice. Along with her, Morarji Desai also became a contestant for the post of the Prime Minister. He was till then Finance Minister and as follower of Gandhian principles, he was implementing the anti-liquor policy. He had utmost faith in moral values. Had experience in the government, as a good administrator. He was also Deputy Prime Minister in Nehru's cabinet. Many, who were opposing Nehru's socialism, were supporters of Morarji. Building and businessmen, land owners, industrialists, were supporting him and so he felt, he had better chances to become the Prime Minister.

Y.B. Chavan, who was Defence Minister and had the support of the army, also wanted to contest. He was a powerful man and a good administrator. In 1967, how to bring the Congress party to power, was the question confronting Kamaraj Nadar. He had full support of the party. If only he wanted to become the Prime Minister, it would have been very easy for him. But he knews his limitations. He does not know English. He cannot speak any other language except Tamil and he cannot participate in international affairs. That is why, he never wanted to be the Prime Minister. He ascertained the opinion of all Congress leaders.

In the beginning, only Nanda appeared to be the lone contestant. Later on, many others joined the pray. Kamaraj himself was asked to be the Prime Minister. But he did not agree.

So, Nanda said, in case, he cannot contest the election, "I will support Indira Gandhi". Atulya Ghosh and the Chief Minister of Rajasthan told Nanda, it is better to support Indira Gandhi. When asked, Indira Gandhi said, she would oblige the Congress leaders especially Kamaraj. But Morarji definitely said he would contest the election in any event. This created an ill will and adverse feeling in the minds of many. In the meanwhile, Charan and Indira consulted each other and came to a decision that one would support the other in case, there was more strength to one of them.

Kamaraj consulted all the Chief Ministers. Many of them favoured Indira Gandhi. So, Kamaraj called Indiraji and advised her "not to talk to anybody and not to make any statement".

Indira was the daughter of Nehru, young in age and active. She was also a minister in the cabinet. Because she was a lady and weak, she would be subservient to him, Kamaraj thought.

Morarji was adamant. So contest was inevitable.

When Kamaraj declared that Indira would be the next Prime Minister, she felt astonished.

Contest was held on 16th January 1966, for the election of the Congress Parliamentary party. Morarji fought tooth and nail to win the support of many. There was much of propaganda and lobbying.

It was also felt that during Nehru's time, power went into the hands of Chief Ministers of states. So, five kinds of people, namely, the chief ministers, the papers, local leaders, state Congress committees and people nearer to Nehru supported Indiraji.

Everyone was anxiously waiting for the result. Many were sitting before the television sets and watching. Some were questioning her about Indira's assessment of the situation. Her only answer was "cannot say so early". One asked her "who will be Prime Minister, is it a male or female"? her reply was "it is not important, whether it is male or female, but who is contesting".

What about your opinion on "woman becoming a Prime Minister representing 48 crores of people", she said "difficult to say".

Indiraji left the decision to the will of the people concerned, whereas Morarji met every Parliament member and was determined to win at any cost.

On the previous day to the elections, Kamaraj went to Morarji's house and made an appeal to him not to contest. "But Morarji said I will surely win" why should I withdraw myself from the contest ? What is the fault I committed ? In what way, I am inferior to her ?

"I am contesting as per democratic procedure. What else is there" he questioned

Indira Gandhiji said "I am not afraid of winning or losing the contest".

On the day of the contest, she visited Samadhi of Gandhi at Rajghat, went to Shantivan of Pandit Nehru and went to her house, did 'namskar' to her mother. She remembered some of the words her father wrote to her from jail "Be Bold! All matters will take care of themselves! If you are bold, you will be able to do anything. Nothing will stand as a stumbling block to you".

Indiraji's Style of Functioning

Indian culture had given a distinct place to woman in the family and in society right from pre-historic times. She is respected as a mother, as a wife and as a sister. Inspire of several onslaughts of civilisation, Indian woman could retain her unique features, through ages.

When Mrs. Gandhi was elected as the Prime Minister of India, the biggest democracy in the world, it was discussed and discussed all over the world, as a speciality.

Critics also were there from different shades of opinion. Can a woman rule ? Can a woman take serious decisions and lead the masses? The orthodoxy pressed their mouths with awe and surprise.

But, Indira Gandhi could prove, beyond all possible expectations her mettle in dealing with difficult problems and varied situations.

On account of her influence, Indian women could get a place of honour. Judging Indian women by their participation in the political life of the country, the American Massachusett's Institute of Technology's centre for International studies gave the verdict that "Indian society is almost certainly less inequitable that the Chinese, Soviet and the American." The study said that the highest participation of women in Indian politics is the result of the influence of Congress tradition in the matter of feminine participation; essentially influenced by Mahatma Gandhi.

The study further said that not merely does India have a female prime minister, women have also succeeded in becoming members of Lok Sabha; some have even been Governors and Chief Ministers of States, Ambassadors, Members of the cabinet and Dy. Ministers and some have held highest positions in the organisations of the major political parties".

A friend of mine from Delhi was remarking once at that time in a context, that "men have stopped looking at a Woman, only as a woman and making comments on her blouse and saree". Thanks to Mrs. Gandhi. Now-a-days a man may try to dominate his wife or sister in his personal capacity. But, he has learnt how to respect a career woman, as a "person" endowed with "intellect" and "Brains".

"I happen to be not merely the daughter of Jawaharlal Nehru" Mrs. Gandhi said "but one who worked with him very closely". Speaking in AICC session at Delhi in 1976; of course, she did not dwell upon her work with Nehru after Independence but she said "So for people, whether of the left or the right, to tell me what people go. There is an allegation prevalent in the country that she could not contribute substantially to the ideology of Congress.

Mrs. Gandhi called for a change in attitudes and method of work in financial institutions to match the changing requirements and hightened expectations of the people. She wanted to instill dynamism and imagination in the Banking system and called for setting aside 'conservative attitude'.

She called for "heart -searching"on the part of workers for the opposition parties, whether rightist or leftist. It seemed rather tragic that all the Congress(O) leaders, including Sri Sanjeeva Reddi, whose nomination for the presidential election triggered of to the Congress split, lost the Lok Sabha seat and got further isolated from country's public life. Mens problems will not be solved unless women's problems are solved. She felt that women held the key to the spread of progressive ideas in any society. She urged women to understand the problems of the nation. Unless women understood the intricacies involve in running their village, state and country, the nation could not go forward. Women are to the mobilised to meet this "great change" she held.

Indira Gandhi succeeded where her father and even Lal Bahadur Sastry have failed. The Pact (called the Simla Pact) that she could enter in with Zulfikar Ali Bhutto in 1971, is a remarkable achievement on her part and finds an honourable place for her among the world statesmen. Combining Mahatma's humanism with Nehru's idealism, she could formulate her own 'firm' to find a solution to the vexed problem. Her strategy in tackling issues is unparalleled.

India was destined to play a prominent role in the affairs of Asia and Mrs. Gandhi has steered the nation successfully to this recognition with her policy of non-alignment and full co-operation with all.

Even while solving the issues of Sikkim and Bhutan, Mrs. Gandhi could display tremendous wisdom.

But, her programmes and policies envisage that she was walking on the right path in the footsteps of Gandhi and Nehru and she is trying to give a new shape to their ideas.

She rebuked the supremacy of male muscle power in the modern context. Times had changed. I do not know how the muscle is there on this hall "she went on" and how men will compare with women in this "this is a challange to critics, who undermine woman's intellect in tackling serious problems".

The Prime Minister also requested her name being mentioned "too often and in every subject". During debate on the 20-point programme, her name had become an additional point under discussion, she remarked amidst laughter. She also said it was not proper to drag her name everywhere and it shows that people want to get rid of responsibility by passing the buck to her.

Trying to speak of the spirit of discipline, she said that when 600 million people shifted from one age to another there were bound to be difficulties. The steps that government had been forced to take were a "painful necessity".

She seems to have her own ideas on women's liberation; as a part of a movement by the "under-privileged". The importance of women's liberation lay, she said, in the fact that women have realised that discrimination was not good for them or for the Europe where women had to fight for the vote and the right for education, Indian women experienced no such problems and even before they were ready to realise about the existence of such laws. Moreover, the concept of freedom is different in the western world and the Indian conditions and concepts are totally different".

"I will go when I complete my job, was the reply given by the Prime Minister, condemning the opposition parties on one occasion and remarked"decisions which will effect life of millions of people cannot be taken in the streets "and she is not going to bow or bend, before she achieves, what she wanted".

After independence, though the country has made some impressive strides in the industrial sector and though agricultural production has gone up considerably, poverty remains to be widespread and visible. Mrs. Gandhi is struggling hard to put the economy in good shape and people are simply wanting to see what she has to say and do, in eradicating this poverty.

Inaugurating the silver jubilee celebrations of Ethiraj College, Madras, Mrs. Gandhi gave a call that "old ideas and habits", which were out of tune with contemporary times should be eschewed. Telling that the "Major task"of education was to help the people step out of 'shackles, ruts and cobwebs and superstitions, abscurantism and "narrow-mindedness", she preached that "what were superficial in our thinking" should be rejected.

Speaking of the special responsibility of women, she said "the task of building the new generation and moulding society" lies on the shoulders of women as men could never do, no matter how much they talk about it?.

When questioned whether she feels the responsibility of leading the country is heavy, she equipped "No". I do not feel it is so heavy because, I feel, it is shared by 600 million people of India.

"It was also voiced in the Mexico city". "Greater role for women in the world affairs means an end to wars".

Speaking at a huge rally in Patna in Gandhimaidan, once Mrs. Gandhi said "A new path, an Indian path to meet our demands has to be evolved and it is not an easy one". "Any country which wants to move from one stage to another, has to face a number of obstacles"; women have a significant role to play. Recalling the critical role played by Indian women during the freedom struggle, women have to serve as a bridge between the rich heritage and modernity. She further continued that mens problems will not be solved unless women's also understand the problems of the nation. Unless women understood the intricacies involved in running their village, state and country the nation could not go forward. Women are to be mobilised to meet this "great challenge".

Indira Gandhi succeeded where her father and even Lal Bahadur Sastry have failed. The Pact (called the Simla Pact) that she could enter in with Zulfikar Ali Bhuttoo, in 1971 is a remarkable achievement on her part and finds an honourable place for her among the world statesmen. Combining Mahatma's humanism with Nehru's idealism, she could formulate her own 'Ism' to find a solution to the vexed problem. Her strategy in tackling issues was unparalleled.

The Prime Minister called "for massive public support in defeating the conspiracy of anti-socialist forces". She also stressed that acute economic disparities between the high and the low-income groups would have to be eliminated speedly for the country's progress towards socialism and in the larger interests of the downtrodden millions.

Revolutions, Mrs. Gandhi said "were of two kinds–violent and non-violent. A bloody revolution did not solve problems because, it destroyed faster than it would rebuild. For this, there is no other path than the path of peace and reason non-violence chalked out by Mahatma Gandhi and it is not an easy path". Very true. The path of transformation of society by non-violent methods had been acclaimed as the best, by the world over especially by all Afro-Asian nations. The very achievements of independence to India, is a standing example that there is no place for the cult of the Bomb and the stick in our hearts. India of Indians the land of Buddha, has shun violence and taken to the path of tolerance.

A new society free from inequality and exploitation can be ushered in, only when there is massive support to the policies adopted by government, from time to time. Mrs. Gandhi who could feel the pulse of the nation, was the only force, who could steer the wheel of peaceful change to progress and modernity and this had been amply proved innumerable times, especially, in critical hours of danger to the nation during her stewardship.

She also raised her voice against the feudal outlook of some officials who sought to contribute to the implementation of certain policies of government.

In an interview *Socialist India*, weekly of the All India Congress Committee(R) (May 30, 1975) committee, she said that introduction of a new spirit was more important than a root and branch reform of the administrative procedure. Asked to indicate her conception of her socialism, Mrs. Gandhi said "socialism may be a dream for some. But, it is a vital necessity for the vast bulk of our people". The masses had participated in the national struggle in large numbers and with enthusiasm because they knew that freedom would lead to emancipation from poverty.

She added "only that society is truly socialist in which the feeling of being exploited has given place to a willing and cheerful participation in national tasks and personal and social objections are not in conflict".

Mrs. Gandhi further emphasised that the measures taken by her government, such as nationalisation of banks and the take over of general insurance, were intended primarily as important advances in the war against poverty and economic disparity.

She said the government had place for special emphasis on the removal of fear "the fear of speaking up and voicing their difficulties".

This is how she could reach the masses and the common man in the street, even a rich rain puller, could repose confidence in her, as custodian of their rights. It is how she endeared herself to the common people in India. These might be many in India, who had no occasion to see her bodily, but the image of her was enough to create a soothing solace in them that were is a woman, who is their mother and guardian and who will spare no effort to bring them recognition and to remove their sufferings.

After all, any man, would like to be recognised and respected as-a human being and the people,who were denied this privilege since ages, rallied round her and her image was enough to instil courage and confidence in them.

Mrs. Gandhi, referring to critics, that democracy was removed from India she questioned "what were the rights of the common man previously".

Her Views on Democracy and Welfare State

Britain is the mother of Parliaments but did anybody in the world consider Britain undemocratic, when was suppressing the rights of millions of Indians ? How many voices were raised that there was no democracy in Britain. She asked and remarked ironically "Britain could remain a democracy even when she was crushing millions of people not only in India, but in other parts of the world". Others can remain a democracy regardless what they do. If the poor man raised his voice, it was not democracy. Mrs. Gandhi continued exposing the hollowness of criticism against India "when land is taken from the rich man, we are doing something that is encroaching upon the rights of the people. But, when the poor people, who have been given land are thrown out, these are few voices against it". This is how she identified herself with the poor man. Sitting in Delhi, in the highest authority she was able to visualise the interests of the poor and the commoners and give shape to their demands and none else could ventilate their grievances better.

It was not as if there was no poverty in other countries. "But one does not hear of the poverty in other country because they are following policies, which are convenient to them (the critics) politically, economically and in other ways". Mrs. Gandhi, in this context declared "we do not meant to follow policies that are convenient to anybody except the Indian people". "Our effort is to set acceptance of the principle of time justice and true equality for people of India. This is what we are aiming to give deeper and purposive meaning to democracy whatever has to be done for that, will be done, regardless of what others say". We can keep our individuality intact, and enjoy the results of democratic life.

The Evening Star, Washington remarked that Indira Gandhi's election victory was a "triumph" but "also a challenge". By making herself the central issue of the election Mrs. Gandhi succeeded in breaking the traditional local voting patterns of the vast nation. "The newspaper said in an editorial".

"Mrs. Gandhi has freed herself of the necessity of dealing with the communists to stay in power. She has received the mandate she hoped for... the Parliamentary majority, combined".

5

Fourth General Elections in 1967 and Mid Term Elections of 1969

The sixties were the most crucial years for post-independent India. Two wars with our neighbours, deaths of two Prime Ministers gave the country a jolt. The emergence of non-Congress governments in eight states, the unprecedented drought, industrial recession, finally the break-up of the Congress party between the rightists and the extremists are the salient features of the story during this period.

Lal Bahadur Sastri, who succeeded Nehru, could rule the country only for eighteen months. After his death, Indira Gandhi, was made the Prime Minister by the then "King Makers" to continue Nehru's policies for some more time to come. She assumed charge as the Third Prime Minister of India on 24th January, 1966. She included all the Cabinet Ministers of Sri Sastry in her cabinet also. It was a time when there was acute food problem in the country. On account of the food zones and on account of the irregularities in the supply of foodstuffs, there was agitation in Kerala State. There was agitation for a separate Punjabi Suba also. She decided to form two separate states of 'Punjab' and 'Haryana' and set out to solve the Nagaland issue.

Mid-term elections were held in 1969 and Mrs. Gandhi toured 16 thousand miles in the country and addressed more than 200 meetings, carrying on electioneering work. Wherever she went, she gathered crowds. She herself won her seat from Rae Baraily in Uttar Pradesh with a thumping majority of Ninety one thousand votes. One important feature of this election was, the opposition parties, mainly the Swatantra and the Bharatiya Jana Sangh fought the election vehemently.

Stalwarts like S.K. Patil, C. Subrahmanyam, Manu Bhai Shaw, Raj Bahadur, all Central Ministers and members of High Command, Sri Atulya Ghosh lost the battle. It was also surprising to note that

Sri. Kamaraj Nadar, the Congress President, got defeated by a student leader. Congress lost the majority, it had in Parliament in 1962 elections and it had to win 33 seats, held previously, thus having narrow majority of 25 seats only.

All the members of the so called 'syndicate' got defeated. They planned to have their candidate as the Prime Minister and wanted to dislodge Mrs. Gandhi. But, the majority of the elected members chose her as their leader and so, she again became Prime Minister, for the second time in 1967. When Morarji proposed her name, after withdrawing from the contest, Jagjivan Ram seconded her name.

This time she did not care more for the opinions of the syndicate in Ministry making. Mr. Morarji was made the Finance Minister with the Dy-Prime Minister's post, Sri B. Chavan (Home), Sri Swaran Singh (Defence), Jagjivan Ram–Food and Agriculture, M.C. Chagla-Foreign Affairs, Ashok Mehta–Planning, Satyanarayan Sinha Minister without portfolio, Fakruddin Ali Ahmed–Industrial-Development, Dinesh Singh - Commerce, M.C. Poonacha-Railways-Dr. Trigun Sen - Education, Dr. Karan Singh - Tourism, R.V. Ra-Transport, Shipping and Navigation, K.K. Shaw - Information and Broadcasting, Dr. Subhag Singh - Parliamentary Affairs, Dr. Chenna Reddy - Steel and Mines, State Ministers like K.V. Raghunadha Reddy, Khadilker, P.C. Sethi, I.K. Gujral, K.R. Ganesh, Prof. Sher Singh were also appointed, Sankaranand, Bal Govinda Varma, Jagannath Pahadia, P.K. Kishen were made Deputy Ministers. She omitted Sri Sanjeeva Reddy this time, in her Ministry but he was later on elected as Speaker of the Lok Sabha.

Zakir Hussain was elected as President, after the completion of the period of Dr. Radhakrishnan. Towards the end of 1967, the term of the President of AICC came to an end and Sri Nijalingappa then Chief Minister of Karnataka was elected as President in the place of Sri Kamraj Nadar, and thus, the voice of the Syndicate finally prevailed. Nothing was discussed about the progressive policies of Congress or any reforms to be brought about, at the time of this change of the President.

Young Turks like Mohan Dharia, Chandrasekhar, Krishna Kant began to make appeal to adopt progressive policies and not to yield to the pressures of the rightist syndicate.

When the 'syndicate' came to know that Smt. Gandhi is no more in their hands, they asked her to adhere only for certain policies waiting for an opportunity to widen serious differences between syndicate and other leaders.

After the fourth General Elections of 1967 and particularly after the mid-term elections of 1969, there was much talk of polarisation of forces inside the Congress as well as outside. The Young Turks began to press for the immediate nationalisation of banks and certain other industries. In this connection, they repeatedly clashed with Morarji Desai, who was a staunch opponent of the policy of nationalising banks. They also clashed with the leaders of the Congress, such as S.K. Patel and Atulya Ghosh and also with Nijalingappa.

In April 1969, Nijalingappa, in his presidential address at the Faridabad session of the Congress, criticised the performance of the public sector, in a manner which gave rise to a controversy as to whether he really believed in the implementation of socialistic policies of the Congress. Nijalingappa declared "I am a socialist to the core but I am an Indian socialist, not of any other brand". He said that he had no particular love for the private sector, but at the same time, he did not think that large units should be started in the public sector merely to suit socialistic slogans. At this Faridabad session, the question of polarisation of forces, within the Congress was also raised. Some even expressed fear that Congress may not be able 'to set' majority at the centre in the next general elections.

But Indira Gandhi depreciated any talk of polarisation within the Congress and declared that such talk arose out of the frustration of individuals, rather than from serious political thinking. According to her, the Congress was and should remain a centrist organisation and should not split itself into rightist and leftist factions.

In this context, it is significant to note that Mr. V.K. Krishna Menon, once upon a time, a close associate of Nehru, could not even gain favour with the Young Turks, after his win from Bengal.

Mr. Chandrasekhar, asserted that on issues like concentration of economic power - the Congress could cooperate with the communists, the SSP and the PSP - so, as to bring about radical. changes in the credit policy of the country, he pleaded for nationalisation of banks and other financial institutions. He criticised Morarji Desai and warned that if people's aspirations were not fulfilled, then some form of violent revolution may break out.

His criticism of economic policies of Morarji Desai mingled with personal criticism and Morarji resented to this and made an issue of it. Mrs. Gandhi had to mediate in between.

Congress, built up, from the inception, as a broad based organisation, which embraced within it, people of diverse political, social and economic views, could not avoid, any longer, conflict between two divergent views. Finally, it culminated in a split in November 1969. Bangalore session of AICC, accepted Indira's plea of nationalisation but rejected her suggestion, as regards the Congress nominee for the presidentship and so, some unpleasant events followed, as a result, in quick succession.

Indira Gandhi, strongly felt that, a group within Congress was not committed to its secular and socialistic policies. The other group was pressing for radical changes. With foresight, Indira favoured nationalisation of banks and sent a note to Bangalore session of AICC. But as soon as the note was read out, S.K. Patel and Morarji Desai opposed the plea for take over of banks and Fakruddin Ali Ahmed, supported Indira's note. At Bangalore, Indira Gandhi's suggestion of V.V. Giri, as Congress nominee for presidentship, was rejected by Congress Parliamentary board, and Sri Sanjeeva Reddy's name was declared as official nominee. She felt the decision "certainly distressing". She made it clear that she would fight against the opponents of her policies inside the organisation and as regards unity, she posed the question "certainly there should be unity, but unity of purpose for what".

On 16th July 1969, a dramatic sequence followed the above controversy and Morarji was relieved of the finance portfolio and the latter had to resign from the cabinet. Making it clear that she did not like to place, the burden of implementing 'progressive programmes' on him, Indira acted in a bold manner and some opposition parties also welcomed the exit of Desai. But, on the other hand, Desai found sympathy from the Jana Sangh and Swatantra leaders. Balraj Madhok, MP and Jana Sangh leader claimed that Indira Gandhi had "begun to pay the communist game openly"and called upon the nationalist forces both inside and outside Congress, "to take concerted steps to foil her designs".

After Desai's exit, there were heated discussions in the country, whether Congress would split into rightists and leftists. In July 1969, Indira Gandhi said that Congress party had not been able to make the required impact on the people that it was going to achieve socialism and that is why, Congress was losing support. She also strongly supported the public sector in contrast to the serious criticisms made by Nijalingappa. She asserted that the attacks on

Public Sector were "misconceived", as public sector ventured into difficult and capital intensive fields which the private sector had shunned.

On 19th July 1969, an emergency meeting of central cabinet was called at which, a decision to nationalise fourteen major commercial banks, with deposits of not less than 50 crores each was taken acordingly, an ordinance was issued.

Efforts were made to put up a single opposition candidate for the presidency. CPI strongly supported Giri. While the CPI and CPM also supported the utterances and measures of Indira Gandhi, and also supported bank nationalisation as also the candidature of Giri for the presidency of the Indian Union. Those belonging to the syndicate were highly critical of her.

Jana Sangh and the Swatantra Party, who opposed Giri, a considered that the presidential election raised ideological questions. In August, 1969, A.B. Vajpayee, President of Jana Sangh, stated that on the question of presidential election, Indian politics had arrived at a cross-road and the Congress was bound to be split into two, from the highest level to the lowest level. In this connection, what Balraj Madhok, said involving in revelling "If the split in the Congress, he said, led to one of the factions adopting 'Nehru line' and the other the 'Patel line', it would help polarization of political forces in the country. If Mr. Nijalingappa takes the 'Patel line' my party will be with him. The split was welcome and good for the country. If Gandhi's will was followed, it would have happened in 1948, leading to the creation of two vioble parties, one led by Nehru and the other by Patel. The present split was acting as catalyst to political polarisation. Though the tussle appeared to be one of personalities, the ideological over tones were unmistakable".

Indira Gandhi claimed that those inside the Congress, who were opposed to the party's programme of a socialistic pattern of society, were carrying on a whispering campaign against her. She launched that she had been described by certain people as a dictator for having implemented the programme set before the Congress by its leaders, fifteen years ago. "If these people had guts, they should have opposed the programme then. Now, when I am trying to implement the programme, I am being labelled as a dictator". She asserted that those, who had once voted for the programme had no business to say anything against it.

She further described bank nationalisation as a 'decisive struggle' between the common man on the one side and a few individuals on the otherside and if the critics were "itching for a fight", then the people of India, also were prepared for a showdown and she would fight back.

On 28th August 1969, Sri Nijalingappa declared that Morarji Desai issue was still open. He also warned against the "mischievous and sophisticated tendency of personality cult" that was developing in the country, which may lead to dictatorship. He said that some people were trying to make use of "catchy phrases and slogans" to achieve their own ulterior ends. On 4th September 1969, Nijalingappa said that communists had infiltrated into the Congress organisation at all levels and he was thinking of some sort of 'screening' process for weeding them out.

In September 1969, Morarji Desai spoke of the danger to the country, if the Congress was split. Though the communists appeared to be the happiest about the political crisis within the Congress, they would, Desai prophesied, never be able to come to power in the country, for in spite of their 'apparent strength', in Kerala and West Bengal, ancient culture and independent spirit of the people would resist communism. Desai referred to the growing indiscipline in the Congress party and said "let the Prime Minister stop in discipline first. Then only, there is meaning in enforcing discipline among the rank and file".

Speaking about discipline, Mrs. Gandhi said party discipline was broken for the first time by Gandhi in 1919, when he gave a new turn to the Congress and transformed it into a fighting machine. She claimed, that by her recent decisions and acts, the Congress organisation, had taken a similar turn and that it was for Congress men to make the best use of it.

On the question of discipline, some opposition leaders, such as J.B. Kripalani and H.V. Kamath criticised Indira Gandhi, J.B. Kripalani contended that the Prime Minister had launched on "an adventurist political career" similarly, H. V. Kamath, PSP Leader said in August 1969, that there would be chaos and dictatorship in the country, if political parties functioned without discipline. He said that the power of Prime Minister has increased, was increasing and must be diminishsed.

In view of the political situation prevailing in the country, Jaya Prakash Narayan, the Sarvodaya Leader, said on 2nd September

1969, that to had come by the Congress would split such a split was necessary, so that a proper coalition Government could be formed at the centre in 1972. Such a split would give rise to a healthy polarisation, otherwise, there would be only an anti-Congress was no ideology.

While people were talking of polarisation and a split within the Congress, Indira Gandhi gave a call to call those, who believed in secularism, democracy and socialism to join the Congress Nijalingappa also gave similar call. He explained that he would welcome J.B. Kripalani - who incidentally, was a most persistent critic of Indira Gandhi - to rejoin the Congress.

Bank nationalisation, on the other hand, created considerable enthusiasm among the people. This measure also increased Indira Gandhi's popularity. But S.K. Patel, talking about her radical promises to the people, said, "the very people, who are showering flowers on Mrs. Gandhi will throw stones at her" when those promises are not fulfilled.

Congress votes were split in the presidential election and Giri was elected President of the Indian Union. Indira Gandhi appealed to the people to participate in the country's march towards socialism. She went on a town of various parts of the country to mobilise public support to her policies.

Many people, especially of the upper strata, were not happy over nationalisation of banks. There was considerable propaganda, that Indira Gandhi had become communist. "Many people have raised"said Indira Gandhi, the bogey of communism. It is strange to see the MC earthyism, which is long dead in the place of its birth, should have now found a foothold across the seas and the contents in India. It shows that those who propound this theory show an astounding ignorance of the political forces at work in our country and the facts of life in the India of 1969....No one can have missed the tremendous psychological change which has come about in this country by this one small step. I do not think, anybody, even the poorest man, would think that this is going tochange his life suddenly or that it is some miraculous event, which has been brought about.

On 28th August 1969, the Union Cabinet decided to set up such a judicial commission. This decision had been hailed by all the Congressmen and they said that this would give a lie to the change of the left communists that the Congress Government at the centre was dominated by monopolists and particularly the Birlas. Indira

Gandhi went on a tour of various parts of the country to mobilize public support her policies. On October 18th 1969, a requisition was signed by several senior readers including Charan, Fakruddin Ali Ahmed, Jagjivan Ram and Uma Shanker Dikshit, where by the Congress Working Committee was requested to commence a session of the AICC, as early as possible to facilitate the election of a new party president before the end of 1969. The requisitionists stated that the acceptance by the Bangalore Session of the AICC of the Prime Ministers note embodying a radical economic programme, created a sense of confidence in the masses.

The kind of change which was widely welcomed by the Nation, generated tensions within the party. On the eve of the Congress Working Committee meeting scheduled for November 1969, Nijalingappa dropped, Fakruddin Ali Ahmed and Subrahmanyam from the committee. So, Indira Gandhi and her supporters in the Congress Working Committee decided to boycott the working committee meeting on 1.11.69, as a protest.

In a way, 1st November 1969, is a turning point in the political history of India. On that same day, two separate meetings were held, one at the AICC office under the presidentship of Nijalingappa and the other at Indira Gandhi's residence. The CWC, under the leadership of Nijalingappa deacided that the requisition by 405 AICC members calling for the election of a new president amounted to a no-confidence motion in Nijalingappa, who had been elected by the plenary session and not the AICC and so, was out of order.

The meeting at Indira Gandhi's residence decided that a special session of AICC would be convened in Delhi on 22 and 23 November 1969 on the basis of requisition of 405 AICC members (The AICC had 708 members with voting rights).

Out of 21 members of the working committee, 10 members each were present at the respective meetings held under the chairmanship of the Congress president and Indira Gandhi. The remaining member K.C. Abraham, president of the Kerala Congress, first participated in the meeting held at Indira Gandhi's residence and then attended the meeting on Nijalingappa's chairmanship. He said he was trying to bring about unity, but he was with the organisation. This situation virtually split the Congress organisation.

This split was complete on 2nd November 1969, when Indira Gandhi, the Prime Ministers, was from the Congress party by Nijalingappa and her supporters. Indira Gandhi, had, the support of the majority of the Congress party, who reaffirmed their faith in her leadership. Towards the end of November 1969, the requestioned meeting of the AICC, met at Delhi and removed Nijalingappa from office as Congress president and appointed in his place Sri Subrahmanyam as the interior president till the holding of the plenary session due to be held in Bombay in December 1969.

The requisitionists Congress, in which Subrahmanyam was elected as interim president, opined that it was the real Congress.

When Subrahmanyam formed the Congress Working Committee, Chandrasekhar was not included in it, but he was given a status as a permanent invitee and inclusion of some others the committee led to controversy.

At Bombay, session, Indira Gandhi, desired that foreign policy had any pro-Soviet that Indira was learning towards commission leaders of the party continued their attack on Indira Gandhi and Kamaraj charged that Indira Gandhi was committing fraud on socialism. Kamaraj even argued that the syndicate, which was opposed by Indira Gandhi, had been founded the instance by Nehru.

There was a clash of personalities and desire to retain power played a major role, in causing the split in the Congress, the clash of ideas and attitudes was mainly responsible for it. Inside the Congress, Indira Gandhi, Jagjivan Ram and Fakruddin Ali Ahmed formed one goup and Nijalingappa, Kamaraj Atulya Ghosh and S.K. Patel formed another group, which was popularly known as the syndicate. Tomorrow the end of the drama, which brought the split, Morarji also was considered to be part of the 'syndicate' though he did not openly come out. After his exit from the cabinet, Desai remarked that he had been the 'victim of the syndicate'.

The opposition parties welcomed the split because they thought they would profit by it. When Nehru and Patel differed, Leftists supported Nehru and the Rightists supported Patel similarly when Indira Gandhi and Desai differed the leftists stood by her and the rightists by Desai.

Before the split, some inside the Congress who were opposed to Indira Gandhi said that she was soft to the communists and was encouraging them.

1977 - Elections : Defeat of Congress

In April 1977, at a meeting of the Congress working Committee, discussions were held about the reasons for the Congress debacle in the Lok Sabha poll. Some Congressmen, including D.K. Barooah, the president, wanted a thorough analysis about the debacle, whereas some others insisted on the resignation of the working committee, after accepting collective responsibility for the defeat. Eventually Indira Gandhi, D.K. Barooah and some other members of the High Command decided on collective resignation by the working committee.

But, Chandrajit Yadav and Vayalar Ravi also, members of the Congress Working Committee objected to this procedure. They said that collective resignation would create a vacuum. Statements were issued by some AICC members saying that the Congress president should resign and a meeting of AICC should be called for. In those circumstances, many thought the Congress was again heading for a split.

Finally, the eaxpanded meeting of Congress Working Committee commenced on 12th April, 1979 prior to the meeting, Mrs. Gandhi wrote to Barooah that she owns full responsibility for the Congress defeat and that she had no canons to defend nor any group to fight against. After the end of 2nd day's deliberations, D.K. Barooah resigned from presidentship of the Congress and Swaran Singh took over as interim president.

6

Verdict of 1977 Elections and a Political Cyclone

Before Barooah resigned, the CWC passed a resolution expelling Bansilal for a period of six years from the primary membership of the Congress for his "undemocratic, autocratic and undignified activities which had damaged the image of the party" and also decided to "reprimand" VC Shukla, former Minister of Information and Broadcasting, on the charge of "Misuse of Power".

Discussions, continued for four days and the committee members analysed the causes of poll debacle. They were frank and quite revealing, one after other criticised the mode of functioning of the party and the Government. B.D. Gupta, the Haryana Chief Minister, stated that he had no power and everything was done at the behest of some persons in Delhi, namely, Bansilal. The President of the Haryana Congress also agreed with this sort of assessment and said that attempts were made by some people to eliminate all honest advisers of the Prime Minister.

Chandrajit Yadav maintained that N.D. Tiwari, the Chief Minister of Uttar Pradesh, ran the front in the state only to please one individual at Delhi, namely, Sanjay Gandhi. K.C. Pant and other central ministers hailing from UP, said that force was used in the implementation of family planning. On the whole, a number of speakers maintained that a group of people, described as the coterie or the caucus did a lot of damage to the Congress.

The question whether the imposition of emergency was justified or not, was not discussed or considered in this meeting. The question of Indira Gandhi, after the Allahabad judgement, has however discussed and A.K. Anthony, the President of Kerala Congress, stated that it was a mistake on the part of Congressmen, to pressurise Mrs. Gandhi, to resign after the Judgement.

Some felt that the type of discussion that took place at that meeting could have not taken place, the excesses and distortions could have been avoided and the election result would have been different. They emphasised the importance of permitting dissent and discussion within the party.

Anyhow, for the first time, after more than two decades, there was a contest for the election of the Congress president in May 1977, and Mr. Kasu Brahmananda Reddy, who secured 317 votes was elected as the president, after defeating Siddhardha Sankar Ray, who got 160 votes and Karan Singh, who got 16 votes. After this election, Brahmananda Reddy was felicitated and there were also slogans to the effect that his victory indicated the victory of Indira Gandhi.

Thus, the controversy came to an end. In February 1977, Charan Singh, Home Minister wrote to 9 Chief Ministers of Congress States, whose Congress had fared badly, requesting them to dissolve the state assemblies and to hold fresh elections.

These states were Haryana, Uttar Pradesh, Punjab, Rajasthan, Sikkim, Tamil Nadu, Tripura, Uttar Pradesh, West Bengal, Pondicherry, Andaman and Nicobar, Chandigarh, Delhi, Dadra and Nagar Haveli, Lakshadweep, Mizoram, Arunachal Pradesh, Goa, Daman and Diu.

A political cyclone in Uttar Pradesh uprooted Congress from the states in North India. Of course various factors contributed to this situation. Many injustices and malpractices in the implementation of Family Planning Programme and for Shri Charan Singh and also with regards to arrests made under MISA and press censorship, were mainly responsible and Mrs. Gandhi expressed sorrow, for these excesses.

The people's reaction to emergency was adverse in Uttar Pradesh and they showed their anger in the elections.

Where these excesses were not committed, people supported Congress. In South India, unlike the North, the Janata Party did not have a well-organised cadre. So, public mind was in support of Congress. Intimation among Congressmen was also less. Electoral adjustments with AIADMK and CPI and others in Tamil Nadu and with the CPI and others in Kerala helped Congress.

On the whole, the verdict in the elections showed that the electorate, though illiterate, are politically awakened. The election also exploded the myth that democracy has a luxury which the developing or the third world countries could not afford. It showed that the democratic values were honoured and people greatly cherished their basic freedom. People voted against certain undesirable trends in running the government.

Indiras Arrest and Release

The manner in which Mrs. Indira was arrested and released was a high drama, turned into a low comedy after the debacle in major states court and the Janata Government had to cut a very sorry figure. It was an "attempt to discredit her"on the words of Mrs. Gandhi.

Mrs. Gandhi was arrested on 4th October 1977, on charges of corruption and misuse of her official position. The CBI did not seek her reward. There was no documentary or oral evidence to substantiate the charges. There was no basis even for believing that the accusations were well founded.

Mr. R. Dayal, Chief Metropolitan Magistrate of Delhi, who held that there were no reasonable grounds for her detention, released her unconditionally.

The Home Minister, Mr. Charan Singh, refuted Mrs. Gandhi's charge that she had been arrested because of political vendetta or witch-hunt by the Janata Government, saying that they were far from truth.

He disagreed with the questioner that the charges were not serious. His tough talking in the press conference justifying the action taken against Mrs. Gandhi, lost much of its punch in the light of the governments maladroit handling of her arrest and release by the Delhi Magistrate.

The superman of the CBI entrusted with the investigation seemed to have forgotten even the elementary rules of jurisdiction in attempting to detain her outside Delhi and in failing to complete the entries in the case diary.

The following is a part of the text of her statement at the time of her arrest warrant.

"I have tried to serve our people and our country to the best of my ability, no matter what the charge or charges now made against me. This arrest is a political one".

It is to prevent me from going to the people. It is an attempt to discredit me in their eyes and in the eyes of the world. I have been concerned not with credit or discredit but with my duty towards my country. Wherever I am, that continues to be my endeavour. This gives an insight into her mind.

Alongwith her, four former Union Ministers and three indus trialists also were held. She made no attempt to be released on bail. Mr. K.D. Malaviya, Mr. P.C. Sethi, Mr. H.R. Gokhale and Mr. D.P. Chattopadhyaya were also arrested along with Mrs. Gandhi, on charges of corrupt practices and misuse of their official positions. Two secretaries to the Government of India, Mr. B.B. Vohra (Formerly in the ministry of Petroleum) and Mr. S.M. Agarwal (Formerly in the Ministry of Communications) were among others who were arrested. The three industrialists Mr. R.P. Goenka of Duncan Brothers, Mr. M.V. Arunachalam former president, FICCI Ltd. are also arrested.

A lean Mrs. Gandhi, clad in a white saree, emerged at 17.30 hrs. from her room amidst shouts of "Indira Gandhi Zindabad, *Desh ki Neta* Indira Gandhi".

Samachar reported that as Mrs. Gandhi neared the police car, the crowd because unmanageable. Mrs. Gandhi responding to the requests of Indian and foreign newsmen and photographers, obliged them, with her usual broad smile before getting into the car.

It was just about 8 P.M. when Mrs. Gandhi was taken away to an unknown destination with a number of police and other cars following her.

When her car was stopped near a level crossing, she got down from her car and when her lawyer looked into the arrest warrant, no formalities were gone through by the police and FIR was not signed by the proper authority. He protested that Mrs. Gandhi could not be taken outside the limits of Delhi city and so, she was brought back. Nobody was clear as to where she should be kept. So, finally she was taken to the Constitution Club and detained for the night in a room. The next day morning she was released when it was found out that there was no valid ground for her detention.

The whole episode gives an inkling into the political vendetta, unleashed against her by the Janata bosses it also proves the small-mindedness with which, they sought to solve the national problems. In the absence of any dedication to the national cause or broader perspectives, what remained was only "Politicing" and incompetence in administering affairs and events.

The very fact that even formalities were not gone through. This shows with what amount of inexperience or inefficiency the Kisan leader, Sri Charan Singh wanted to lead the Home Front.

The Janata Rule

Four sizable parties - The Jana Sangh, the Bharatiya Lok Dal, the Congress(O) and the socialists merged for the specific purpose of forming an anti-Indira Front and for replacing the Congress, in power. In this process, they lost their distinct ideologies, though not their personalities. But a same political colour and culture was not developed organisational structure was also not built up. No political or personal loyalties were observed. Each and every dignitary, thought in his own way and thus no identity of cause or purpose, could be established.

Janata Fails

Formulation of Janata type of government, would have achieved something concrete, to the benefit of the nation, if only the leadership had the courage of conviction or the sagacity to think in terms of the welfare of the masses and the longer interests of the nation. Better organised Jana Sangh member with the backing of the well-disciplined RSS cadres, was forging ahead and the other constituents did not have organisational hold among, either its constituent members or on the workers at the grass root level.

Split in the Janata was inevitable; Charan Singh,with his ambitions to become the head of the nation, had to depend on Don-quixotes like Rajnarain and formed the Lok Dal. Jana Sangh had to depend on Jagjivan Ram as its leader finally. The socialists in either group got totally isolated and have lost their relevance. Proud of personalisation: Absence of well organised party system brought to the forefront personalities only, finally the leaders began to blame each other and try to gain a point over the other. The silent masses were watching the 'big tamasha' helplessly. In general, party legislators and other functionaries were not able to appreaciate or approve the style of functioning. This turned out to be a strange phenomenon. The whole matter turned out to be a family frend. Rank indiscipline and bickerings became a feature of everyday functioning.

Stab in the Back-Desai

Describing the manner in which Mr. Charan Singh (S) had brought about the fall of his Government at the centre as 'a stab in the back'. Mr. Morarji Desai, said without any further do about these matters, "I would confidently leave it to the judgement of history as to who is to be blamed for the acts of omission and commission.

What has happened in recent months would shortly lapse into history and the historians will, objectively without being affected by the dust and din of the contemporary scene, assess the part played by individuals".

Recalling that a serious issue of the dual membership was made for the first time, Mr. Desai said the "question should have been raised in the beginning of the formation of the party. RSS can by no stretch of imagination be described as a political party".

The Janata Party Chief Mr. Chandrasekhar, made it clear, that he was not quitting his post, though he had recently, thought of it. After his call on Jaya Prakash Narayan at Patna Mr. Chandrasekhar made an appeal to 'defectors' to return to the Janata. When asked, whether he was of the view, that the defectors had betrayed the people, he said that they had broken the pledge taken at Samadhi of Mahatma Gandhi that they would work for party's unity. When questioned about the desertions from the Janata party to form Janata(S) and whether they would repesent a split or defection, Mr. Chandra Sekhar shot back to the newsmen "write what you like-split or defection".

Thus the Janatas ambition could not be fulfilled. Broad national perspectives were not given due consideration and they were set aside, conveniently individual clashes reigned over all other considerations. It was a show of petty mindedness and lack of vision.

Janatas Achievements and Inadequacies

Even though Janata entered the third year in office, Mr. Desai and his colleagues could not devote more purposefully to essential task of reestablishing its credentials for providing the country with a stable government. Despite its comfortable majority in the Lok Sabha, the party was not sure whether it would remain in power for a full term of 5 years, with all the internal rivalries and contradictions.

The Janata bosses, who highlighted the mistakes of Mrs. Indira Gandhi, during emergency could not realise that reshaping and revitaling the nation is of paramount importance. They could not even keep the large party interests, above the lot of factional policies. Mr. Morarji's Stewardship of the government, had been singularly in holding the Janata constituents together, in the face of their running factional fights. After the first flush of enthusiasm, they had no direction, whatsoever, they failed miserably in moulding the destiny of the nation.

Not only the critics, even the admirers can look upon the Janata crisis, primarily, as a crisis of identity. The anti-emergency vote could not give it a distinct character or coherent philosophy to continue in government. The party's credibility in the eye of the people had been declining step by step. Morarji could not offer effective alternatives to the so-called monumental follies of Indira Government.

Morarji's rigidity and self-righteousness could not make him a strong man. He had not endeared himself even to his well-wishers, who expected better performance from him.

Finally, Desai had to bow to pressure and resign, after stubbornly resisting all the repeated pleas of his senior colleages to step down and save the government.

'The' most funniest part of the whole story is the incapability of the Janata Government in taking a decision, even after receipt of the Shah Commission's report. Legal luminaries were consulted and finally nothing came out and the whole thing turned out to the simply a force'.

Apart from this enquiry, the following utterances were made by a senior judge of the Supreme Court Sri Hegde.

Mr. Hegde, who resigned following supersession in the appointment of new Chief Justice said that the wrong done to the independence of the Judiciary and the cause of democracy is very serious and that the people's confidence in the independence of Judiciary is shaken.

Another charge levelled against Indiraji was that her agents were trying to build up a case against him, since her election appeal. He also came out with a proposal that "judges should be selected by an Independent Agency and not by Government".

Another kaleidoscopic drama of succession of power from Morarji, to Charan Singh was spectacular and the wonderful strategy played by the Congress (I) and its leader is remarkable. The way Mr. Charan Singh installed himself in office as Prime Minister, is the low comedy packed with surprises, and his supporters keeping their fingers crossed and hoping for the best on the vigilant manoeuvres of the rival Janata leaders to outlist them, is noteworthy. With the Congress (U) joining the Ministry, the picture is complete. The way the Congress (I) party had withdrawn support to Charan Singh's Ministry is another turn and Mrs. Gandhi's role in capably handling the affairs during this period adds another feather to her cap.

Mrs. Gandhi Emerged as the Saviour of the Nation

The way Mr. N. Sanjeeva Reddy, announced the mid-term poll and averted the political crisis facing the country is also remarkable and as a keeper of the conscience of the nation, he proformed his sacred duty. Mrs. Gandhi finally emerged as the saviour of the nation. Landslide victory of her party in 1980 elections paved the way for the glorious come back of Mrs. Gandhi and she, at the helm of affairs was destined to take the nation on the right path. The events in Delhi left all parties confused and divided. The only beneficiary was the Congress (I). Mrs. Gandhi's strategy was clear. She took interest in dismanlting the Desai Government and had it replaced by a new set-up, which, she knew, very well, would not lost long. Therefore, she had to throw the Congress (I) weight behind Charan Singh.

Azamgarh and two earlier elections in UP have caused tremor in the political circles of the country. There was a descent in the popularity graph of Janata Party. The victory of Mrs. Gandhi's candidates demoralised the Janata leaders.

Mrs. Gandhi's hectic campaign in Azamgarh was a significant factor. She addressed scores of well attended meetings. The poorer sections and women folk attended in large numbers. A 'frail woman', who was sought to be sent to jail by the Janata bosses, without power could attract crowds. Her appeal to the uncommitted rural electorate had an impact and her presence worked sympathy in them.

If at all, people were unhappy with the Janata, they would have for Mr. Chandrajit Yadav, the Congress candidate, who had earlier represented this seat he had, no doubt wide contacts and popularity and also had a strong cadre for him. Instead, a rank outsider, Mrs. Mohsina Kidwai, was elected by the Azamgarh electorate in perference to Mr. Yadav. If it has to be explained in terms of an expression against Yadavs (The Janata Party candidate - also an Yadav was 77 years old Mr. Ram Bachan Yadav).

To put it in one sentence, the defeat of the Janata candidates in the bye-elections in UP had shaken the party leadership. Internal quarrels, caste feelings, poor administrative record have added to make the political situation more unstable.

One of the biggest handicaps of the Janata Party was the absence of any organisation at the district or lower level. There was a total vacuum, with the former constituents winding up their frame work. No clear cut policy or plan worked out to either implement cherished goals or to fight elections. The defeat in the by elections also, did not induce any serious thinking within the Janata Party.

Morarji on BBC

The Prime Minister, Mr. Morarji Desai, on a visit to UK, while speaking in an interview on BBC, said that violent disturbances and tensions in India were not new factors but were there for many years. They were suppressed forcibly and no papers published them. The sharply rising phenomenon of rising disturbances "is a reaction from the silence of the grave which took place during emergency for nearly two years". When asked whether the disturbances were politically inspired, Mr. Morarji said "many of them were politically inspired".

On the question of launching prosecution against Mrs. Gandhi, for the misuse of power personally, he said, he did not want to be vindictive but the process of law will be there and that will not be compromised in any manner. Pointing out that Mrs. Gandhi", was the Janata Governments main opponent, Mr. Desai further mentioned that he was doubtful about her coming back to power as easily or quickly as is made out by some on account of her win in bye-elections.

"Her victory will also be a danger to democracy", he defined.

About Soviet involvement in Africa, Mr. Desai said that it was not just a question of one country dabbling in other people's affairs; it was a habit of the superpowers, which does not disappear quickly.

When asked about the statement by the leader of the then Tory party, Mrs. Margaret Thatcher that the future Tory Government would like to orastically reduce the number of coloured immigrants entering Britain, Mr. Desai said any form of discrimination should be condemned.

Interview to Voice of America

In an interview to Voice of America, on the eve of Mr. Desai's visit to UK, the Indian Ambassador to US, Mr. N.A. Palkhivala expressed his belief that the PM's visit was politically significant and the President Carter generally shared with Desai, common ideals, because, both have faith in God.

On Relations with China

As regards relation with China, Mr. Morarji Desai said that he was not worried about the slow progress in the normalisation of relations between India and China.

His Views on Domestic Issues

Answering questions on domestic issues, Mr. Morarji said if the atmosphere of violence grew in the country, the Government might have to consider reasuming detention powers. On prohibition, he said that Government had the right to limit freedom in the interests of the larger sections of society. Asked if he would give his moral support against "suppression of human rights" in the Soviet Union, he said his principle was not to interfere in any country".

On Relation with Pakistan

When asked whether he would make an appeal, on humanitarian grounds, to spare the life of Bhutto, Mr. Morarji said that he could not sit in judgement over a Government's action in its own country according to their Law. "They also asked me about Mrs. Gandhi. I said I will not hang anybody".

The half hour press conference, held in London with correspondents arguing with each other and the Prime Minister sticking to his right to counter - question newsmen, threw much light on his personality and his ideology dealing with several matters.

Role of JP on Vital Issues

JP's advice was sought on vital issues. The party president, Mr. Chandra Sekhar, who called on Jayaprakash Narayan, sought his advice on broad national issues, alongwith Madhu Limaye. The party chief said that they would try to implement Mr. Narayan's ideas on the problems of involvement of people in developmental works, economic problems, local interest in some places, unemployment. But he said, he never sought the advice of Mr. Narayan on party affairs, stating that Mr. Narayan was above party politics. Regretting some violent incidents in Bihar, he said that Janata Party believed in and committed to Panchayat Raj and the process had to be completed soon.

7

Pre-emergency Days and Situation in India

In a political situation cynically identified by its intrigues, nefarious deals and opportunities it was becoming increasingly difficult to serve the rural masses, rising unemployment, industrial closures, inflation, monopoly super-profits demanding further burdens on an already impoverished people, was the common scene in India.

There was mounting opposition from all corners.

The left opposition, the socialist party, the CPI (M) and the CPI (ML) though divided from each other sought to disrupt the functioning of Government machinery. There was mass discontent and indiscipline everywhere.

(1) J.P. Narayan advocated a return to economic and political Gandhianism, identifying centralisation and corruption as the source of the people's woes. In fact, these two factors could be simply grasped, as they were indent,and there was a clarion call against the so called "misrule". JP called his movement as a "total revolution". There was a procession in Delhi on March 6,1975, with Singh, Atal Bihari Vajpayee, Badal, Chandra Sekhar and many other leaders. Amongst the hundreds of thousands of marchers, there were RSS volunteers and the Jana Sangh. In fact they were the slogan makes; 'Desh ka Neta' ? Jaya Prakash. Andhera Ka Roshan - Jaya Prakash! Sat Mil Ke Bolo - Jaya Prakash?- Any one gifted with a little foresight could have seen the shape of things to come. Indira Gandhi and JP, who should have been on the same side, fighting the fascist forces, lifting their head, lose at logger heads and those busy destroying each other. What would be the outcome of this conflict ? It would be nothing but chaos and the only beneficiaries would be communal forces.

JP's call for "total revolution" had richly contributed to a sorrowful state of affairs.

JP, who was in his sick bed, rose to lead the Janata to victory and he was also acclaimed as the Lok Nayak and the saviour of the nation.

But the Janata conglomeration proved to be a total failure. It was proved beyond doubt.

I do not know how history will judge J.P. But one thing is clear, the people, who now heaped adjectives on J.P., did not think of him before they, now, tried to exploit him, simply no doubt. They called him "confused" muddle headed, indecisive, inconsequential and reactory. He is undoubtedly a misser of buses. He is a good man, an honest man, an able man and a brave man. But leadership was thrust on him, by men, who were neither honest, nor able or straight forward to become leaders themselves by fair means. His qualities were high-lighted, not out of regard or affection for him - but to achieve their selfish ends.

JP. was not a pacifist. He was a *krantikari* and he did not believe in 'Ahimsa' as a "nation-wide struggle" from June 1975, to press for Mrs. Gandhi's resignation in view of her failure to get 'unconditional stay' of the operation of the Allahabad Court's verdict, setting aside her election.

Representatives of Congress(O), Jana Sangh, Bharatiya Lok Dal, Socialist Party and Akali Dal, held a meeting and decided to start 'Quit India' stir from June 29th 1975. Lok Nayak, Mr. Jaya Prakash Narayan also was present.

They set up a Lok Sangharsha Samiti (People's Action Committee) under the chairmanship of Morarji Desai, to conduct the movement all over the country. Representatives of CPM and DMK were also present at this historical meeting but Mr. Mehta, President, Congress(O) said that they would convey their formal association with the movement, some time later.

Mr. Mehta announced action programme also for the first week beginning with 29th June. Opposition parties would hold rallies and mass meetings at the state and district headquarters upto July 6th, to educate public about the current situation. Leaders would address meetings. Prime Ministers to hold demonstration everyday from June 29 to July 7, to press resignation demand, Mr. Mehta said.

All opposition members of Parliament including those of CPI, met on July 6, to decide future course of action, to be adopted by them on the Parliament Front.

AICC (O) headquarters at Jantar Mantar Road, would be the headquarters of the Samiti and Nanaji Deshmukh, (Jan Sangh leader) would be its secretary and Mr. Ashok Mehta, the treasurer.

Mr. Mehta expressed the hope that people would "overhelmingly" respond to their movement.

Complaining against what he described as "deliberate, conscious and despicable" efforts on the part of the government to exploit TV and AIR to brainwash the people, Mr. Mehta added this would be opposed.

Mr. L.K. Advani, the Jana Sangh President speaking at Bangalore, suggested that if the president failed to summon the monsoon session of Parliament, opposition members should assemble and discuss about the serious 'political and Constitutional crisis' arising out of decisions of Allahabad High Court and Supreme Court. He demanded that the President should summon Parliament since a crippled Prime Minister could not paralyse the Parliament.

Sarvodaya Leader appealed to the Chief Justice of India, Mr. A.N. Ray that he himself should not hear Prime Minister Indira Gandhi's appeal against the Allahabad High Court verdict. Addressing a mass rally organised by the five non - CPI opposition parties, he made it clear that he was advancing this plea not due to lack of faith in Mr. Ray or his impartiality. Since Mr. Ray became Chief Justice after the government had superseeded three senior judges, people might entertain doubts even if Mr. Ray did justice.

Further, Mr. Narayan said that he was making this appeal to Mr. Ray 'as an ordinary' citizen of India. In his 80 minute speech, punctuated with repeated cheers, Mr. Narayan said if Mrs. Gandhi broke the convention of convening the Parliament, it would amount to her going the fascist way step by step. 'Only awakened public opinion can save the country from this threat' he said and added "Mrs. Gandhi must realise India is neither Bangladesh nor Pakistan where such developments would be tolerated".

Mr. Narayan said, it was all the more necessary for Mrs. Gandhi, to lay down office after the Supreme Court's rejection of her plea.

He asked the people, to look beyond declaring the resignation of Mrs. Gandhi. They had to prepare themselves for the Lok Sabha election and ensure that the Congress should not come to power again.

He praised the Young Turks for their stand in the given situation and expressed surprise as to why senior Congress leaders like

Jagjivan Ram and Y.B. Charan are keeping quiet, why were they afraid of Mrs. Gandhi was she a tigress? Silence at this moment is a disservice to the nation as well as party, he added.

Mr. Narayan "deliberately" reiterated his appeal to the police armed forces and other Government employees not to obey the "illegal and immoral"order of the Government and challenged. The then Home Minister (Sri Brahmananda Reddy) to try him for his treason. "The day JP turns traitor, there will hardly be any patriot left in the country" he remarked angrily.

Referring to the FICCI resolution urging Mrs. Gandhi to continue in office, he said that the "Indian Capitalism" stood solidly behind Mrs. Gandhi, to protect her. But she had temerity to accuse others of being reactionaries. This exactly was the tactics of "Goebbels" he added.

The stronger words he used in criticising Mrs. Gandhi and the CPP, only show with how much of venom, he wanted to preach people to rebel and how much of hatred he wanted to dispel.

I had an occasion to listen to Mr. Jaya Prakash Narayan, when I was a student at Madras. We attended a meeting held in Sarojini Devi Hall in the year 1956. He had come to Madras to speak on Gandhi Jayanti celebrations. In very soft spoken words, he spoke by Freedom Struggle and also "socialism". Nobody could get a clear policy of his socialism by his words. I doubt, whether he himself had any clear picture about his socialistic ideas. He calls it "total emolution".

Mr. Jaya Prakash, with his stature, as a patriot, could not contribute substantially to the ideology of Congress at anytime. Nor could he take any active part in any programme and prove his dedication to the nation. He remained a silent spectator or an 'easy-chair' politician throughout his life. But his words could have some considerable impact on the masses, by virtue of his previous image.

His antagonism towards Indira's rule seems to be purely on personal grounds and ! do not know what was his goal opinion in differing with her or what his alternatives were ? He never made himself clear to the people. Later his utterances could not prove an alternative to the Congress Government and the conglomeration of parties, could not rule the Janata in the Janata type of way. Jaya Prakash's choice of the leader also proved amply that he was a mere tool in the hands of a few and there was no democracy either in the style of functioning of the Janata Government or in the conduct of party bosses.

After the Allahabad Court's judgement and the conditional stay of the Supreme Court, there was so much of tension in the air and among the member of Parliament and journalists. There were heated discussion, arguments. Everywhere Mr. Krishna Aiyars 23 - page order did not allow Mrs. Gandhi either to vote or to draw allowances. Reading in between the lines Mr. Kuldeep Nayar a noted journalist (*Indian Express* dt: 26th June 1975) said that "a conditional stay is a cloud which is bound to cast its shadow on the Office of Prime Minister. It is a ability with which Mrs. Gandhi will have to live".

Another funny allegation of Mr. Nayar is like this, "the fact that a party which depends on the landed aristocracy to 'catch' votes and collect funds for elections only talks of progressive steps. Quoting the World Bank's report that the Land Reform have been mainly on paper Mr. Nayar points out that "it is an open secret that every economic policy or decision has a price tag". This shows the double pronged propaganda carried on in the country at that time. On the one hand, she is branded as a supporter of landed aristocracy and on the other hand, she was criticised as a torch enemy of landed aristocracy and a friend of the poorer masses.

Referring to an editorial in a local newspaper that "still there is time for her to resign with grace and dignity" he said, "If she goes now, she will do so without grace and dignity".

Mr. Narayan said he had been looking for an opportunity for an All India Struggle and were was the one as the issue concerned the whole country.

He called upon the people to gherao the Information Minister for allowing AIR, to do "personal propaganda" for Mrs. Gandhi.

Is it not possible for the people to challenge the partisan policy of AIR and take steps to paralyse its functioning, until it changed this policy", Mr. Narayan asked.

The above utterances would give an insight into the mind of JP. The tone in which Sri Jaya Prakash instigated the people and the parties is clear.

But Mrs. Gandhi pointed out that the 'Indira Hatao' campaign started by the opposition parties, was not something started only after the Allahabad judgement. They had been making sustained attempt since 1969 to dislodge her because she took to a programme to bring about radical socio-economic changes.

Addressing a mammoth rally organised by AICC, in which lakhs of people parties participated, Mrs. Gandhi declared amidst thunderous cheers that she would continue to serve the country "till the last breathe of her life".

The opposition attempts to get rid of her by "fair or foul means" were the product of a deep political conspiracy involving powerful internal and external forces, she said and also added there was no question of any deviation from the chosen path of Congress Socialism. The whole attack on her by the vested interests was clearly aimed at frustrating her policies.

She strongly denounced the opposition attempts to exaggerate the difficulties and be little her achievements, by fomenting an atmosphere of pessimism.

Expressing that there was so much of latitude for free expression in India to the opposition and to the press in India with all its traditions, she said that nothing was done to suppress dissent. Many foreign leaders were surprised at the freedom allowed and the way she was abused day in and day out was a clean proof of such freedom.

In her view, this freedom was being grossly abused, not only to run her down as an individual but also to demigrate the office of Prime Minister even at the cost of lowering the country's dignity and reputation.

At the international level, the significant achievements of her Government, have secured for India an honoured place in the commity of nations.

The Congress Parliamentary Party, with unanimity, expressed its "fullest faith and confidence" her leadership and affirmed the view that "her continued leadership is indispensable for the nation".

Referring to this support of the CPP to Mrs. Gandhi, Mr. Jaya Prakash Narayan said the point at issue was not whether Congress MP's had faith in Mrs. Gandhi's leadership but whether there was rule of law in the country and whether it applied to all equally high or low. The CPP's resolution was another instance of "unabashed political immorality"of the Congress leadership and of its "mischievous attempt" to "mislead the people", he added.

Jaya Prakash Narayan also said that Mrs. Gandhi "must go" as Prime Minister as her rule had ruined the country's economy as well as its public and political life. "Her continuance in office will debase further not only the political coinage but also everything else that the ordinary Indian citizen still holds dear". She had degraded the values for which "Swaraj" was fought and won at so much cost. He called for a dignified and effective compaign of mass education so that the cherished values of life and our democratic institutions were saved from "fascistic machinations".

His line up argument was that the mass media under the control of Congress and carried on "Goebbells Propaganda" to mislead people, to the great detriment of democracy.

Indira - Symbol of Resurgent India

It was felt to be a great tragedy of national magnitude if Mrs. Gandhi were today to lay down office. The Chief Ministers of Congress ruled states met the President and presented a memorandum that "Mrs.Gandhi symbolises in herself the resurgent India and the aspirations of the people; particularly the poorer masses and the minorities. When the country is passing through severe economic strain, when communal, subversive, divisive and disruptive forces are out to create conditions of chaos and confusion and when there are threats of external aggression by forces hostile to us, the nation needs her leadership, and guidance.

Her stepping down from the office of Prime Ministership, would bring about conditions of instability not only at the national level but also in various states".

Therefore, Mrs. Gandhi must and should continue as the Prime Minister of India, in the interests of the nation, they felt. The Congress has had the privilege of her leadership to guide the destiny of the nation. In fact, she was destined to lead the country in her own way. Indira made it very clear on several occasions.

Speaking in the Congress Parliamentary Party meeting she said she would not oblige the opposition by resigning and giving up the fight for the implementation of the party programmes in the midst of present crisis facing the Indian people. Addressing the assembled MPs, she said in a raising voice. "It does not matter what happens to me but it does matter what happens to the Indian people". Her response to the crisis would not depend on what the opposition wanted her to do or say but on what her Congress party and people wanted her to do.

This shows, with what amount of identification with the cherished goals of her party, she had been working.

A national emergency was proclaimed by the President of India on 27th June 1975, in the face of a "deep and widespread conspiracy" that had been brewing from a long time in the country, in the words of Mrs. Gandhi. In a speech addressed to the Nation, Mrs. Gandhi said that "the President had to resort to this extraordinary step because the nation's integrity demanded firm action". A situation which weakened the capacity of the National Government to act decisively inside was bound to encourage dangers from outside". The forces of disruption in the country by preventing duly elected Governments from functioning. This situation was watched with utmost patience for long. No Government can allow the country's stability imperilled". After a hurriedly summoned cabinet meeting at 6 A.M. in the Prime Minister's residence, the president issued the proclamation under Article 352 (1) of the Constitution declaring that "a grave emergency exists whereby the security of India is threatened by internal disturbances".

A number of preventive arrests were made by the central and state governments.The centre directed the state governments Union Territories to use the emergency powers for the maintenance of law and order and for keeping up the unity of the nation.

Views and Comments

Emergency was declared in India twice before. Once in 1962 and 1971, following external aggression. But the emergency of 1975 was proclaimed to meet a threat to the internal security of the country.

People at large hailed the emergency, as the advent of a new era in national life and this should be utilised to bring about an atmosphere of self-discipline; all people would join in a common endeavour to fulfil the aspirations of the masses.

Relentring the charge that she was a fascist, Mrs. Gandhi asked which leader would have tolerated so long. "The consistent compaign of falsehood, columny and violence". Citing the utterances of Sri Jayaprakash Narayan and Sri M.R. Masani, soliciting intervention of the army to save democracy in India, Mrs. Gandhi said "The opposition used to hear its own voice and that of a few newspapers and imagine it to be the voice of the people".

Mrs. Gandhi said "that democracy demanded self-restraint on the part of everybody, when individuals or groups did not learn to exercise self-restraint, Constitution had to tell them where to stop".

She described that emergency created an atmosphere where "it is easier to implement, what we wanted to do".

Indira Gandhi's Thesis for Building up a New Era

Even before the proclamation of Emergency, Indiraji was operating an anti-inflationary strategy and measures, which required some extraordinary will power such as price fixation for paddy in 1979 and wheat in 1975, in spite of the opposition of chief ministers of some states and political parties.

She was asked (Aug. 25) "What do you think, your emergency has achieved that could not have been achieved in a less radical manner ? Her reply was The people have had a shock. And they have realised that they have certain obligations towards the nation towards themselves because this is not forms, for the Government. It is for themselves....So, this new feeling and it is even enthusiasm, it is not just discipline. This can involve people and therefore it is a very important slip in democracy- the participation of people at all levels The Big Business need fear. The common people just need a feeling of involvement and participation", "creative people have nothing to fear".

The second point in her strategy was to define three objectives, which "should command general acceptance, cutting across conventional party lines"(July 13, letter to Chief Ministers, July 22 Lok Sabha etc.)

The third point in her strategy was to squarely locate responsibility on the Chief Ministers for establishing credibility of our political and administrative structure in the eyes of underprivileged sections (July 13) stems have been specifically listed for holding the states and the centre accountable.

The fourth and purposive primary element in the strategy was "to restructure attitudes of responsibility to the nation and self-discipline for building a new India and involvement of all sections of people in identified formidable tasks (For example rural poverty for the bureaucracy) as well as complex and small tasks for all sections of the people.

Indiraji, after receiving the functioning and capability of the administrative structure and public services, could catagorise, three primary gaps. Gap 1 - The sectoral, departmental planning and administration or management have been identified as anti-growth factor. Gap 2 - The attitude gap in the public services. Gap 3 - Management of personal policies.

She prescribed the need for a new concept of over all management (for example, making the poor productive, presentation and integrated development of basic resources like land, forest, water.

In her own words, this concept as well as the role of public services and personal policies mainly constitute the main element in her implementation strategy.

Another element mobilisation of the central government and its agencies including the public and nationalised sectors. Another one is the use of emergency powers under the Constitution for

(a) presenting roles of chief secretaries in the matter of centre-state relations and follow-up of objectives and implementation of economic programmes.

(b) Chief secretaries role regarding massive investment sectors like irrigation and power.

(c) Chief secretaries role for controlling misuse of powers and corruption.

Talking of human resources, she said "the country needed not only increasing capacity but making maximum use of human resources. In this task, labour relations and labour participation played an important role. There were important to not merely to keep labour quiet, but because it was only when a person felt involved and realised his own role in fighting the difficulties, which the country faces, that he did a better job"."In our system, economic growth could not be achieved and sustained unless we convinced our people that we were also fighting for social justice. The workers should not be regarded merely as production units, but as human beings. That was really the purpose behind the idea of greater participation of workers.

Before emergency during a period years, Government had attempted to lay down priorities to simplify procedures. Speaking on this subject, Indiraji said "Own accent should be on efficiency in the use of resources - financial, material and human. This is no time for slackerers or inefficiency in any sector of national life. Industry can no longer insist on a return to the easy days of earlier....years Excellence does not imply extranagance .... Among other things the reduction of costs calls for the curbing of the present tendency to pass off-expenditure on personal consumption as business expenses. This practice is at the root of the conspicuous consumption which has brought the business community into some disrepute.

Another strong point of her strategy was to make a cautious attempt (i) to sift elite-level Congress party members, who may not be responsive to or be working against the economic programme and (ii) to locate elements who are committed to the economic programme and place them in implementation or follow-up official-cum-non-official groups down to the block level.

When prime Minister was questioned if there was any guarantee that the 20-point programme, would be implemented, she said, "we are trying harder and there is a new spirit of discipline and morale .... We have begun doing things in right earnest".

R.K. Karanjia, Editor, BLITZ, presented an analysis that the Congress party was ill-equipped ideologically and politically and those were too many lobbies representing vested interests like landlords, industrialists, trading classes. It had been dragging its feet, "what is being done to shake up the party and give it a new orientation", her answer was "The Congress does have landlords, industrialists and traders, but it has also a large number of industrial workers, artisans, kisans, landless labourers, teachers, lawyers and doctors. I mean, we have all sections and this is the strength of the Congress. It has been so broad based. There are conflicts and there are obstructions, but I think we just have to meet the situation.

She was asked to mention the agency for implementation. The agrarian part of the 20-point programme, which deals with the enforcement of land ceiling distribution of surplus land and house sites, abolition of bonded labour, mitigation of rural indebtedness, fixation of minimum wages for cultural, labourers, implies a versitable rural revolution but a revolution requires an effective agency. What is the agency which will implement this project ?.

Prime Minister replied "This programme involves the entire central government, the state governments bureaucracy as well as every agency which the government has, I do not think there can be any new agency".

"We do want, however and are trying to have far greater people's involvement, popular participation (*Blitz,* Aug. 23).

"We chiefly hope that the people will get a sense of responsibility, so far they had been acting irresponsibly because the opposition kept on saying all the time, 'Government does not do this'. But the Government cannot do everything. It can only guide, the things have to be done by the people themselves." The day the emergency was declared, suddenly the people did feel that it was their responsibility and they had to do something.

"We want to create an atmosphere where the whole public provides a watch dog committee and gets involved, committed, in what is happening. The people of the village, whether they are officials or the local people know, what are the wrongs. What has to be righted or what is being done well they make the best watch dog committee.

8

Political Situation in India from 1967-76: Some Major Events

Lal Bahadur Sastri invited Indiraji to join his cabinet. She was reluctant to join. She wanted to leave political field and take up social service. "But Sastry was particular of her joining and so tried to convince her to take up ministerial post. At last, after much persuasion, he could convince her.

He knew pretty well that she was in touch with the heads of all nations, and so she would be able to serve better if she was a member of the cabinet. Because, he never visited any foreign country, Sastriji felt that she would be of great help to him.

He offered her the Foreign Affairs ministry. But she did not agree. She chose the Information and Broadcasting Ministry at last.

Soon after she took over as minister of Information and Broadcasting, she left Teen Murty Bhavan and came to live in No.1, Safdarjung Road.

She improved her contacts with the people who ever came to her, she was developing nearness and was listening to them patiently.

They used to place before her several issues confronting the nation. She was carefully passing on, all of them to the government for their solution. That is why people began to like her.

As Information and Broadcasting Minister, she remodelled the whole department.

Unless radio and television are improved, they cannot reach the uneducated millions and they cannot be made aware of their problems, she felt.

Till she became the minister of the department, radio was only the mouth piece of the government. But later on, it was made an instrument for the use of the opposition parties also.

As Minister, she visited foreign countries twice. In Russia, after Kruschev, Kosigin came to power and he also declared that their country would maintain friendly relations with India, as in the part and invited Indiraji to visit their country.

After her return from Russia, Indira Gandhi, went to America to participate in the inaugural celebration of Jawaharlal's memorial.

In 1965, when Commonwealth Prime Minister's conference was held in London, Sastriji did not attend. He felt, it is better if Indira attends such a conference, as she had attended several such conferences along with her father, discussion was held on this topic and finally, and decided that a delegation consisting of T.T. Krishnamachari and Indira, should go to London.

When she was in London, several old friends met her and she revised their contact with them.

As Minister Information and Broadcasting, she made radio sets available to people at cheaper rates and hours of working in the day were also increased.

But in no time, she could detect that Sastri was not putting Nehru's politics into practice. During his rule, the employees took the upper hand.

The economic resolution passed in the Durgapur Congress, she supported and could win the favour of all Congress workers. She realised in no time, that Nehru's politics were set aside and she was weak, she would be subservient to him, Kamaraj Thought.

Morarji was adamant. So contest was inevitable.

When Kamaraj declared that Indira would be the next Prime Minister, she felt astonished.

Contest was held on 16th Jan 1966, for the election of the Congress Parliamentary Party. Morarji fought tooth and nail to win the support of many. There was much of propaganda and lobbying.

It was also felt that during Nehru's time, power went into the hands of Chief Ministers of states. So, five kinds of people, namely, the chief ministers, the papers, local leaders state Congress committee and people nearer to Nehru supported Indiraji.

Everyone was anxiously waiting for the result. Many were sitting before the television sets and watching. Some were questioning her about Indira's assessment of the situation. Her only answer was "cannot say so early". One asked her "who will be Prime Minister, is it a male or female"? her reply was "it is not important, whether it is male or female, but who is contesting".

What about your opinion on "woman becoming a Prime Minister representing 48 crores of people", she said "difficult to say".

Indiraji left the decision to the will of the people concerned, whereas Morarji met every Parliament member and was determined to win at any cost.

On the previous day to the elections, Kamaraj went to Morarji's house and made an appeal to him not to contest". But Morarji said "I will surely win" why should I withdraw myself from the contest ? what is the fault I committed ? In what way, I am inferior to her ?

"I am contesting as per democratic procedure. What else is there" he questioned.

Indira Gandhiji said"I am not afraid of winning or losing the contest".

On the day of the contest, she visited Samadhi of Gandhi at Raj ghat, went to Shantivan of Pandit Nehru and went to her house, did 'namskar' to her mother. She remembered some of the words her father wrote to her from jail "Be Bold! All matters will take care of themselves! If you are bold, you will be able to do anything. Nothing will stand as a stumbling block to you".

She entered the Parliament House with some determined thoughts. It was 10.40 a.m. The central hall was fully packed with photographers, press persons, television personnel and some thousands of prominent people.

She straight away went to Morarji Desai and shook hands with him. Gallaries were full. All the 526 Parliament members out of 550 of the Congress Parliament were present. The whole situation was tense.

People standing outside the Parliament House were guessing in their own way.

At 11 O' clock sharp, on the advice of Kamaraj, Hanumanthayya, the Chief Minister of Karnataka proposed Morarji's name and a member of Rajasthan by name Tikaram Paliwal supported him. Indira's name was proposed by the acting Prime Minister, Sri Nanda and her name was supported by Sri Neelam Sanjeeva Reddy.

Nothing had to take place.

At that time, Sri Diwan Chamanlal, a member of Rajya Sabha made an appeal to Morarji to withdraw from the contest to facilitate election unopposed.

Supporters of Morarji, began to shout loudly.

By 1 O'clock voting was completed. Ballot Box was kept before Kamaraj for counting. Y.B. Chawan asked Satyanarayana Sinha to sing a song or tell a story to break the silence. Sinha laughtingly said"nobody causing when every one is hungry".

It was 3 O'clock, Returning Officer, Sri. G.S. Pathak, "I declared Smt. Gandhi got elected". Indira got 355 votes and Morarji 169 votes. "She could win with thumping majority and the country was hers".

As soon as this was heard by people after the announcement of Mr. Pathak, they began to shout with Joy. Indira's neck was full with flower garlands. Members came foreword to grant her. Indira walked, from the midst of the crowd, to Morarji to take his blessings.

Afterwords, she walked to the platform, wherefrom Nehru was speaking all these years and spoke for a while.

She went home amidst big crowd and people throged her house also.

When Narayana Menon came to greet her, she cited the poem by Robert Frost which he wrote on "a person not wanting to be a ruler".

King said to his son thus
"This is enough for me; This kingdom is yours afterwards
I am leaving by tonight
Lo Receive this crown".

The son not knowing what to do, did not receive that crown - This was the poem.

On 24th January 1966, Indira Priyadarsini took oath as Prime Minister of India in Rashtrapathi Bhavan, at 2.15 p.m. Thus she became the head of the largest democracy in the world.

A woman becoming a Prime Minister for a country like India, was a matter of shock and surprise for many in the world.

Gaurdian, a British newspaper wrote "In history, no woman could shoulder such responsibilities. A Democratic country like India somp such power to any woman". "She has shrewd intellect. Good moral courage. It only she could show administrative capability many supremacy in the world, would become pale" the paper wrote.

Pravda, the communist newspaper in Russia, wrote "she is Nehru's daughter. So, his talent would be present in her also". Russian Prime Minister Kosigin said "In Soviet Union, all respect you. You are an important person among the political leaders of India. I believe you will follow the same policies of Nehru" and sent a message.

On 26th January she spoke over the All India Radio, addressing the people as follows.

"I will humbly try to solve the problems confronting us. The policies of Gandhi and Nehru are able to give us the necessary moral courage. It was proved many times that India is great.

Coming months are difficult for us. We have to face many problems and solve them immediately. Because of drought conditions, there is famine in many of the states. We have to stand by those people.

When we are less in our food production, it is inevitable we have to depend on other countries. Then they will try to put some conditions and make us subservient. To come out of this situation, we have to increase our food production.

We do not want war. We want peace. Avoiding the war, we have to wage war on poverty. We have to declare war on illiteracy, education and we have to provide food, clothing, shelter, education and health for all people.

Those who are economically weak, those who are in need of social justice, they are in my mind. To protect them and to better their conditions, I will try my best.

I am tied down to democracy, secularism, planned development, social welfare and good relations between the countries.

Let us have faith in our future and walk forward. Let us declare that we have the skill to build our bright future. We are all sharers in this great task. Let us prove ourselves that we are worthy citizens of a great country".

This talk of her over the radio, moved the entire nation.

When Indira Gandhi was elected, Kamaraj said one word. "This election is only temporary. We have to elect the Prime Minister once again after elections".

So as to win in 1967 elections with great majority, Kamaraj wanted Indira Gandhi to be the Prime Minister temporarly that is only a few months. It was only temporary arrangement, he felt perhaps, (till the elections of 1967).

But Indira could understand his intentions. She wanted to take drastic steps and to win the hearts of people.

She also felt that those Congress leaders who could vote for her many turn out to be dangerous to her. In the guise of givings suggestions, they brought pressure on her. But she never yielded to them. To run administration itself was a big problem for her because of their old policies. She could not proceed further.

As soon as Indiraji became Prime Minister, she had to implement Tashkent declaration, opposition parties insisted that our army should not leave places occupied. There was much of propaganda that Tashkent Declaration is harmful to the country "Indiraji could withstand all this criticism and could implement Tashkent declaration and fulfill all the conditions.

Because of the war, the economic condition of the country deteriorated. Production of foodstuffs got lessoned.

America stopped all help, when there was war between India and Pakistan. This caused much harm to the country. Indiraji went and met Johnson. She could convince him about the necessisity of help to India. She could convince the senators of America. She could get supply of food grains to India. That way, the problem of food supply and to same extent, economic problem, she could solve.

Because of the language problem there was trouble between the Sikhs and Hindus in Punjab, It reached upto Delhi and it increased day by day creating havoc. Indira Gandhi went to Chandni Chowk and called both the parties and could convince them that such quarrels are not good for anybody. She came to the office and immediately decided to divide Punjab into two different states and thus the problems of the state were solved and peace was restored.

There was anti-Hindi agitation in Tamil Nadu. Indira Gandhi saw that English speech on the Independence Day was translated into Tamil and again broadcast over the radio.

There was famine in West Bengal. Blackmarketeers created more problems and food grains were hoarded in black markets. Leftists organised strikes, Bands and the city was in misery. Indira Gandhi went to Calcutta, convened meeting with both the parties and restored peace and harmony.

She toured NE India, held discussions with Naga leaders and restored normalcy.

She went to Britain, France and Mosco and improved relations with them.

Indira Gandhi became a Prime Minister when India was facing lot of problems. Her own people, belonging to her own party did not cooperate with her and did not encourage her policies.

State Governments were not working as per the wishes of people. There was rampant corruption.

There was anti-Congress feeling among the people. It was very difficult for her to get the support of her partymen.

There were drought conditions in the second year also. Because the states had more freedom, it was not possible to take out food-grains from one state to another. She had to bring wheat supplies from America, Canada and Australia and had to save the country from famine.

Those who supported Morarji, during the time of her election, started propaganda that Congress did a blunder in electing her. Because she received help of 500 million dollars leftists criticised her that she was mortgaging the country to America. Above all, the very leader, who favoured her election, turned out to be against her. Her independent spirit, he could not appreciate. He expected that she would be a pawn in her hands. But, when she began to take independent decisions and assert her position, he got angry.

With Rajagopalachari's encouragement, Swatantra Party was formed. They opposed the policy of collective forming. Dravida Munnetra Kazagam a regional party became strong and they started fighting against Hindi.

Communists got divided into two different units. She supported Moscow where as the other supported China.

There were many serious problems in the country. Famine on the one hand, hunger on the other hand, were two major problems, facing the country, there were language differences between the states. There were opposition movements in hilly areas like Assam. Planning was not in accordance with actual auditors. There was slackness in running of the industries. There was unemployment.

Indira Gandhi had to struggle hard to solve the problems. Because there was no cooperation from the party bosses and the members of the ministry, she could not solve them. But, she decided to face them boldly.

President of Egypt, Mr. Nazar and President of Yugoslavia, Sri Tito came to India. They held discussions on all the issues of the world and came to a decision that America should leave North Vietnam. This statement brought name and fame to her.

Indira Gandhi wanted to rebuild India with great strength. Her trials began to yield good results. So, her reputation was doubled in foreign countries and this became a cause of inconvenience and hatred to her opponents. But she decided to go ahead with firm determination.

1967 elections were fast approaching Firoz was representing Rae Bareilly constitutency Nehru helped the movement of ryots there. So, she decided to get elected from Rae Bereily and wanted to meet the Congress workers there. When she got down there, thousands of people gathered there and it turned out to be a big meeting instead of a small worker's meeting.

All the people were discontented with the performance of the leaders after the death of Firoz. So, they deputed her to represent them in the elections. Sivasanker Singh of Dalman village requested her to plan for more borewells and for more water canals and to have a bridge on Ganga river and to renovate the railway station of Rae Bareilly- Dalman, spoiled at the time of Pakistan War. She promised them to do what all they wanted.

There were 16 Muslims in every hundred of people. They showed lot of interest in Indiraji and as many as 1,50,000 people gathered around her, when she rose to speak.

Whole addressing the gathering, especially women, she said "There is famine in the country. Because of the wars with China and Pakistan there was loss everywhere. We are giving more importance to agriculture sector in planning. High yielding varieties of grains will be used to bring more production."

People felt happy and there was applause Sucheta Kripalani, the Chief Minister of UP and President of Congress, Sri Kamalapathi Tripathi were with her throughout her programme and requested her to represent Rae Bareilly.

Afterwards, she travelled upto Allahabad. It was the first time for her as a prime minister to visit that place. Throughout the 8 miles distance people gathered around her and received her with flowers and bouques and gave her ovation. Slogans of "Indira Gandhi Zindabad, National Congress Zindabad"went into the skies.

It was not only the situation in Ahmadabad. Wherever she went, people gathered four times more than expected and there was stampede also. She criticised the opponents very vehemently and that those who criticised Congress have no sense of responsibility. They are encouraging violence. We are followers of Gandhi and we are tied down to the policy of non-violence and so, let us condemn the acts of violence. With simple words, we cannot produce crops and we cannot reduce the prices. We have to work hard and increase production.

There she travelled 10 lakhs of people travelling in one day in Gorakhpur, Maharajganj, Kusinagar areas. She could identify the problems of people wherever she went and lots of women gathered for all her meetings, as a special feature.

As election propaganda was intensified it was evident how much of glamour Indira had. When she went to Bihar, people thronged the Airport and she had to address 5 lakhs of people. "Congress is stronger now. Except Congress, there is no other party which can keep India united and can remove poverty" she said.

Addressing the youth, she said "the future of the country depends on you. Prove your worth by serving the people and the country".

When voters were only 73 millions in 1952, it reached 242 millions in 1967. Peoples demands and aspirations also increased. Women learnt to vote by themselves without depending on men.

It was possible only in India, to live under the influence of one single person for 20 years. The country had to face many problems like religious quarrels, border disputes language differences but in spite of all of them the country was progressing.

Lal Bahadur Sastri had good relations with members of Parliament but not with the people. His period also was short. But, after Indira's arrival into the scene, she built up contacts with the people and she could instil new courage and inspiration in their minds and could lead them forward.

But, the opposition parties were noted in bringing down the Congress.

"Now is the time to defeat Congress for all the faults that Congress committed, now is the best opportune time to punish them. For their, we are prepared to join hand with anybody and do any sacrifice" said A B Bajpai, the secretary of Bharatiya Jan Sangh.

"Congress is weakened. There is no craze among the people towards Congress. But opposition parties are also weak. There is no unity among them. If the present position continues, like in the last elections, the opposition parties will suffer" said Madhu Limaye, of Socialist Party.

But they carried on personal propaganda against Indira Gandhi and tried to lower down her importance.

Soon after the announcement of the elections, all the opposition parties declared war on Congress and tried to organise agitations. Fifty thousand on communists organised a big demonstration in

Delhi, from Red Fort to Parliament House. Jan Sangh organised big rallies in Uttar Pradesh, Madhya Pradesh, Rajasthan against Congress. Jan Sangh people wanted to bring abolition of cow slaughter issue to the forefront once again.

In Jayapur, when Morarji Desai, was speaking, opposition parties created disturbance and so the audience fled away.

All the meetings of D P Misra were disturbed. In places like Ratlam, stones were pelted. Morarji was even wounded in Nimalghir in Assam and so meetings were banned there.

In Bihar, when Jagjivanram wanted to speak stones were pelted Congress flags were burnt and the caps on the heads of Congress volunteers were thrown into the air and they were molested. So, the meeting had to be stopped.

In spite of all disturbances Indiraji boldly carried on election propaganda for forty days.

In all the places, she was warmly welcomed and women offered 'Arati' and garlanded her. They applied 'tilak' on her forehead.

Her tour in the Telengana districts, especially Karimnagar, was memorable. In a meeting at Karimnagar, she said "If a tree does not give good fruits, does anyone cut it. We will give it more fertilisers and more water and make it fertile. As farmers, you know all this. So, you have to strengthen Congress. Then you will get good results". The words worked wonderfully on the farmers present there. Those leaders who got disappointed at Hyderabad, felt happy when they saw her touring in Telengana districts they thought that on account of Indira Gandhi, Congress got strengthened.

When she went to Tamil Nadu, she replied to all the queries of press persons. A reporter from West Germany took out a total film of that meeting.

She could attract the attention of the students more. She emphasised that there was no question of taking out English. Kamaraj also travelled along with her in Madras State.

Referring to the unity of the opposition parties, she said "Even if nine disabled people come closer, can they walk better than a normal healthy person".

Congress workers felt that her place among the people is memorable.

She went to Karnataka, toured 600 miles and addressed twenty-two meetings. She inaugurated Tungabhadra Canal Project.

In a meeting, she said "Don't think that the present friction is in between the parties. Congress is wanting to run the country on a new path. There are revolutions in the economic, social, technical and scientific fields, which can bring about a total change. But opponents are wanting to take it backwards".

In a meeting at Kittur, she said "Just as Chennamma fought against the British Government, our women should wage war against poverty, ignorance and lethargy. As Gandhi said, unless women come forward, the country cannot prosper" she added.

When she went to Kerala, she criticised the communists vehemently. She seriously condemned their attempt to create enemity between the Government and the army." Our army is great. Patriotic. Nobody can misguide it", she said.

In Goa, there was so much of friction. Some wanted it to be merged with Maharashtra. Some wanted to keep and maintain present status quo. Indira Gandhi took a firm decision that" Goa people should decide what is to be done. The Central Government will not interfere with their problem". This argument seemed to be convincing to all the parties in Goa and so, Congress could see more strength in Goa.

Puri Sankaracharya was fasting so as to bring pressure on the Government to abolish cow slaughter. His fast for 59 days brought about disturbed conditions in the country. This turned out to be more injurious to the interests of Congress in the coming elections. Jan Sangh in Madhya Pradesh, Rajasthan and Maharashtra, which christigated the fast, was gaining strength.

Indira Gandhi toured all over Rajasthan and also Chittodghad where she said "Ranapratap's" valour and bravery should not be forgotten. We may be committing mistakes. We are also achieving progress. Those who find fault with us should not forget our progress.

More and more women attended her meetings and listened to her with rapt attention.

Indira Gandhi visited Jayapur, Gwalior and Orissa and addressed several meetings cautioning the people against voting for the opposition and what will happen to the country if they come to power.

Like this she toured all the areas, giving replies to all the problems created by the opposition. Though she was heckled and ridiculed in some places she could continue her travel undoubtedly.

Before the results came out, Newspapers began to imagine, whether Congress can come to power even if Indira Gandhi wins.

Before 1967 elections, some of the Congress leaders, vexed with Congress policies, walled out of the party and started their own parties-in the name of Jana Congress in Orissa, Bangla Congress in Bengal, Jana Congress in Assam, Jana Paksha in Mysore. Thus, there were 12 regional parties in sixteen states. Some were afraid that these regional parties may disturb the vote bank of Congress and so Congress party may get defeated.

But Indira Gandhi was not afraid of these parties. She knew that it is natural before any general elections.

There was also another speculation among people whether Indira Gandhi would be the Prime Minister, even if Congress wins.

Is it possible for the members of the syndicate to make Indira the Prime Minister. She was made use of before the elections. Now, they may not allow her to come to power again, some thought.

The statements made by some leaders were not favourable to her.

"Atulya Ghosh, the leader of the West Bengal Congress party said" Let us wait and see. How can we predict now itself ? "I like some to contest. But they must be willing to compete. If she wants to stay on, I have no objection. I do not know whether she is willing or not". That was his version even though Indira Gandhi made it clear that she was willing to contest for the Prime Minister's post.

When Kamaraj was asked about her selection he said, "Don't ask me". On the invitation of this Russian Prime Minister, he went to Russia and came back. So, his prestige was enhanced. He was of the view that Mrs. Gandhi will not win without his support.

S.K. Patil another Congress leader said that Act is not a problem to be discussed now before the elections.

I cannot say I am unfit for the post of Prime Minister. But dont't think I am contesting in this election only to get elected as Prime Minister. But in the selection of the Prime Minister, I will have my role without fail and this I can say emphatically".

The representative of scheduled castes in the Congress party was Jagjivanram. He had considerable voice and strength in the Congress party. When asked about his views, he said "I cannot say now itself. I have not quit politics. Nobody asked me so far about this."

Then Home Minister Sri Y.B. Chauan said The present Prime Minister may continue. She can give leadership to the country. Our future and the country's future would be safe in her hands.

When Morarji was asked, he said, "If I had thought like Charan, I would not have contested for the post".

Any way elections were over. Counting was completed. Very stunning results came out. Out of 16 states, Congress lost in 8 states. In the centre Congress could win. Leaders belonging to the syndicate like Kamaraj Nadar, Atulya Ghosh and S.K. Patil got defeated. Biju Patnaik in Orissa and Sanjeeva Reddy in Andhra also got defeated. Jana Sangh could win in the Lok Sabha seats of Delhi, in the Metropolitan Council and in a corporation.

It was a personal success to Indira Gandhi and in a way defeat for Congress party.

Soon after, the results came out, Indira Gandhi declared that she would contest for the Prime Minister's post. Morarji was also getting ready for the contest. He said, "when there was a contest for the leadership in the past, elections were coming nearer. So, many of the Parliament members were afraid of Kamaraj Nadar, thinking that they may not get tickets for the election. But this time it is different. They have no fear for another 5 years".

Some wanted not to have the contest. Morarji was asked to be the Deputy Prime Minister.

Congress Parliamentary Board met and decided to have the contest on 12th March 67. There was so much curiosity among Parliament members of the Congress party.

When Kamaraj was asked to comment on the situation, he said "wait and see", "whom do you support" was the next question. "All are the consulted" was the reply. "Last time you have taken initiative" they asked. He said "Those days were different".

From this, it was evident that many of the syndicate members were against Indira Gandhi. Though they were defeated, they were waiting for an opportunity to defeat her, the syndicate members wanted to assert their position once again.

This time, D.P. Misra, C.B. Gupta, Nijalingappa got united and wanted to work against Chavan and decrease his popularity. But Indiraji strengthened her position, with the support of Chavan, Ashok Mehta, Subrahmanyam and Dinesh Singh.

Kamaraj observed the situation and met Morarji and Indira and tried to convince them. Though adamant in the beginning, Morarji accepted to work as Dy. Prime Minister. That was how the contest was averted. All congratulated Nadar for averting the crisis.

1967 elections have proved, in a way, that Congress party was losing confidence of the people. It had lost hold in eight states. In the absence of Indira Gandhi and her Charisma, Congress would not have had that much of majority in the centre, some observers felt.

Why Congress had come to the stage ? Because Government was not working properly, people lost faith and there was also lack of publicity for the good works done by the Government, and there was no attempt to develop Congress as a dynamic force, some of the cabinet colleagues felt. Indira Gandhi took confidence of all the reasons for such state of affairs. Groups were formed in Congress. One group was trying to smash the other group. Both the groups failed to go to the people and work for them.

Congress had been passing very valuable resolutions. But they were as resolutions on paper only. They were not implemented properly. For their implementation, several in the Congress itself were obstructing.

Government was spending thousands and lakhs of money on planning but its results were not reaching the poor. Loans given by government, facilities, created by government were reaching the higher strata of people instead of the poor.

Even those people who are elected as representatives of people belonged to the upper classes and so, they were not bothered about the problems of the downtrodden.

On account of the above reasons, Congress was getting weakened Indiraji felt. Unless there is liaison between the organisation and the people, there cannot be any benefit, she felt.

A wide gap between her and the syndicate developed.

In Jabbalpore AICC Congress, held on April 1967, she was wanting to propose nationalisation of banks, to lay limitations on urban property, land reforms to be speeded and to abolish privy purses. S.K. Patil, who was the Finance Minister was opposing all her plans. Though no Congress leader openly opposed her policies, but in implementation, they were opposing her.

From 1968-69, Indiraji could not take any firm decision. In the meanwhile, Sarvapalli Radhakrishnan's term as President came to an end. She wanted to make Zakir Hussain the next President. All the Congress leaders opposed this idea. But she could win and make Zakir Hussain the President. With this, syndicate members temporarily, were mellowed down, but they never put a stop to their attempts.

In 1968, presidentship of Kamaraj came to an end. She wanted to dislodge him but she could not do it successfully as Sri. Nijalingappa, belonging to syndicate, get elected.

After she returned to Delhi, from Bangalore session of AICC, she removed Morarji from Finance portfolio and so, he resigned. On 19th, at the dead of the night an ordinance was issued nationalising fourteen banks. She was expelled from the party.

Nijalingappa was removed from the presidentship of the party and Congress Working Committee was formed by her. That is real Congress, she declared. Congress of 84 years history, got divided into two divisions. Those who supported Indira were called members of "Indicate", while others were called "syndicate".

Indira Gandhi gave full freedom to all the members to vote as per their conscience. Neelam Sanjeeva Reddy got elected.

Indira's Congress was called the "New Congress"and Nijalingappa's Congress was called "Old Congress". There was the emergence of "young Turks"also

She encouraged youth and appointed them in key positions.

Jag Jivan Ram was made the President of her Congress.

India, a poor country, could not pay some crores of ruppes as compensation to the ex-rules. She wanted to abolish these privy purses by bringing out an ordinance. But, it was defeated in the Rajya Sabha with one vote. She thought of another method. Through a special ordinance by the President, she could abolish 550 ex-rulers. They went to Supreme Court and got their payment proposal revived.

It was not an easy task for her, to knit a socialist society, when there were reactionary forces all around, working against her.

So, on 28th December 1970, she declared about general elections to the surprise of the opposition parties. Nobody could understand her strategy when she had majority in the Parliament.

She had to depend on other parties to implement any of her policies. So, she wanted a thorough change and she declared fresh elections.

She contested from Rae Bareilly and Raj Narain also contested there as her opponent. She conducted election propaganda for two months and she travelled throughout the length and breadth of the country.

Old Congress, Jan Sangh and Swatantra Party formed a "grand alliance" and worked against Indira Gandhi. She could win 90 out of 100 seats in Parliament and every member of the new Congress could win with lakhs of votes of majority. Except Morarji, all the other members of the syndicate got defeated.

Formation of Bangladesh

Formation of Bangladesh was another feather in her cap. Pakistan consisted of 2 different parts called East Pakistan and West Pakistan. East Pakistanis were talking 'Bangla' (Bengali) language whereas West Pakistanis were talking Urdu. The two parts were some hundreds miles apart and most of the rulers of Pakistan were from West Pakistan. They were exploiting East Pakistan and were developing West Pakistan only. They wanted to impose Urdu language on East Pakistan which they did not like.

Pakistan was ruled by Yahyakhan who was a military man. Soon after Mujibur Rehman got elected in East Pakistan, there were disturbances. Several thousands of people migrated to India. In 1971 February, Awami League declared East Pakistan as separate Bangladesh. Yehya Khan began to fire on the people migrating Indira Gandhi took pity on the women and children migrating to India. Those who were coming to India, had to be protected, even though they were Muslims. Jan Sangh also supported her move. There were heated discussions in the Indian Parliament on this situation. When Indira Gandhi was trying to talk to Pakistan Government to prevent willings of Bangladeshis, China was criticisng Awami League.

Indira Gandhi requested for help from U-Thant, who was Secretary General of UNO at that time. But Pakistan Government objected to this, saying that it was their internal affair. Pakistan army arrested Mujibur Rehman and took him to West Pakistan.

There was much of agitation in India about spending crores of rupees on the refugees. Some wanted her to send them back. But, Indira said a political solution is formed out for the issue, it is not possible.

Yahya Khan alleged that what all was happening in West Pakistan was due to Indira Gandhi.

In June 1971, Yehya Khan wanted to talk to Indira Gandhi. But "till Mujibur Rehman who was in the custody of the Pakistan Government, talks were not possible" she said.

Except Russia and Yugoslavia, no other condemned the acts of Pakistan Government. Soviet Prime Minister Kosigin went to

Pakistan to prevent war. Indira Gandhi went to Europe and America, to request them to interfere in the problem. But they were not favourable. On the other hand, the number of refugees were increasing day by day. The money to be spent for development purposes in India had to be spent on the refugees.

Pakistan Government was interfering with the towns of western India and so emergency had to be declared.

Indira Gandhi reconfused the independence of Bangladesh. Yahya Khan who called her "that Woman" had to compromise with her, when she declared stoppage of war on the border.

Soon after the end of the war, Indira took up distribution of Banzar lands to the poor. She laid stress on increasing production of Good Grains.

Indira Gandhi brought a bill in the Parliament to nationalise all the insurance companies. Bharat Iron and Steel Company was nationalised and run on proper lines.

IT sector was given more importance in the industrial development. People belonging to the lower income groups should be given facility of employment, she felt and for this purpose, she formed a housing corporation.

Indira Gandhi was implementing some developmental projects and confirming her rule in the country.

In the meanwhile, Raj Narayan filed an election petition against Indira Gandhi in Allahabad High Court. Its enquiry went on for four long years. Finally in May 1975, the Judge of the High Court, delivered a judgement against her.

Her election was set aside and she was debarred from participating in any election for six years.

This judgement came as a bolt from the blue not only for Indians, but all in the world. This could temporarily withhold the history of India.

What were the reasons given for issuing the judgement against her ? There were ten allegations against her. Eight were dismissed by the judge himself. Two were said to be proved.

Yashpal Kapur was working in the Prime Ministers secretariat. Being an employee, he assisted her election is one of the allegation. In fact, Yashpal started election propaganda on 7th January and resigned on 13th January. His resignation was accepted on 25th January. So, being a gazetted officer in Government, he should not help any candidate in the elections and so his work, was against election code, Sinha felt.

Another allegation was that for erecting stages for Indira Gandhi's election meetings and to arrange loud speakers, state employee's of Uttar Pradesh were made use of and taking the help of Governmnet employees was an offence, as per the election code, Sinha felt.

These were small matters purely technical. Not only election meetings, for any meeting which the Prime Minister attends arrangements would be made by the Employees of Electricity Board.

It would have been an offence if she had brifed the electorate or arranged vehicles for coming to the polling booths. She had not committed any such mistakes.

After hearing the Judgement, Indira wanted to resign. But Congress leaders did not accept this proposal. An appeal was made in the Supreme Court as per the provisions of People's Representation Act.

A meeting of Congress Parliamentary Party was convened and the matter was discussed thoroughly. Senior leaders like Yaswanth Rao, Charan, Swaran Singh, Jagjivan Ram, Barno attended and decided that she should not resign as people are pinning all their hopes on her. A resolution was passed accordingly.

Many leaders and experts advised her to file an appeal in the Supreme Court.

Poor people from all the corners of the country wanted her not to resign but the opposition parties took this opportunity and started agitation that she should resign.

But communist party (LC) only supported Indira Gandhi.

Opposition parties met at Rashtrapathi and asked him to take resignation from her. Of course, they were trying to inconvenience her and not to allow her government to function.

Under the leadership of George Fernandez, All India Railway workers union started a strike. There was famine in the country everywhere. People were suffering on account of the strike, it was not possible to transport foodgrains from one place to another. Business men increased prices and began to blackmarket the food stuffs.

The strike was put down. Opposition parties started bad propaganda. "Saying you all believed that she is the saviour of poor people. See, how antagonistic she is towards labourers".

Indira Gandhi was not afraid. She gave more weight to the interests of the people.

Smugglers began to collect money selling goods at very high prices. Because the opposition parties could not support their agitation, they approached Jayaprakash Narayan.

He started the movement of "Total Revolution" in Bihar. He instigated people against the Government. All the anti-progressive forces joined together supported his movement, but, it was not successful.

One Sangharsha Samithi was formed with Nanaji Deshmukh as Secretary under the presidentship of Morarji Desai. Their aim was only to remove Indira from power. "Indira Hatto" was their sole purpose.

20 point programme was started by Indiraji. Even Jayaprakash was arrested. When elections were declared, Congress party lost in all the states of North India. Even Indira Gandhi got defeated.

Jayaprakash Narayan and Kripalani brought all the opposition parties, except the communists, under the umbrella of Janata Party. Even Jagjivan Ram's Congress democratic got merged in it and finally, Janata Government was formed at the centre, Morarji as the Prime Minister.

In 1969 elections, Congress could win 41 seats in Andhra Pradesh out of 42 seats. But it was totally swept in the North.

Charan was elected as the leader of the Congress, Parliamentary party on the advice of Indira Gandhi, but he did not choose to support her. When emergency was declared, he was in the cabinet and he also gave his consent. But, he never gave any reply to the criticism levelled against her.

After Congress got defeated, there were some leaders who thought that politically, Indiraji has no future. One of them was Dev Kant Barua. Till recently, he was very close to Indira Gandhi. In 1971, when Congress got tremendous success, when somebody said that it was "Indrajal", he said "No, it was Indira Jal" "India means Indira, Indira means India", he said. Such a person turned out to be antagonistic to him.

Siddarth Sankar Ray was another such person. He was one of the persons, who were very close to her. In fact, it was he who advised her to impose emergency in the country. As he a person turned out to be an opponent to her. Thus, many of the Congress leaders felt there was no use of being with her. They began to leave the Congress party.

Under such circumstances Indira wanted to bring about change in the leadership of the Congress party. With her blessings, Kasu Brahmananda Reddy became the president to the All India Congress instead of Barua.

Janata Party people promisesd to the people in the elections that they would restore all the freedoms lost. They declared that they were lovers of freedom. Under Indira's Government they released all the smugglers and blackmarketers who were in jail. They even made George Fernandez a cabinet minister, relieving him from the dynamite case.

From the next day, they came to power, Janata party people began to do anti-propaganda on Indira Gandhi and on her son Sanjay. This was useful to Maxists. They felt that Indira and her sons are evil forces and that unless they are destroyed, there is no salvation for the country. They thought of creating an impression that all the Congress people were corrupt and they have misused their power to destroy the country. They concentrated mainly on this propaganda, to weaken the Congress party.

Janata Party people gave promise to the people during election period that they would change Article 356 of the Indian Constitution, to impose president's rule, much against the will of the ruling state government. But, they never took any action on this. Charan Singh, who was the Home Minister then, asked all the chief ministers to resign rulers they should do voluntarily, he otherwise would dismiss them, he threatened.

Because Congress got defeated in all the states, those state Governments have no right to continue in power, he said.

In both the Houses of the Parliament, Congress people expressed their discontent on this proposal. The Chief Ministers refused to resign. Even then, Charan Singh dismissed State Governments in Uttar Pradesh, Punjab, Bihar, Orissa, Haryana, Himachal Pradesh, Rajasthan, Madhya Pradesh, West Bengal. He even found fault with the Vice President, who delayed matters in doing so.

Janata Party people said that they would discourage the policy of changing parties, soon after they came to power. But, they began to encourage such changes. They admitted those Congress leaders who left Congress into their party. In Maharashtra, when there has

Congress rule, they broke the Congress party and made Sharad Pawar as Chief Minister of Maharashtra.

They used Gandhi's name to come to power. But later on, they resorted to all tactics to strengthen their party.

They produced a photostat copy of a draft before the Speaker, that in the name of Menaka Gandhi, Sanjay had sent twenty-five lakhs of rupees to be deposited in the Switzerland Bank. They started propaganda that Indira Gandhi and her son have amassed crores of ruppes and that they are struggling hard to save it and keep it in the Banks. Congress people said it was a blatant lie and it had to be proved after thorough enquiry. After enquiry, it was proved that the allegation was baseless.

They formed some commissions. Shah Commission was one of them. Mathur Commission was another to look into the affairs of Maruti Company.

One Nagarwala had drawn sixty lakhs of rupees from State Bank of India and on this matter, enquiry was sought to be conducted by Jagan Mohan Reddy, a retired justice.

To lower down the prestige of Indira Gandhi, in the eyes of the public, was their main purpose in appointing such commissions.

The two Congress Chief Ministers of A.P. and Karnataka, Sri Vengala Rao and Deva Raj Urs also were not spared. They appointed commissions of enquiry.

A criminal case was filed on Yashpal Kapur, who was maintaining the accounts of the central Congress election committee. K.R. Dhawan was also involved, saying that he had taken away thirteen crores of rupees from the above account and paid it to somebody.

Another criminal case was feild on Bansilal that he had misused the funds of Youth Congress. Thus, every thing was done with a vindictive spirit and the newspapers also were giving publicity to all alleged misdeeds.

When Shah Commission sent summons to Indira Gandhi to appear before the commissions, Indira Gandhi refused to appear before them. "See, see, she has no belief in democratic procedures" was their propaganda.

Congress people wanted the commission to be abolishesd, as it was working under the guidance of Janta Government.

Vengalrao, the Chief Minister of Andhra joined hands with Brahmananda Reddy. All the Congress people came to know that Brahmananda Reddy and Chavan became opponents to Indira Gandhi and those who could not adjust with them came out of Congress party and formed a new Congress, under the leadership of Indira Gandhi. Thus Congress party was again split up.

Subrahmanyam, Pai, Raghuramayya gave evidence before the Shah Commission that Indira Gandhi misused her power Brahmananda Reddy was asked to resign but he refused.

The people, observing all these developments got angry and their anger was exhibited in the elections of Andhra and Karnataka. Indira Gandhi's Congress won with great majority. Candidates of Vengala Rao and Brahmananda Reddy got defeated. 200 of them lost even deposits.

3 cases were filed against her and attempts were made to assasinate her in Delhi, Mathura, Bhuvaneswar, Chicago.

Some Congress leaders suggestesd to her that she must get elected in a bye-election as member of Parliament to withstand the antagonism lashed out against her.

She was requested to stand in Chikmagalur which was vacated by Chandra Gowda. Though Devaraj did not like this idea much, he had to agree as there was no alternative. They decided Veerendra Patil as their representative of Janata Party.

Wherever, she went she was accosted as "mother". She could win with great majority.

Significance of Chikmagalur

The decisive victory of Mrs. Gandhi, in an electoral battle at Chikmagalur, signifies a new turn in the political situation in the country. She went on foot to even corner villages of Chikmagalur constituency and she addressed more than 200 meetings. Mr. Veerendra Patil was selected as the candidate of Janata to contest from Chikmagalur as against Mrs. Gandhi. Some of the central ministers of the Janata concentrated on this election and made all possible efforts to defeat Mrs. Gandhi.

In fact, this bye-election of Chikmagalur attracted the attention of the whole world. But Indira Gandhi carried vehement propaganda that if Janata Party continues in power, any longer, the country would go to dogs and would emerge as a threat to democracy.

On 3rd November 1978, Mrs. Gandhi was declared to have been elected by a majority of 77 thousand votes.

Chikmagalur Win

11th November, 1976, was the day when the people of Chikmagalur gave their ultimate judgement against the forces of reaction and highlighted the place for Indiraji in Indian politics.

It was the stunning victory of the battle. Janata leaders were once again realigning and hatching conspiracies for the total elimination of the leader of the Nation but the masses of India gave their verdict in support of her policies, at a time when the Prime Minister of India was put to indignity and lowered her prestige in the eyes of the nation and the world.

The country was in imminent danger of the breakdown of democracy and the Parliamentary system. After all, the Prime Minister is not merely a chairman of the council of ministers. He or She is a leader of the nation, and framer of policies, embodying the aspiration of the people.

In a democratic set up, there may be discussions, differences on some view-points on several issues, but the Government should function with consensus. It is on their point that the personality individuality or leadership of the leader comes into picture. The Prime Minister should be capable of not only running the Government but must also lead the nation Indiraji had her definite policies to lead the nation.

The malady of the Janata was lack of leadership rather unity of purpose. It was an unholy alliance of divergent idealogies and confusion of different concepts. Their only one-point programme appeared to be personal villification and political vendetta against Mrs. Indira Gandhi. Janata suffered from the decease of inaction and decision. There was breakdown of administration.

At that crucial time, the forces of progress, democracy secularism and socialism rallied round Indira Gandhi and to say in one sentence saved the nation from degeneration Indiraji's triumph in chikmagalur was expected by all, who knew her well. People felt that were was a single person, Srimathi Indira Gandhi, to sustain democracy and to keep up the norms of social justice. She was considered to be the saviour of the people from darkness, poverty, inequality and misusing of life.

Throughout the country, there was provocation of communal forces during Janata rule. If things were allowed to move in the same manner for some more time, there would have been a blood revolution in the country.

If the Parliament war made an instrument for satisfying political revenge, it is nothing but dictatorship. That would be a dangerous trend to put an end to all democratic norms.

Janata Government was the other name for the degeneration of democratic norms. Its component parties were working at cross purposes for personal and class aggrandisement. In every branch of administration, there was total chaos and confusion. There was no law and order in the country.

People realised the need to vote in favour of the Congress(I) party for the survival of democracy and for the upliftment of the Backward Classes, Scheduled Tribes and Scheduled Castes.

In, Chikmagalur bye-election, all the top-ranking leaders of all the political parties from the Himalayas to cape comerin stormed into the Chikmagalur constitutency and so it is historically an important event.

Election details of Polling

A little over 76 per cent of the total electorate of 5,95,393 voters of Chikmagalur Lok Sabha constituency have exercised their franchise in the bye-election for which polling was held on 5-11-76, recording an improvement of about 9 per cent over the last General Elections to Parliament in Chikmagalur constituency.

2,4290 were men voters and 2,10,164 were women. Tariheri assembly segment in Chikmagalur district topped the list by recording 79.20 per cent polling. Nadar and Belthangady segments stood next to Tarikeri, recording 78.32 and 77.01 per cent polling. While in Priner, the percentage of polling was 76.27, it was 76.25 per cent in Sringeri unit. Karkala and Mudigeri segments witnessed 74.03 and 72.55 per cent polling respectively.

Election Results

In spite of the malicious propaganda of the press and the opposition leaders, Indira Gandhi won the election by a margin of over 77,333 votes over Mr. Veerendra Patil, her nearest rival.

Some opinions on her success :

- Sri Chandra Sekhar hoped "she will change her style".
- Fernandoz - "Our failures led to her win".
- Sri Patil took defeat in sporting spirit.
- Morarji Desai - "Her victory will not hit Janata Party".
- Mrs. Gandhi - Thanked the electorate.
- Indiraji's triumph in Chikmagalur was confidently expected by all, who have understood her, Dalit log, Harijans, backward classes have been politically determined to vote for "Garibi Hatao" a call given by her in 1970.

Her majority could have been much larger if only her campaigns had greater transport and linguistic communication and if the unfortunate lamented but recidental death of a lady had not been politically exploited. All those that tried to reply her and ban her from participating in politics have been disappointed and Janata's vindictivity, unParliamentary tactics are dismissed by the public as fasistic. Democracy, Dalit - Look and political tolerance have won.

9
Movement of Indira Hatao The Grand Alliance

The Congress Plenary Session, held at Bombay in December 1969, resolved to abolish privy purses, to nationalise the bulk of the import trade, to take steps for the early nationalisation of general insurance and to implement land reforms. The question of excluding the right to property from the chapter on fundamental rights in the Constitution was also raised but no decision was reached on that point.

The demand for amending the Constitution began to gain strength after February 1970, when the Suprème Court declared that the provision for the nationalisation of the fourteen major banks was ultra vires, because the compensation provided for the same was in adequate. In view of the Supreme Court decision, the Central Government brought another bill in Parliament, for the nationalisation of these banks, which provided for the grant of more liberal compensation.

So as to enable the banks to work in a dynamic and innovative manner the attitudes of conventional and conservative banking had to be changed and emphasis was laid on rural masses and their upliftment.

The traditional insistence of collateral security or documents of land ownership will be self-defeating such methods would rule out millions of small farmers and tenants. The banker must become the friend, philosopher and guide of the farmer, by providing him technical assistance inputs, etc.

In the mid-term election manifesto of the Congress, it was said that "as a result of certain judicial pronouncements, it has become impossible to effectively implement some of the directive principles of the Constitution".

For this poll, Congress did not enter into any electoral under standing with any political party. But it called, upon the people to cast their votes overhelmingly for the Congress, so that a strong, stable and progressive government could be formed, at the centre. The Congress(O) fought the Congress in alliance with Jana Sangh, Socialist Party and the Swatantra Party. This four party alliance contested the election.

1971 - Election

The princes and industrialists fared equally badly, in this election, contrary to earlier expectations. The three Raj Matas of Gwalior, Jaipur and Jodhpur and the Maharajas of Baroda, Bikaner, Kota and Rewa have won. The rulers of Dhrangdhara, Bharatpur, Tehri - Gadwal and Narsiinghar have lost. Similarly Mr. K.K. Birla, Mr. Naval Tata, Mr. R.R. Moraska, Mr. D.N. Patodia, Mr. N.K. Somani and Mr. Kamala Nayan Bajaj have lost. On the whole the outcome of the election had been, total rejection by the people of the obstructionist tactics of a few interested persons and policies.

Mrs. Sirimavo Bandara Nayake, Ceylon Prime Minister, commenting on Mrs. Gandhi's victory at the polls, said, that Indira's teaming millions had pinned their faith in her and given her an absolute mandate to continue to rule according to socialistic policies and programmes.

"New deal at Delhi" the "biggest peaceful revolution in the world" "a model for the third world countries", "Indira on the doorstep of a new era"- these are some of the comments in the French press on the outcome of India's general elections.

The Paris newspapers, which were relatively discret about the poll while the compaign was on, have suddenly published a spate of articles on the "New India" that, they believe, is likely to emerge from the Nation's Verdict.

The Pro-Government "Lie Figaro" wrote thus. "The triumph of Mrs. Gandhi's moderate and pragmatic thesis over the extreme left-wing and reactionary adventures, places India in an original position in relation to other big nations. Neither an ally nor an enemy of Washington, Moscow or Peeking, the Prime Minister appears to be the veritable leader of the countries of the third world".

Highlighting the "Indian Experiment", promises of promoting socialism adopted to Indian conditions-where the right to private property will not be abridged in reducing inequalities have been singled out as evidence of the originality of the Indian-experiment "If she succeeds," the conservative *L'Arove* writes, "India could serve as an example to the developing countries. In the same breath, she could establish herself as a greater leader than her father", the journal adds.

On the other hand she toured the country, calling upon the people to unite for "Garibi Hatao" and to join hands to fight poverty.

The results of 1971 elections showed that the trend of the people was reversed from the fourth general elections in 1967 and they voted for the Congress and for a stable government at the centre the results further showed that the Congress had been able to win the hearts of people and to raise hopes amongst them, that it would implement the declared policies. The bold steps taken by government, in connection with the freedom struggle of Bangladesh, generated a sense of pride and confidence among Indian people.

The following table shows the particulars of seats contested and seats won by various political parties, along with the percentage of seats won.

Table

Party	*Seats Contested*	*Seats Won*	*% of Seats Won*
Congress	2,529	1,927	70.00
Congress (O)	870	89	3.27
Jana Sangh	1,233	104	3.82
Swatantra Party	307	16	0.59
CPI	330	112	4.11
CPI (M)	467	34	1.25
SP	659	57	2.10
Other State Parties	456	114	4.18
Independents and Others	5,177	270	9.91
Total	**12,028**	**2,723**	**100.00**

Grand Alliance

Another important feature in 1971 elections was that a grand alliance was formed by different groups to fight the Congress. These groups had different ideologies but they were united, in their belief to prevent Congress from coming to power. The Grand Alliance suffered reverses in Parliamentary election. In 1972, state elections also, it did not fare better. The economic situation in the country deteriorated because of inflation and scarcity. In 1974, when elections were held in Orissa and Uttar Pradesh the Grand Alliance wanted to use the economic situation for their advantage but the Congress could improve its position and could form governments in both the states.

In 1973, various groups and parties began to organise different kinds of agitation. In Gujarat, an agitation was launched against corruption and high prices and this ultimately led to a demand for a dissolution of the elected state assembly. Finally, the Assembly had to be dissolved. In Bihar state also, under the leadership of Jaya Prakash Narain, a similar agitation for the dissolution of Assembly was launched.

In October 1974, Sri Dev Kant Barooh became the Congress president and he took initiative in Uttar Pradesh for the Congress leaders. Political programme adopted at Narora stated that similar training should be held at state level and district level, that youth training camps and youth rallies for the defence of democracy should be held and conferences of agricultural workers should be organised in all districts and Congress Seva Dal should be revamped and strengthened.

Narora Camps

The economic programme at Narora camp included a crash programme for the distribution of non-alienable house sites to, Harijans, Girijans in the rural areas, revision of scholarships to poor students, creation of a separate agency for providing credit facilities to the rural masses, extension of public distribution system for supply of essential commodities, dehoarding drive against black marketeers, a programme of slum improvement and the organisation of the agricultural labourers and the rural poor etc. When Congress was busy organising Narora type of training camps, certain parties like Jana Sangh, Congress(O), Socialist Party and Bharatiya Lok Dal engaged themselves in various movements. Jayaprakash Narayan gave leadership to these movements by speaking against corruption and partyless democracy.

Congressmen opposed Jayaprakash Narain's movement for the dissolution of elected bodies saying that it is an attack on the country's democratic institutions. The CPI also criticised Jayaprakash Narain's movement that such a move would only help the growth of undemocratic and fascist forces.

This movement was however continued and intensified after 12th June 1975, when the Allahabad High Court delivered judgement in the case that had been filed against Indira Gandhi, challenging her election by Raj Narain, judge held the election to be invalid but also granted an absolute stay of the order for 20 days or till an appeal against the judgement was filed in the Supreme Court, which were earlier.

Jayaprakash and some opposition parties like Congress(O), Jana Sangh, Socialist Party and Bharatiya Lok Dal, demanded the resignation of the Prime Minister, after the judgement of the Allahabad High Court. The Congress Parliamentary board, the Congress Parliamentary party and the organisational governmental wings of the Congress in different states, reaffirmed their faith in the leadership of Mrs. Gandhi and requested her to continue in office.

After an appeal, the Supreme Court, passed an order on 24th June 1975, that Indira Gandhi could continue in office, as Prime Minister without any restrictions, but as a member of Lok Sabha, she should have no right to vote until further orders or till the disposal of the appeal. Jayaprakash, Congress(O), Jana Sangh, socialist Party and Bharatiya Lok Dal, continued their demand for the resignation of the Prime Minister and they further wanted to launch a nation wide compaign of *satyagraha, dharna, gherao* and various other forms of civil disobedience in support of their demand from 29th June 1975.

Jayaprakash's movement in Bihar included boycott of schools and colleges and of all examinations for one year. Social boycott of MLAs as also their *gherao*, so that they may resign, a no tax compaign, boycott of courts, establishment of parallel governments and parallel courts namely, Janata Sarkars and Janata Adalats. In June 1975, his movement for a revolution, a total revolution was launched.

In May 1975, at Vijayawada, he asked students "to start a Bihar type of movement with dharnas before the state secretariat, gherao before assembly, satyagraha before courts and defiance of prohibitory orders".

He further said that a revolution could be successful only if the army and the police rebelled. In June 1974, he asked policement to "disobey" illegal orders given by their superiors.

In December 1974, Morarji Desai, gave a threat of staging a dharna inside the Lok Sabha chamber. In June 1975, Morarji Deshmukh, the Jana Sangh leader, stated that there had to be a Delhi Bandh to compel the Prime Minister to resign. On 25th June 1975, at the Ram Lila Grounds, Jayaprakash said "Nanaji had given a call. I have travelled throughout the country in search of the struggle.....how can I keep out of it.....Friends... civil disobedience will be of varied types. A time may come when it may be necessary to derecognise the government. We would derecognise them. We would not cooperate with them, not a paisa of tax shall be given to them". I am prepared for a treason trial.

10

Period of Emergency and Her Power of Planning

Indira Gandhi had to perform the unenviable task of making the fast changing system, work successfully without allowing it to collapse. This could be achieved only by two methods. Either by achieving results in quick succession by drastic steps or by acceptable process of economic development, in a normal way, but with the required dynamism and sincere effort. Our economy is still sluggish. Millions and millions of people are living below the poverty line. Under such circumstances, a leader, who wants to run on the right path, has to lay down a fairly sound infrastructure. In a vast continent like ours, problems are many and also varied. Mrs. Gandhi, being a shrewd woman has paved the way, for eradicating poverty and for making the country proper.

'Garibi Hatao' one of her slogans, could reach the masses in no time. Being a national leader with the necessary sagacity and image, she could put forth her programme of "Garibi Hatao" with the necessary zeal.

Even her sharpest critics like Sri Madhu Limaye of the SSP, (Samyukta Socialist Party) conceded that she is the leader on the Indian scene. People want a change but are not clear in what direction to move and how. Taking into consideration the basic issue and malady conforming Indian society viz. poverty; her two assets were her integrity and her uncanny sense of timing, she did not even care to disown a person, who does not fit in her programme which kept everyone guessing. Probably this was one facet of her personality, which was very disconcerting to her friends and foes alike that opened her to the change of being autocratic and dictatorial. She was not bitter or revengeful. But she could claim to be the personification of the aspirations of the backward and the downtrodden. Though she did not know what poverty was as she had never experienced it, she could understand the evils of poverty and the moorings of the needy and underprivileged sections of the society. Unlike others with a human heart and a motherly heart, she was open about many other things and that is why she made many enemies. "No government can afford to ignore the urges of common people. After all democracy has its basis on those very urges and if any government flouts them, it is pushed aside and other government takes it over" Jawaharlal Nehru said, Mrs. Gandhi could understand the time spirit of the above words and it will be a serious mistake, to underestimate her power of planning.

What the country needed was an economic, social and moral revolution and the 20-point programme was intended for achieving it. After all, creating a new society was a joint endeavour of all. Sacrifices on the part of those, who have the ability to do so, are required after the dissolvement of Parliament in 1970.

In a special broadcast to the nation, Mrs. Gandhi said "There comes a time in the life of a nation when the government of the day has to take an unusual step to cut through difficulties in order to solve the problems, with which the country is behest. Underlining that the poll is only to keep pledges, she made it clear that it was found necessary, to seek a fresh mandate from the people, so that a speedier and more resolute advance to the proclaimed goal of a just social order could be achieved".

Speaking of the opposition from vested interests and political enemies, and of the far-reaching consequences of the social and economic reforms contemplated by her Government, she mentioned about a new deal for the impoverished millions of India.

Emergency had meant more engagements, more people to meet and longer hours of work for Mrs. Gandhi. The Prime Minister's house became an open house, as she remained to be the most accessible Prime Minister in the world. Callers on her included students, editors, MPs, social workers and so on. She started her work by 8.30 AM and by that time itself, her lawns were full with several groups.

She was not hyper-sensitive to any personal criticism but she reacted sharply to the smallest criticism that was levelled against the country and its self-confidence.

One could see democracy in operation, very clearly from her group discussions. Voice of the people was freely heard and the people from any remote village could freely discuss any point with their elected leader.

She returned to her residence for a short lunch break and she was in her office, to meet more and more visitors or diplomats. She participated in public meetings or functions in the evening and returned home afresh after a hard day's work. The Prime Minister's working day stretched from eighteen hours to 20 hours and she worked past midnight. What was the secret of this tremendous stamina ? To quote her "the harder one works, the more one can do. The best way is to like what one does and find fulfillment in work. Then one can also be more relaxed while working harder".

Intervening in the debate in both the Houses of Parliament, Mrs. Gandhi lashed out at the opposition and said, there could be no return to the pre-emergency days of total license and political permissiveness".

She said the declaration of emergency had to be made to frustrate the attempts of certain opposition parties to destroy democracy. In the peculiar conditions of India, a balance had to be struck between the political rights of the individual and the economic rights of the millions. "We have to evolve a political system in which the right balance is struck between the two", she added.

In her speech in the Rajya Sabha, Mrs. Gandhi said "nobody wants this type of situation to continue for ever in the country". She warned the opposition that govenment could not allow unconstitutional and violent methods it adopted in the recent past to discredit the government.

She said that government's action was not against any person or party. It was Pro-India and Pro-Indian people and solely designed to some democracy from those who sought to destroy it.

Rebutting the charge that she was a fascist, Mrs. Gandhi said "which leader could have tolerated so long to the consistent compaign of falsehood, calumnly and violence". She quoted extensively from the writings of some leaders to show their lack of faith in democracy.

She also cited many utterances of Jayaprakash Narayan and his close associate, Mr. M.R. Masani, soliciting the intervention of the army to save democracy in India.

Mrs. Gandhi referred to the agitation launched by the opposition in Gujarat and Bihar marked by violence and intimidation of elected legislators. She said that the final campaign of the non-CPI opposition parties to paralyse the government after the Allahabad High Court judgement only marked in the culmination of their deep-laid conspiracy.

Observing that some opposition friends were preaching socialism and radicalism, she said that she had never claimed to be a doctrinaire socialist. She had her own version of socialism and her own vision of what Indian society should be like. She was moving towards that direction steadfastly. It might be slower but it was the surer way to achieve the objective, she added.

Fascism did not mean mere repression or were of excessive force by the police or imprisonment of people; it was falsehood, the whispering compaign and finding scape goats, she said.

She said it was time now for all to think seriously about basic matters like democratic functioning and democratic institutions. "Political liberty and political rights exist only so long as the political order remains. A state of anarchy can only lead to quick erosion of every freedom and political right of the individual. In any modern democracy, the question of economic betterment on social justice could not be separated from proper functioning of democracy".

11

Post Emergency and Later

Though emergency was ratified by Parliament, the question remained whether emergency was validly declared. After Jagjivan Ram resigned from the Congress in February 1977, he stated that the cabinet was not informed about it. Charan Singh, Home Minister of the Janata Government, stated, on the basis of records, that the cabinet had approved of the emergency not before but after its declaration.

But, the propriety of declaring emergency was an issue, much discussed, in 1977 Lok Sabha elections, which the Congress lost.

Major development after the finalisation of the Fifth Plan in September 1976, was announcement of elections to the Lok Sabha, in February 1977 been extended upto March, Parliament was dissolved and Elections to the Lok Sabha were held in March 1977.

After the elections were announced, the emergency was relaxed and Morarji Desai and many other political leaders, who were in prison, were released. Political meetings were allowed.

On the eve of the March 1977 Lok Sabha Elections, the Congress(O), Jana Sangh, BLD, and the Socialist Party announced the formation of the Janata Party, with the blessings of Sri Jayaprakash Narayan, who had been working for the unity of the opposition parties, as against the Congress. These parties stated that they would contest the elections under the name of the Janata Party and under the symbol and flag of BLD. They also claimed that after the elections they will dissolve themselves and formally of emergency and denounced all the steps taken later on in continuation of it. They described that "The country had passed through a nightmare of fear and humiliation, reminiscent of the days of foreign domination". They charged that the Government had resorted to "coercive force and compulsion to firing and terror" in the family planning drive and fulfil "sterilisation quotes". They regretted that habeas corpus was taken away and a "pail of fear was thrown over the country and the rule of law ceased to exist".

Jayaprakash Narayan, Acharya Kripalani - the senior most erstwhile Congressmen and also Smt. Vijayalakshmi Pandit, aunt of Mrs. Gandhi, supported the Janata candidates, toured the country propagating that the elections offered the last chance to the people to reverse the trend towards dictatorship and authoritarianism and the struggle against the ruling party.

The Janata Party in her manifesto declared "That it is a choice between freedom and slavery, between democracy and dictatorship, between abdicating the power of the people and asserting it, between the Gandhian path and the way that led many nations down the principle of dictatorship in stability, military adventure and national ruin".

Referring to the activities of Sanjay Gandhi, Janata Party claimed that during emergency an extra Constitutional centre of power was built up who was permitted to wield power without the trammels of legality or accountability. It said that the party aim was the establishment of an open government in a free society. It promised that it would lift emergency, restore fundamental rights and freedom, repeal the MISA, release all political prisoners, enact laws to ensure that no political or social organisation that opponents and loyalify followers and foes, served as a bitter pill for many ailments. The fact that there was hardly a murmur of protest, was ample proof that the people did not regard emergency as an evil. On the contrary, a vast majority of people sighed with relief schools, factories, shops were opened. Strikes, lock-outs, gheraos, hooliganism came to an end. A sense of discipline prevailed throughout the length and breadth of the country. Every one was mindful of his or her own duties and responsibilities. Nehru was no believer in partyless democracy and for the success of democracy, organised and responsible parties were essential, he held. For a massive democracy like that of India, ideological commitments provided through political parties, are still more important for the efficient running of the government, he felt.

Against Groupism in the Party

Nehru always welcomed differences of opinion within the parties but he neither encouraged nor aligned himself to any such formations. Though he differed fundamentally on various issues, with Congress leaders like Gandhi, Patel and others, "his differences of opinion never resulted in groupism".

No leader can take the country on the path of success and progress, unless he had the solid popular backing.

He faced vast audiences with the feeling of a friend, he went straight to them, trusted them to the maximum extent in spite of their backwardness and indisciplined behaviour. He talked to the crowd also. The presence of all the basic prerequisitions of a democratic political set-up is not an insurance of democracy in itself. India with a totally different social and economic background from that existing in the western liberal democracies, started off with full-fledged political democracy and faced many problems from the beginning. Nehru himself witnessed the emergence of certain forces on the Indian scene which emanated from different sources and posed great threat to her democratic character, stability and national unity. It is not feasible to deal with all of them, were, in this context and so I am not able to extend.

Judiciary

It is a relic of the colonical era. Due to the multi-lingual, multi-religious and multi-cultural character of the Indian society, and an under-developed economy, there are many challenges to the functioning of democracy.

Unfavourable Conditions

Agitational approach and growth of violence in public life :- Democracy provides full scope for the expression of dissent, protest and differences of opinion. But, when people resort to violent agitations, demonstrations, fasts, threats of immolation and the like frequently, the very basis of democracy is seriously threatened. The structure of a democratic society would crack up with the adoption and frequent use of undemocratic means to achieve political ends. There might be genuine grievances of people against the government, but that does not entitle every one, who feels sore, to take law into his own hands. Extra-Parliamentary pressures have a place in a democratic set up but their frequent use and the attempt to secure policy changes through non-action, is the surest way of undermining political democracy.

Democracy and violence are incomputable and the attempt to settle problems by violent methods is not democracy, but something which is the very reverse of democracy". Violence means a complete denial of any idea of ordered progress.

Nehru, was a product of the Indian Renaissance and the Indian National movement. A life so varied and so deeply involved in the great freedom struggle and the mind receptive to main thought currents of India, can hardly be assessed in a few lines. But his untiring efforts in reshaping India are unparalleled. But the comments on his life and work by political thinkers, scholars, commentators, theoreticians, diplomats, world dignitaries are many and varied. He lived up to the high ideals of democracy, though he was branded as "popular dictator" and less of a democrat.

To him, Gandhian doctrines appeared to be idealistic and far from realities prevailing in India. But both understood the spirit of India and talked in consonance with the "Conscience of India". He believed as a way of life and as a basis of social structure. He gave a broader definition to democracy when he remarked "Democracy is not only political, not only economic, but something of the mind - it involves equality and opportunity to all".

A country most inexperienced in self-government and a people untrained in the processes of the functioning of democracy really need certain special defences against danger of disruption and disintegration.

The Janata Party and the CFD entered into an election alliance to fight the Congress. CPI, welcomed the statement of Jagjivan Ram about the deviation from democratic norms in the functioning of the Congress party.

The Congress party maintained that the Janata Party was not really different from the Grand Alliance of 1971 and 1972. Congress also claimed that the Jana Sangh dominated the Janata Party but the real force behind the Jana Sangh, was RSS; a communal organisation and the Socialist Party, which gave a call for Railway strike at a time when the country faced great economic problems, could not take the country forward. These parties had, in fact, conflicting programmes and ideologies.

Mrs. Gandhi maintained that the country made rapid progress since emergency. She referred to the production of 121 million tons of foodgrains and to the industrial growth of 5.7 per cent and to the loss of per capita income of 6 per cent in that year and also to the accumulation of 2,500 crores of Foreign Exchange. Its abuse in the interest of any individual or group, amend Article 356 of the Constitution, to ensure that the power to impose President's Rule in a state was not misused for the benefit of any ruling party, introduce electoral reforms, repeal the amendments to the representation of the people's Act, which had redefined corrupt practices and had placed electoral offences of certain people beyond the scrutiny of the court, restore the authority of the judiciary, safeguard the integrity and independence of the bar, assure the right of peaceful and non-violent protest, abolish censorship and end harassment of newspapers, journals, publishers and printing presses.

After the Janata Party started its election compaign, on 2nd February 1977, Jagjivan Ram resigned, to form Congress for Democracy (CFD) alongwith H.N. Bahuguna, ex-Chief Minister of Orissa also joined hands with them. These CFD leaders claimed that they left Congress party and told the people that benefits that accrued on account of the 20-point programme and referred to the progress of the country, in spite of the Bangladesh crisis, severe drought and the attempts by some opposition parties to obstruct the functioning of governments.

12

After Her Re-election in Chikmagalur

After her win in the election, Mrs. Gandhi announced that Chikmagalur election is like any other election but is a clear indication of the fall of Janata. Her trip to London, on 14th November 1978, Mrs. Gandhi went to London to inaugurate a steel unit and also participated in the 89th birth anniversary of Pandit Nehru. She was given a tumultous welcome and she spoke of the poor people in India and their dutiful life, which symbolises the civilisation, carried on from generation to generation.

She began to tour the length and breadth of the northern country from February 1979. Her charisma did not fade out and people attended her meetings in large numbers.

She spoke of the larger interests of the nation and encouraged the people to work unitedly and to keep up standards leaving petty differences.

Fall of Janata

On 11th of July 1979, Sri Y.B. Chavan, leader of the opposition, introduced no-confidence motion in the Parliament and while doing so, he spoke of the imminent danger to the secular ideas preached by Sri Gandhi and Jawaharlal and because of the internal differences among the Janata rulers, they themselves are ruining their government and also the nation.

Practically, there was no coordination of any sort between the various departments and there was decline of law and order situation in the country.

Raj Narain's story was an episode and he quit the 'Janata', along with 20 others. Ravi Ray, Gnaneswar Singh etc., resigned from the cabinet on 12th July and Bahuguna, Ram Kinkar followed them. With this, the strength of the Janata Party in the Parliament fell down to 225.

Morarji had to resign in the end, though he resisted from doing so in the initial stages. On 15th July, Morarji resigned and the President asked the opposition leader to form the government. But, Charan Singh, who had only a strength of 75 in the Parliament made it clear that he cannot form the Government. Later on, leader of the Janata (S) Sri Charan Singh was asked to form Government, to which he agreed. On 29th July 1979, Charan Singh's cabinet took an oath and Sri Y.B. Chavan, S.L.N. Misra, Bahuguna, Biju Patnaik, Ravi Ray joined his cabinet. Later on, Mr. Brahmananda Reddy, K.C. Pant, Dr. Karan Singh, Hitendra Desai, T.A. Pai and C. Subrahmanyam joined as Central Ministers and some members of Anna DMK also, joined the cabinet. But, Sri Charan Singh could not prove his strength and so he was on the look out for support.

The very Charan Singh, who told stories that he would conduct enquiry against Indira Gandhi, as Nazi criminal, had to request her to give a helping hand and Mrs. Gandhi immediately extended her support unconditionally and without joining his cabinet. She knew pretty well, that no government can live longer, without popular support.

On account of the wonderful strategy played by Mrs. Gandhi, Charan Singh had not only to resign, but also to request, the President of India, to hold fresh elections. On August 27th president dissolved the Lok Sabha and fresh elections were called for. Charan's government continued as care-taker government.

Finally, on 26th October 1979, Mr. Shakder made an announcement that from 3rd to 6th January, elections would be held for all the 542 seats of Lok Sabha.

Indira Gandhi, made a whirl wind tour of the whole country and recognising the Indira wave, several senior Congress leaders who differed with her, even joined Congress (I).

Election Manifesto : 1980

On 1st December 1980, Mrs. Gandhi released the election Manifesto of the Congress party and she carefully worded it with great forethought. In it, the uncertainly caused by the Janata Party in the country was highlighted. Janata Government, which could rule the country for only 28 months, could not continue in power on account of its own weaknesses and this was well brought to the notice of masses. Any government formed at the centre, should be capable enough to run the government and should have definite ideology to rule. It must have its own, social and economic policies, should have the numerical majority and should be able to withstand the upheavels or any eventualities. They may be caused in course of time.

Giving such guarantee that her government would be able to give a stable and strong government at the centre to protect the nation from any danger. Mrs. Gandhi made an appeal to one and all to vote for her policies.

Making it very clear that she was not enamoured of power, Mrs. Gandhi said buiding up a strong India, was her single aim. Instead of solving the problems of the people, the Janata Regime only concentrated on internal squabbles and took to a policy of indictive spirit to punish her and other members of her family. Because the image of India is being tarished in the eyes of the outside world, Mrs. Gandhi, apprised the people that it was a testing time for the people, to decide whether they wanted Janata or Congress, stability or instability.

Mrs. Gandhi contested from Rae Bareily of Uttar Pradesh and also from Medak of Andhra Pradesh.

She addressed hundreds and hundreds of meetings and people waited for her arrival with rapt attention. They wanted to see her and to listen to her. Her Charisma astonished all.

By 9th evening in January 1980, results started pouring in and Mrs. Gandhi won with great majority in both the constituencies.

On account of the total wave of Indira Congress, Janata Party was swept away and in several constituencies, total strangers to the political line were elected in the name of Indira Gandhi. Youngsters without any experience, also won the election battle in her name! It was indeed a vote for her ! for her 'Hand'. It was an individual success for her and for her party. After 33 months, she was again voted to power !! This was unique in the annals of history.

During the time of Janata rule she was subjected to so much of harassment and was made a party in several cases and so much of bad propaganda was made against her, but in 1980 elections she could win the appreciation of the people in an unprecedented manner.

On 10th January 1980, she was elected as the leader of the Congress Parliamentary party and she took an oath as a Prime Minister, for the second time on 14th January 1980 in the Rashtrapati Bhavan.

Addressing the people over the Radio, she said that the prestige built up by Congress in 30 years, was ruined in 30 months by the Janata.

She never wanted to waste her time in taking vengeance on those, who were responsible for her vilification she only said that her party was not made up of small-minded people. Her attempt, was to build up a new society, a new India.

In the International sphere, she wanted to revive the policies adopted previously and to build up the dignity lost and the External Affairs Ministry had been called upon to take drastic steps to that effect. Policy of non-alignment had been strengthened and we see today the quick results of such a policy. She arranged a conference of foreign ministers of all Non-aligned nations at Delhi and it was grand success. After the Cancun Summit Conference, she convened a third world conference and the deliberations proved quite encouraging. In a way, she was trying to built up a resurgent India, on the path, of achieving its goals.

On account of the wrong policies, adopted by the Janata Government, the economic order in the country was made topsy turvy. After assuming charge of the Prime Minister, the first job she did was to frame some sound economic policies to set right the economic situation. The budget, she presented spoke of her anxiety to help the weaker sections of society and to lift the public sector to its original status. Six more banks like Andhra Bank, Vijaya Bank, Corporation Bank, Punjab and Sind Bank, Oriental Bank of Commerce and New Bank of India, were nationalised.

Especially, in the field of science and space technology India had decided to achieve rapid progress and the launching of 'Aryabhata' was a feather in the cap of Mrs. Gandhi.

If we review the whole situation in the country, at that time, there was over-all improvement in all fields and the policies followed by Mrs. Gandhi also, were proving highly successful.

India was no more considered to be only a developing country. The world was looking to her as a nation making rapid strides and it had reached a stage, where it could be leading to several other developing countries specially the west was giving her weight.

In the previous years, India's poverty and life of its millions of people, with several problems, was much talked off. But now, the marvellous success of the Green Revolution could solve the food problem and India need not look to the west, for any help, for feeding its masses. This could be possible within a small time - say two decades,due to the untiring efforts of the agriculturists and the scientists. This Revolution could win the appreciation of the World Bank experts even.

Several steps were taken to develop small scale industries in the rural sector and in the coming decades, the very picture of rural India, may change on account of this, the experts felt.

Since the common man was not yet educated, certain mob mentality has taken hold of us. What we need is good training and right education in the appreciation of ethical values, which are the foundation of a healthy society. These principles are more than philosophical platitudes, a way of life on which depends the courage and integrity of the nation. Every one of us must make it his or her earnest endeavour to translate certain beliefs into personal convictions and commitment. Then only the country can prosper, she felt.

The Gandhian Revolution heralded freedom from unjust tyranny, on the basis of human right and dignity. Another revolution is yet to be fought. It is against the subservience of inner unjust forces, which stifle man's liberty. When everyman can free himself from the inordinate ambition for power and greed his aspirations for a better world will blossom forth, equality and fraternity of all men. This is no easy task. It requires concerted effort, courage and tireless attempt.

Ultimately, it is the work of the spiritual strength, without which, we will be small people trying to tackle big problems. Men must, first of all, be liberated from the bondage of our apathy and selfishness.

We must build up a new India, of our dreams.Democracy is an experiment but it is up to us to make it a successful experiment. I hope the guidance, we get, will pave the way for a better India.

In one sentence, Mrs. Gandhi making it clear that democracy was murdered by Janata, she asserted herself and made it clear that she had not deviated even by one millimetre from the ideals of Mahatma Gandhi and Nehru and she only stood for modernisation of the country and for a synthesis of the old and the new.

13

What will Happen to India after 100 Years ? Peoples Reaction

India in future say after a hundred years ! This was an interesting question discussed vehemently in a friend's gathering recently, which I followed carefully, but without any participation.

Ramu was asking, with youthful zest, thumping on the table– can we achieve what we are wanting now, even after a hundred years? In fact what is our cherished goal? What is the ideology behind the ruling party namely the Congress? Can Mrs. Gandhi deliver the goods? What is her strategy ? Is intelligentsia thinking over the future of the nation ? Are the middle classes participating, rather getting involved in the programmes taken up for the betterment of the Nation ?

Nagesh put a stop to Ramu's current of thoughts, by interrupting him. "Mr. Ramu, could you ever think of one thing. These are well-laid down of policies by Congress-to build up a socialistic pattern of society - to safeguard democracy by guaranteeing one and all, equality before law and order. The gap between the precept and practice remains always, in any given society"-Nagesh was continuing in his usual voice in a balanced manner.

But Ramesh rushed in with his vehement arguments. Look! My dear friends, I want to make it very clear to you one thing. I do not have any apprehensions or misapprehensions about the achievements of ideals. I am only worried about the methods being adopted. Why these reservations on commercial basis ? Why this exploitation of so-called upper classes - I call it only exploitation - because, they are neglected and are lacking in facilities - So, they are flooding to other countries in search of jobs and other opportunities. Is this not a loss to the nation ? Is the aim, to produce sub-standard professionals and men in other fields ? The Nation is sinking. Is this not be temple phenomenon. Is it not the duty of any right thinking man, to raise his voice against this ? I ask - he took away his glasses and rubbed them, put forth his arguments our social order is disturbed. It takes time for the new order to take its shape. What will happen during this transition period ? From the other side, Are the Harijans, Girijans satisfied that government is doing something - though not great things for them ? Are they not raising voices sometimes against the government ? That is how discontent is created. No section seems to be happy. That is why, I say, it is not happy atmosphere for a nation to prosper ?

Mohan interrupted at this point by his counter arguments. Look here ! you seem to be a sadist. Look around and see for yourself, what amount of awakening is there among the masses. Go to the villages. There is tremendous impact of government policies. Of course the implementation may not be as effective at all levels as expected and there may be some delays and lacunae in implementation. But, can you say that the whole policy is wrong who is to take care of the downtrodden, neglected and none else than the government. It is simple and glaring that is what Mrs. Gandhi is doing ? Then why do you criticise all her economic policies ? Srinath an expert entered the discussion by his sobre arguments. It is better to fix up economic levels and do help people, instead of giving preference to some on the basis of caste. This classification is leading to some fissiparous tendencies and some sections are feeling that they are neglected. This is not a healthy sign. All poor people may be like economically. But some sections, neglected from some centuries, do not have the necessary moral calibre or the necessary background to view things in a broader perspective. It is not enough to make them economically sound. They must be taught certain decent norms of life. Who will do this ?

Who else,

"This Government"- suddenly replied and Ramu at this juncture. Srinath laughed and said "can the Government do all things. Can moral transformation be brought about Government alone. It is the duty of the intellectuals and the right-thinking men in the society. It is a slow process. It is not easy to change persons", he said "you may be seemingly right Srinath ! But can people afford to wait till something is achieved ? It is an age of rising expectations. People want, food, clothing and shelter. Even these basic things of life are denied to some people. Will they keep quiet, till some miraculous change comes over. Does it not again lead to friction, chaos and disturbance in society ? asked Komali, with her shrill voice, in an innocent, feminine way.

"Komali! what you say is also correct. But, you should not think of immediate things. In fact you and I are ordinary people. The policy-makers, rather the builders of the nation, should think of matters in a broad perspective, keeping in view the future of the country. I am worried about the nation after a 100 - years. If the present trend continues, the nation may be somewhat different. But reservations are only for a period say another 10 years to come. Later on, when they are also educated, they may even stand in open competition - interrupted Mohan.

What guarantee is there that there will not be any further reservations after ten years. Can you educate millions and millions of illiterate masses within a decade - This was Ramani's view.

"If necessary, reservations may be continued to achieve the desired goal"- said one voice.

"This is where I differ with you. Think of a broad plan. There are nations which have launched on universalisation of education and they have achieved - said another voice. Some drastic changes are necessary to achieve quick results. Do you mean to say that Mrs. Gandhi is not aware of all these things - raised the third voice. Nobody, else it is she who is moulding the destiny of the nation now. She is the single leader, in fact. As a builder of modern India - a great nation, I am afraid that she is not aware of certain facts - asked Ramu 'again'.

I do not have any difference of opinion or doubt her genuinesse. She may be alright. But what about her followers ? What about the men around her ? Are they believing in her and her policies or are they around her simply because she is in power, Are they committed souls - committed to the nation's cause and development? or are they simply self-centred people who pursue their own interests ?

Think of the days of the freedom struggle. Leader identified themselves with the cause. They wanted to give what, they had- their time, energy and even their lives. They sacrificed everything. They never wanted anything in return. They never sought any positions. But now, people are crazy about positions. They are running about for power. People want money, recognition - what not - at the cost of service - continued Ramani ! "True. But, you should not lose sight of one thing. Times are changing. Situation differs. Now, we are trying to build up something new, a modern nation. We had only one goal and we fought the British. We achieved independence. Now, the situation is different. We have to bring about alround development of all sections and also to bring about a cohesion or a synthesis of thought to protect the nation. This is indeed a greater task,"grinned Viswanath, with his elderly look– as a writer and as a columnist. He continued to say "visualise things in a different set-up. We have the necessary freedom. We have the necessary will to build up the nation. We have the necessary ambition also, to achieve things in a quick pace and to take our rightful place in the commity of Nations. But, what is it that is preventing us to do things, without any discontent from any quarter. Why, we are not able to achieve things quickly? Why the benefits are not reaching the right person? Why are the middlemen being benefited ? Something is wrong somewhere. Some serious thought be bestowed on this."

The personality of man is undergoing change superficialities and self-interests are outweighing the 'ideals'. In fact, this is a serious threat to the nation. This is where, we are a failure. "A man entrusted with a job is not able to do his bit honestly. He is trying to utilise the opportunity given to him, to use for his own ends. Unfortunately a sense of national outlook has not come over. It is not built up even, from grass root level.

Think of the younger generation. Do they have any basic values of life ? They are born after independence. They do not know the difficulties of living in slavery. Our culture or heritage is not having much impact on them. Even deep-rooted sentiments are not there.

We have suffered enough, as a nation in the past. We have seen chairs, we have witnessed famines and devastations, we have lived in scarcity of everything. But, could we have that urge to build up wealth, to strive for nations cause - unfortunately that sectioned outlook has come over. Each thinking in terms of his own class or community. The National character must be built up and each one must put up his or her own bit to achieve this.

"But, sorry Mr. Viswanath who should do this ? The Government or the people themselves ? asked Srinath."All concerned. People like you and I. I mean the intellectuals, the writers, the economists in fact the thought makers among the people - are responsible. They have their major share in this gigantic task. Society changes on the opinion of some opinion-makers and they should be right thinking men. The masses follow them consciously or unconsciously. This is what is happening in any country.

Alright. Coming back to the point on which we differed namely- what will happen to India-after a 100 years - what do you want to say ? This time Ramani and Komali combined their voices.

Viswanath corrected his throat and changed his looks and began to say - Nobody can predict or prophecy. The Nation will evolve its own character. A new economic order may set in and pave way for a new social order.

But our strategy should be such that we do not lose sight of certain basic and fundamental thoughts of our nation. In achieving a particular order, we should not forget our very national character. In the name of equality, we should not sacrifice rich traditions - said Mohan.

Nobody wants it- continued Viswanath. We have to protect our identity.

Can Mrs. Gandhi lay down the necessary basis for this bright future, asked Nagesh, this time, with his usual procrastinating tendency. Of course, she is striving hard to involve people in nation building activity. She wants to change the life pattern of people and make the nation richer and is trying to find out solutions to several problems in her own way - concluded Viswanath, with superior airs.

This little discussion of some friends, throws light on the topics currently discussed in the country in any group or gathering. But, how are the people in power thinking ? How is Mrs. Gandhi thinking?

It is a general saying that intelligentsia should play a major role in the national life. But who are these intelligentsia ? The writers, lawyers, the teachers and the elite of the society ?

Mrs. Gandhi, herself, while addressing a writer's conference at Bombay said that "something is missing in the intellectual life of India". She also said that we do not see the zeal to light social evils.

But what is their percentage ? When compared to the larger masses, they would be certainly less in number. People are no longer in the habit of following a few thinkers. The new trend seems to be to think for ourselves and to take a decision in one's own way. The younger generation are no blind followers. Still in the villages, the elders, who can command some respect, are controlling the youth the opinion makers in the village community should themselves be properly oriented, so as to suit the changed circumstances.

The glare of living reality is such that the old are not able to lead the new generation. Feudal ideas are still hanging on heavy. There must be a proper orientation and proper direction. Independence, without any norms, is meaningless.

Leaving apart some undeveloped areas, caste is not considered to be a taboo.

When we look back to the decades of freedom struggle, we see leaders, with high sense of dedication and sacrifice. They brought respect to the posts they held. With undawnted courage, they shed their lives. They were not self-seeker's with lofty ideals, they fought like warriors.

But, times have changed. This is a criticism rampant that self-seekers and professionals are ruling the masses. A sort of new culture, entirely different from what it was in earlier days, is getting involved incidentally. The lower strata of people are buiding up a new culture, on account of their enlightenment, on account of their education and social status ? But, the so-called elite, hither to, are getting frustrated. They lost their roots and their sentiments in the modern context and feel depressed on account of total neglect. If we view things in one way, the whole effort is to lesson in equalities and disparities prevailing in different sections of society. In other words, it is trying to improve standard of living. Indiraji made a serious effort to bring about the required change in the minds of people. In fact, I think, she was facing her biggest challenge.

Her action and thought would leave a stamp on history.

India, with a great history and heritage, India, the great country, the land of Buddha, was once upon a time, a teacher of the Buddhist philosophy to the whole world. India's civilisation antidates the Romans; it has its own identity and mission. India's history extends back to thousands of years. But in the material world, what has been accomplished is less than what is to be done or achieved.

But, a new era of international status for India seems to be in the offing. Mrs. Gandhi's words will have far - reaching consequences. Anyone, who judges things with a broader prospective will not fail to notice that Indias weight is independent of its material strength and the ideological influence required by India is as imposing as material power would be.

A rural leadership emerging in the rural areas, is prepared to welcome new technology and they have the benefit of modern education also. With this background, it is not an easy task to bring about the required change. It may take some centuries to create rural elite but the thinkers and writers should raise their voice in bringing about an effective change in the outlook of the villagers by their writings.

In this context I think, it is proper to quote the example of Hongkong, which I had the fortune to see in 1979. Hongkong, wherein, education was universalised only 20 years back, is now having the largest number of youngsters working in every field. It is now turning from cotton textile manufacturing to highly sophisticated industries. Singapore is no longer a warehouse for the products of other countries. It is manufacturing its own goods and is attracting world market. Formosa, occupying only 0.37 per cent of the territory of China and with less than one-fiftieth of its population, does half as much foreign trade as Peking. Thailand and Malaysia have taken Japan as economic giant as model and are progressing in every field. What is due to ?

Some say there is wide gap between the policy and the practice. Some fear that India is facing a crisis of character. How far is this time ?

The written with more insight and intense feeling than other fellowmen, are to give a directive to the countrymen. They must affirm the basic ideals and beliefs and should give voice of the inner-most urges of the people. Without intellectual effort, social change is not possible.

Man of action, i.e., the litter of the soil or the man working in the mill, cannot live in isolation with the man of thought and innovation.

In any phase of history of the nation, writers have been powerful instruments of change. Our Constitution is guaranteeing freedom of thought and expression to every person. We have to go a long way in taking the nation to that direction.

Poverty is still a curse on us and we have to wage a relentless battle to remove poverty.

Illiteracy is yet a drawback. But in the last two decades, there has been explosion of human consciousness and people are trying to solve their problems. This must find a place in the minds of written and they must give a proper directions and perspective to the thoughts of the people and should produce literature, that can inspire, encourage people and lead them on the right path in politician.

In a country where minimum qualification are not prescribed for contesting the elections, the politically ambitious ones are likely to resort to all kinds of malpractices, first to win the battle of elections, thus causing a fall in the standards of public life.

So, there is greater need today than ever before for an informed, enlightened and conscious men and women to enter into public life and to enliven politics by commitment to society not as a short-cut to personal gain, but as a sincere endeavour to improve the quality of public life.

Dissent from and defiance towards authority is much inevidence in India today and this unhealthy trend should be put an end to.

Excessive reverance to property rights is putting our penal code into conflict with the peasants, the working classes, slum-dwellers etc. A bond of good behaviour is expected from a man, who has no obstensible means to livelihood.

The slogan of more production is there and more is being produced. But the wealth that is produced is cornered by a few. This leads to inevitable discontent.

In a hurry to bring out quantitative changes, sub-standard man and women, with less calibre and dedication are being produced.

Noble ideals with which the war of Independence was waged and won, should be maintained it is fatal to any country with a democratic system to let politics degenerate into a last resort, for the drop-outs in other walks of life. They should not be interested only in the spoils of office.

Unfortunately a feature of post-independence era had been that almost all the major political parties have been unhospitable to younger elements. Probably, they did not want to lose the battle, taking chances. The result is, the olders ones, with their outmoded and outdated ideas continue to rule. In the pre-independence days, participation in politics was considered and respected to be patriotism and now it has come to the level of being looked down upon as hypocrisy and adventurism. Again politics must be made respectable. A sincere endeavour to improve the quality of public life should be made.

The elite cannot afford to be 'silent'. A 'changing situation' demands a change in attitudes and ideas. They must develop keen sense of the past and a keen observation and care for the future. They must in fact preserve the foundation of Indian method of expression.

There is also general saying that the middle class in the society, are neglected or not given their due place. Why this sort of discontent? How far this is time value ? It is to be judged from a broad perspective. Are the middle-classes - rather the elite - resisting any change ? Are they not changing, in accordance with the changing times ? Are they static ? Are they reactionary forces ? Why not wilful cooperation come forward from their side ? Why they are not able to break special barriers ? These are all some of the ideas over which, some serious thought should be bestowed by all concerned. Their resilient attitude should be changed and they should be made to actively participate in the work being taken up, for bettering the lot of the underprivileged. For this a national character and national outlook should be built up.

Who is supposed to do this ? Can the politicians do this ? It is only the pioneers and innovators of intellect and originality, that can do this. Only when the political system is run by people with knowledge and self-confidence, can this atmosphere be built up. Only, when promising young men and women, enter public life, by combining personal advancement with an honest and dedicated involvement in the processes of the country's socio-economic evolution.

Eradication of poverty also, will be possible only by hard labour and continuous effort. The have-nots have to put forth their mind and soul and should contribute to the maximum extent, to this effort. The role of the 'haves' is also there. But, when there is a clash of optitudes, it may be difficult also to continue the struggle, peacefully.

When political life and intellectual life in the country have close contact, they get enriched. When one is separated from other, two different worlds are created.

Science and technology have changed tremendously the life of man, though in the material sphere. But, the core of man, remained still unchanged. Unless a new man, who can face the changed situation is created, no amount of progress, would be worth-while.

Our music and dance are in the traditional form whereas our poetry, drama, painting and architecture have broken with tradition and yielded to the western influence and took to European forms. In India, all writers, so to say think, all artists are applying their minds to preserve the spirit of man and the content of civilisation.

The writers with more insight and intense feeling than other fellowmen, are to give a directive to the countrymen. They must affirm the basic ideals and reliefs and should give voice to the innermost urges of the people. Without intellectual effort, social change is not possible.

Man of action, i.e., the tiller of the soil or the man working in the mill, cannot live in isolation with the man of thought and innovation.

In any phase of history of the nation, writers have been powerful instruments of change. Our Constitution is guaranteeing freedom of thought and expression to every person. We have to go a long way in taking the nation to higher levels.

Poverty is still a curse on us and we have to wage a relentless battle to remove poverty.

Illiteracy is yet a drawback.

But in the last two decades, there had been explosion of human consciousness and people are trying to solve their problems. This must find a place in the minds of writers and they must give a proper direction and perspective to the thoughts of the people and should produce literature, that inspire and encourages people and lead them on the right path / with a sense of achievement.

14

Indira Gandhi's Contribution to Women's Cause

India was till recently the only country in the world, ruled by a woman. Mrs. Gandhi, being at the helm of affairs of the nation, had no doubt overtly, contributed to the cause of woman. How far could she do this, is a question, of course, to be answered not in a single sentence. Her very presence have encouraged women to chart out a new destiny for themselves.

There are some women who are the most successful business persons. Among women are top-notch doctors, managers, managing directors, chairpersons, successful lawyers, industrial and public relations consultants. As well there are creative people and artists too.

It is now time for us to see how far men are able to accept such a situation. For some centuries, the principle in India accepted by one and all was that woman should live in reflected glory only. But now men find a different scene. Women are rising to glorious positions out of sheer intellect and hard labour. But, there may be men who find that being recognised as the husband or son or brother of a prominent woman is humiliating. To accept woman's achievements, a husband or a brother needs to be a towering personality. He must be able to rise above the atrocities of a tradition-bound society.

A woman, on the other side, also has to stand up and face the present storm of social change with grace and charm and should prevail like a giant among lesser men. This, the Indian woman, mostly a career woman is able to do, in spite of odds.

Wives, in general, are also not treated as glorified Ayahs. A super-successful wife may be a rarity, but common men are beginning to learn the art of treating their women as equals. This is a great applicable characteristic of the present day society, though the pace of progress is slow. Gone are the days when woman was only treated as a shadow. Of course, there are still millions and millions of women, who are living in utter ignorance and poverty. This is the other side of the coin. The message of equality is not reaching them in the proper perspective. Their destiny is yet to be moulded in the proper way. Several welfare schemes, covering these illiterate womenfolk living in the corner villages and tribals are especially in receiving attention of government and they are planning to make them enlightened. Of course, this is a gigantic task, which cannot be achieved overnight, with a magic wind.

Thanks to the woman Prime Minister, who could bring about the magic of change, by her silent work. She was considered to be the 'only man' in the cabinet by some politicians. From the point of view of a historian, we are passing through very critical times. When the present phase undergoes a change, a necessity will be born, everyone felt. Indira Gandhi had in her an image of the"mother". She was the saviour and the 'giver of individuality to the masses. An ordinary rickshaw puller in a small town, in Mahabubnagar, a silent district in Andhra Pradesh could think of Mrs. Gandhi as his ' Amma' a lady sitting in the highest chair, some thousands of miles away in Delhi. When interrogatead by me just before the historic 1979 elections. Once a rickshaw boy tells me that he could own a rickshaw on account of the loan given to him by a Bank, which was his long cherished dream. I could see cheer and joyful tears in his eyes, when talking about his 'Amma' who treated "Them as individuals".

What had 'she' done actually for women ? some question !

When we see brave women going ahead neck to neck with men in highly competitive spheres, can anybody fail to see that Mrs. Gandhi gave women a fair deal. Of course, the magnitude of problems and the complexity of situations associated with women as wives, mothers and workers is so overwhelming that no one person, as such, can do very much for improving the prevailing conditions as they exist.

Legal instruments are many but what they contain is limited to a few lawyers and social activists. Awareness of their existence is not there among the commoners.

It is a well known fact that it was during Mrs. Gandhi's tenure in office as Prime Minister that Indian Parliament has passed laws on issues like liberalising the laws of divorce, strengthening anti-dowry measures, raising the age of marriage, medical termination of pregnancy etc. But much depends on the will power of women, who can avail of the opportunities created by law.

In her own words, Mrs. Gandhi was a "Prime Minister", not a "feminist". She had to deal with the problems of women as a Prime Minister, not as a biased person.

It is generally argued that even in India, where a woman is ruling, women are being treated as second class citizens. To some extent, this may be true. It was not the fault of the law but of society, the framework of which is not very congenial.

All said and done women force in India are not an organised sector. Women's time and energy is wasted in still unproductive activities.

The very fact that women are raising their voice against the injustice done to them, is a positive contribution of Mrs. Gandhi to Indian womanhood. Hitherto women suffered submissively, but now they are gaining confidence in themselves and learning to fight for justice.

What is needed is change of attitudes, not only by women towards their problems, women towards women and men towards women. Mrs. Gandhi's rule in this venture is historic. Her style of functioning had tremendous impact on the thinking process itself and on its current trends.

Mrs. Gandhi was handling the destiny of a democratic nation, where more than 50 per cent of the population constituted women, and in fact they were the people who have voted her into power with a tremendous mandate and utmost confidence in her.

The prosperity of a nation lies not only in the hands of government, but in the hands of the people, where men and women work side by side and shoulder to shoulder, for a common purpose.

Speaking about what she had done for the nation, includes what she had done for women. Mrs. Gandhi herself said once ' I do not regard myself as a woman alone but as a person with a job.'

She had taken up the giant task of changing the traditional society into a modern one. She had undertaken immense responsibility for the underprivileged and the women in distress. She was trying to bridge the gulf between the rural women and their urban counterparts through informal education.

But the pity is women themselves consider and believe that they are weaker sex. There are some women luminaries, who could discard inhibitions and rise to important positions after taking inspiration from Mrs. Gandhi. In the International arena she was a Prime Minister, much sought after, more so in the third world and this fact was enough to show that women can also become effective and successful in the outside world, provided they have the necessary zeal and ambition. Indian society also is not averse to their rising to positions of respect and responsibility. This sort of indirect contribution made by Mrs. Gandhi to the uplift of women and changing of mental attitudes of women in India and elsewhere cannot go unnoticed and history has to record her service in golden letters.

Mrs. Gandhi, probably, may not be able to do so much as she wished to do for women. Time and again, she had come out openly, by raising her voice on taking stern steps to eradicate evils prevailing in the Indian society and to mobilise public opinion against the injustices being done to women.

Some suggest that a separate Ministry should be formed to look after women's causes. What is required is, perhaps, more and more services made available to working women, more so the rural women. Hostels for working women in every taluk and town is a must and creches run by government are a dire necessity. More and more socio-economic schemes are required to improve the conditions of women. Small scale industries should improve the conditions of the low income groups and women should play a more important role in running them. If facilities are at their doorsteps, women may take up part time jobs like in Western countries and some may even acquire skills in the job market.

Providing such facilities may not be a great task. But, bringing about transformation among some political and vested forces, is a gigantic task. This cannot be achieved overnight or by a single person.

Strong views should be knit up to prevent atrocities like trafficking in women to the Middle East and other countries from Bangalore and Hyderabad. This sort of in human and ghastly phenomenon, is a blot on our national character. Women are not there chattels to be sold in the market, as any other commodity ! This trend and upsurge must come spontaneously from women especially and from the Indian public.

Are women able to move freely ? Can women assert and live by themselves, without anybody's protection. Can a woman in public life live with honour and dignity ?

There are some of the questions, like any other man which no one can answer. A healthy atmosphere should develop, of its own accord and women should, rise, assert themselves and standup with confidence to withstand the ordeals and to shine. It is not an easy thing for a woman to achieve this in a male dominated society. But slowly, menfolk are also realising and are learning to reconcile with the situation. It is now for women to assume their rightful place. And also how is the women's turn to make out the best of the bargain !

Gandhiji says about women's education in "India of my dreams"- *Harijan* - 27. 2.37)

"I believe in proper education of women. But I do believe that woman will not make her contribution to the world by mimicking or running a race with men. She can run the race, but she will not rise to the great heights, she is capable of, by mimicking man. She has to be compliment of man". Bapuji tried to exhort women, to develop a social outlook, broader than family attachment and to this, he advised them to cultivate inner mental development. To help serve all

"Women hold the key to swaraj
Become expert in your work
Lead a pure life
Falsify the common notion
that women are timid and weak".

Such were the finer sentiments with which Gandhiji preached equality of women. Later on, Panditji, brought out all the necessary laws to lift the status of women in India. To quote a few, the special Marriage Act of 1955, the Right to Property Act are milestones in the progress of women. When the (1955) drafts came up for discussion in the Parliament, even the hardened traditionalists could not vote against, though they grumbled and fretted and fumed in lower tones outside. On account of the towering personality of Nehru, several progressive measures were taken for the awakening of women. Future generations will not be able to forget easily the service rendered by Bapuji and Panditji to the cause of women. Indiraji took the torchlight to the nook and corner of India and spread the gospel throughout the width and breadth of the country.

Kaka Saheb Kalelkar writing an introduction to says "Gandhiji became a Woman" for the purpose of uplifting women. He had in an extraordinary manner developed a woman's heart in himself. So, he was able to reach the hearts of women". He further says "with the age of Gandhi, begins a special age of the awakening of women in our country".

Gandhiji, speaking about the constructive programme said "My greatest hope is in women. They want a helping hand to lift them out of the well, in which they have been kept. The slightest thing will work wonders. They made a record contribution during the *satyagraha* of 1931-32. So little work had been done among them. They are waiting to be organised. They have the capacity for suffering evoked by non-violent effort and they suffer silently. Are we going to fulfill that hope, is the question before those of us, who are in a position to lend that helping hand for our own sake, no less than for the country and the world".

Gandhiji's utterances and writings on behalf of women's cause, could evoke a responsive chord in every well wisher of humanity and even in the most hardened conservative. "Women pure, firm and self-controlled as Sita, Damayanti and Draupadi would command the homage of society as they have done through ages these immortal heroines of fore".

Thus Gandhiji, a passionate lover of humanity, a foe of injustice in whatever form or sphere, espoused the cause of women. In everything he had preached, he began a reform of his own. With his masterly fen, he used every platform, throughout his long life of service, preached against the wrongs done to women, in the name of law, tradition and even religion. He spoke about *purdah*, widowhood, dedication of girls to temple, prostitution, early marriage, dowry system, economic bondage, marital slavery of women".

"I am uncompromising in the matter of women's rights. In my opinion, woman should labour under no legal disability not suffered by man"- with such lofty ideals, Gandhiji made it a convention to have a women's session in every AICC and passed resolutions to liberate women from bondage and slavery. Smt. Rajkumari Amrit Kaur, Smt. Sarojini Naidu did pioneer imaging efforts made by the Congress organisation and contributed to Gandhiji's thought and action.

Since then, several women's organisations came into existence and continued their efforts to educate and to liberate women.

Now, after having traversed a period of trial and hardship, we have come to a stage, when it is no more a taboo to educate a girl. Nowhere it is being discussed, whether education or employment is a 'necessity' for girls. It is taken for granted that Indian woman can adjust with the changing situations, with respect and dignity. Indian culture, being what it is, has imbibed the idea of a woman entering into public life, with utmost grace and charm. The modern woman is able to mix up her 'career' with family life.

'Family life' is still the basis of Indian way of life unlike in western countries and so a career woman has to struggle hard to assert her dual role efficiently.

Who can make a more effective appeal to the heart than women ? Education does not mean literacy, but it means building up of character and development of necessary skills for everyday living. Nobody objects to this, thought if properly interpreted. Slowly, the gap between the urban areas and rural areas is also getting lessoned and the village folk are also realising the importance of socio-economic change.

What remains to be done is creation of more and more opportunities.

When one recollects the days of great national awakening, specially of women's awakening in a tradition-bound society like ours one feels astonished at the enormous amount of work that people put at that time. It was a time when we worked wonders. That was possible on account of dedication and identification with the cause. The same spirit and the same amount of dedication are required to bring about the transformation of society in a steady manner and everyone has got a role to play in this gigantic task, irrespective of his/her position or economic level.

15

A Purely Personal View of Her Personality

In 1971, it was an election held after the Congress split. Mrs. Indira Gandhi set the tone for the poll through a compigning theme "Garibi Hatao". It was a good manner to outwit her detractors who tried to personalise the election with slogans such as"Indira Hatao"and it paid off well.

'Six years later, 1977 elections were held under the dark shadow of the emergency and marked the end of one party, with the installation of the first non-Congress Government at the centre. Three years later, Mrs. Gandhi was returned to power. It was victory built amidst the endless within the Janata Party. Her dealth in 1984, saw the emergence of her son Rajiv, with the election that heralded the promise of hope; the emergence of a brave new India and the promise of a clean and an efficient government that not only worked but "worked faster".

1991 election saw a return to the Congress(S) Rajiv was assassinated during the compaign and the Congress(S) won 270 seats but failed to win a simple majority. P.V. Narasimha Rao became the PM in an election that signalled the growth of BJP (117 seats).

Indian National Congress (I)

—Election Manifesto 1983.

After three years of confusion, between 1977 and 1979, people turned again towards the proven, dedicated and dynamic leadership of the Congress and Smt. Indira Gandhi in 1980. The affairs of the nation were put back on the rails. Economy was pulled out of stagnations planning was resumed. Weaker sections and minorities developed their confidence in government that it would give them the necessary protection and help.

Election Manifesto of Congress (I)

The people of Andhra Pradesh, Karnataka and Tripura are due to elect their State Legislative Assemblies next month. The Indian National Congress - I appeals to the electors of these three states to vote for its policy of defence of integrity and sovereignty of the nation and fight against communal, separatist and divisive forces, inculcating the spirit of Swadeshi and self-reliance, the development of scientific temper and spirit, the strengthening of the Gandhi-Nehru framework of national and international objectives; in short, national unity, national strength and national progress. They should reject parties and individuals who preach narrow loyalty to region, caste and community.

From the beginning the Congress has been a party for freedom and democracy. Under the inspiration of Mahatma Gandhi it became a friend of the poor and the weak and the symbol of secularism. Under Jawaharlal Nehru it became an instrument of peaceful economic transformation. Under Smt. Indira Gandhi's leadership the Congress has helped the nation to make further progress towards social revolution. The country is stronger and economically more dynamic than ever before; all sections, particularly the minorities, the Scheduled Castes and Tribes and the weaker sections, have greater opportunities than at any other earlier point in India's history. The Congress-I Government has paid special attention to the problems of women and the disabled and taken steps to improve their condition. The world recognises India as a force for peace and international goodwill. Country after country has come to grasp India's hand of friendship.

The Indian National Congress is the world's largest democratic party and a unique repository of a whole people's trust. To no other party have a nation's electorate vouchsafed their affection in the manner the Indian people have done to the Congress. The Congress has stood with them in their difficulties ; it has led the nation to victory and safety during invasions; it has given them a faith and a vision.

The strategy of planned development initiated by the Congress has laid the foundations of self-reliant economic growth. The country has attained self-sufficiency in foodgrains and ranks among the first ten nations in the world in the matter of industrial growth. Indian scientists and technologists are held in high esteem throughout the world, for their notable work in many advanced areas, such as space, communications and oceanography.

After three years of confusion between 1977 and 1979 the people turned again towards the proven, dedicated and dynamic leadership of the Congress and Smt. Indira Gandhi in 1980. The affairs of the nation were put back on the rails; the economy was pulled out of stagnation; inflation was checked; planning was resumed; science and technology were once again assigned importance; the Twenty Point Programme was revised and reactivated for achieving greater production and helping the poorest sections; the faith of the minorities and weaker sections in Government's concern for their protection and upliftment was restored and India's links with the non-aligned and friendship with all nations were refurbished. In short, the period of obscurantism was once again replaced by an age of reason.

Wholesale prices had risen in 1979 (when two non-Congressmen were Prime Ministers) by 22.7 per cent. This figure came down to 16.2 per cent in 1980, 5.4 per cent in 1981 and 3.3 per cent in the 11 months of 1982. The production figures in important sectors in the last two years are as follows :

		1980-81	*1981-82*
Food Grains	(Mill. tons)	129.87	132.0
Coal	(Mill. tons)	114.0	124.9
Cement	(Mill. tons)	18.55	20.91
Electricity	(Billion KWH)	111.6	122.9
Railway Freight	(Million tons)	195.9	220.4
Movement Irrigated Areas	(Mill. Hects)	55.1	57.7

The gross national product, which grew by 7.5 per cent in 1980-81, registered a further increase of 4.5 per cent in 1981-82. Even though international trade has been in the grip of difficulties, our exports rose last year by 7 per cent in terms of volume. A stirring symbol of the resurgent self-confidence of the nation in the recent IX Asian Games held in the Capital. They demonstrated how the country is capable of doing things in a big way. They were a triumph of India's organising abilities.

The commitment of the Indian National Congress to the basic interests of the Indian peasantry has always been deep and abiding. During the past two and half years, the farmers of the country have felt reassured and have shown their appreciation of the government's policies by producing record harvests. The farmer has received remunerataive prices for his produce, while the consumer has been protected through a vastly enlarged and strengthened public distribution system.

On the advice of government, the Agricultural Prices Commission has kept in mind the costs of inputs and also brought about a more equitable relationship between agricultural and non-agricultural prices.

In 1982, widespread drought has caused a set-back to our plans for increasing agricultural production. Large number of people have been hard-hit by erratic behaviour of the monsoon. The Central and the State Governments have taken prompt and effective steps to provide relief to people and to protect their incomes. The Congress-I will carry out fully its resolve to render every possible help to the vulnerable sections of the people who are facing this natural calamity of unprecedented magnitude. The manner in which drought relief work has been organised reaffirms the deep commitment of the Indian National Congress-I to policies and programmes designed for the upliftment of the weaker sections of the community.

Two years ago government announced some modifications in industrial policy. Our objectives were fuller utilisation of installed capacity, higher production and productivity, greater employment generation, correction of regional imbalances through special programmes to develop industrially backward areas, promotion of agro-based industries, equitable opportunities for investment and dispersal of small and growing units in rural as well as urban areas. After declaring 1982 as the productivity year, industrial licensing was further liberalised to refix capacity on basis of best production-a totally new concept. Government is also in the process of finalising certain further incentives for priority areas in selected lines of production and industrial location. The new Industrial Policy has already yielded significant results. Despite some difficulties that have arisen during the current year, all possible mesures, including liberalisation of credit, have been taken to maintain the momentum of industrial growth.

Government has provided for a massive investment of over Rs. 97,5000 crores in the Sixth Plan. It has formulated regional and sub-regional development strategies, particularly programmes for backward regions and hill areas. Vigorous action is being taken to mobilise further resources for development. At the same time, successive budgets of the present Congress(I) Government have provided many reliefs. In view of the international situation, high priority has been given to the evolution of a National energy policy.

Coal production is being stepped up. Oil exploration and exploitation are being intensified. In fact, within two years the total domestic production of crude petroleum has doubled. New organisations have been established to suggest alternative energy resources and to explore the resources of the seas around us. A mid-term review of the plan is being undertaken to provide more resources for critical sectors of the economy such as oil exploration and production, coal, railways and power and irrigation.

In January, 1982, Government announced the Revised 20-Point Economic Programme. The Revised Programme takes note of the achievements of the original 20-Point Programme in 1975. It is a comprehensive plan of action to bring relief to the poor sections of the land and also to give a thrust to points of growth. This programme is to be carried out throughout the country, effectively and in a time-based schedule so that our pledges to the toiling masses of the people are fully redeemed.

The heightened respect in which Nations hold India today was evident in the discussions Prime Minister Smt. Indira Gandhi has held with world leaders during her visits to the United Kingdom, the United States, the Soviet Union and the countries in the Arab World and in Africa during the year, as well as with major political dignitaries who visited New Delhi, and in the unanimous request by non-aligned nations that India would pay host to the Seventh Summit Conference of Non-aligned countries in New Delhi in March, 1983. It will be India's endeavour to consolidate the non-aligned movement. We are also determined to improve our relations with our immediate neighbours, viz., Bangladesh, Bhutan, Burma, China, Nepal, Pakistan and Sri Lanka, and also to make our voice heard in two of the major international problems of today–disarmament and reduction of disparities between developed and developing nations.

The Indian National Congress has served India for nearly a century. It is the people's custodian of the national inheritance of the struggle for freedom and for social and economic emancipation. The Gandhi-Nehru framework of policies and programmes alone provides a basis for the nation's continued progress and prosperity. These policies have been tested time and again, as indeed has the leadership of the party from Mahatma Gandhi to the present day. The Gandhi-

Nehru framework of policies has been enriched and taken forward by Prime Minister Shrimati Indira Gandhi through various measures and initiatives taken by her. The nationalisation of banks, insurance and coal, the strengthening of the pivotal role of the public sector, rapid strides in the development of oil resources, the 20-point programme for continuing the fight against poverty, the revival of the National Integration Council, the major initiatives in the field of foreign policy which have protected national interests while at the same time buttressing peace and international cooperation, have enriched the legacy of Mahatma Gandhi and Jawaharlal Nehru.

Not all our problems have been solved, Indeed, each successful step throws up new problems, in addition to the old. The battle for ending poverty is a long and arduous one. Similarly, the task of consolidating the unity of the nation required continuous vigilance. Fissiparous tendencies have not disappeared. Indeed, both external and internal forces are busy fomenting movements that have a tendency to weaken the fabric of national unity. The challenges to the secular foundations of the Indian society come from various quarters. Pernicious ideologies, which are destructive of communal harmony, continue to be propagated by the R.S.S., Jamat-e-Islami and other communal organisations. Dangers to national security have not adated. The induction into Pakistan of a sophisticated weaponry has revived tensions in the sub-continent. Therefore, the challenge of development, the challenge of protecting the unity and integrity of the nation and the challenge of safeguarding our independence in a troubled international environment create formidable tasks. Our people have successfully overcome many hurdles. But more, much more, remains to be done. In the elections that we face, we seek a renewal of the mandate for carrying forward the work the Congress has done in the three and a half decades since independence.

Meanwhile, the opponents of the Congress and of Smt. Indira Gandhi have also been active and aggressive. Refusing to learn from their rejection by the people, they are creating communal trouble, fanning violence, stirring up provincial and regional passions and stocking the forces of fascism. They are trying to hamper industrial production. They are unable to put forward any clear cut programme or policies. They have only been indulging in the politics of character assassination. They have, therefore, to be fought by the determined forces of nationalism.

The total irrelevance of the programmes of the opposition parties is shown by the fact that although they have nothing whatsoever in common ideologically, they are prepared to join hands with one another on the basis of rank opportunism and a totally negative approach, such unprincipled combination, pose a real threat to democracy since, in the very nature of things, they promote divisive and unwholesome trends.

Defence of democracy sounds strange from parties that launched a vendetta against Shrimati Indira Gandhi and used their brute majority to nullify the verdict of the electorate in expelling her from the Lok Sabha. Systematic suppression of opponents, on numerous occasions through physical violence, has characterised the record of these parties when in power. On the other hand, the Congress-I and its leaders have consistently upheld democratic practices and institutions even in the face of serious reversals. If Democracy functions vigorously in India today, credit goes not to those who have used falsehood and calumny to denigrate our leaders but to the painstaking efforts of the Indian National Congress. We are firmly committed to democracy not because it is an instrument of power but because it is the basic prerequisite for the unity and progress of the country.

The Congress-I stands for a strong Centre because that alone would ensure the integrity of the Nation. However, the strength of the Central Government is based upon the strength of the States. There is no conflict between the two. Only within the framework of a planned economy can regional development proceed in a scientific way. Regional aspirations can be satisfied through dynamic development of the national economy. Therefore, the broader national perspective is indispensable for solving problems of backward areas and regions. Congress-I has consistently pursued a policy of channelling resources to areas that have lagged behind in development. Regionalism as the basis of political action can have no meaningful contribution to the solution of the basic problems of the people. This fundamental fact has to be clearly grasped. Otherwise, progress and stability in the wider sense will be jeopardised.

Congress-I appeals to the people to be fore-warned of the dangers ahead and to stand by the forces of integration under its banner. It urges the people to defeat the fragmented, opportunistic and destabilising opposition groups so that the process of social and economic transformation is not weakened.

Congress-1 seeks the mandate of the people for maintaining stability, for the unity of the nation, for orderly economic and social progress, for a better future for the poor in village and in cities and for self-reliance as befitting a great nation. With Shrimati Indira Gandhi as its leader, the country is moving forward towards its cherished objectives. In this dangerous decade of the eighties when the world faces the terrible prospect of extinction by a nuclear holocaust, as well as economic disaster by shortsighted policies of some rich nations, the same voice of India, as symbolised by the Indian National Congress-I and effectively articulated by Smt. Indira Gandhi, needs to be strengthened for the good of humanity as a whole. Support and admiration from other countries have been forthcoming in ample measure, matched by equally solid support by the people of India. This is as it should be and should continue hereafter. Congress-I therefore invites the people of Andhra Pradesh, Karnataka and Tripura to accelerate this process by giving it their over-whelming support.

Of course every election has a significant theme or characteristic. First three elections held in India, after attaining independence were only for affirming and reaffirming faith in the Congress party which was in power. 1967 elections took a different turn, but the support of the voters, Congress (I) could again come back to power.

After Rajia Sultana, Indira Gandhi could prove her capacity to rule such a vast country like India. As per significant steps were in the right direction, she could achieve some remarkable rights and overcome all odds and could bring about the needed change. Her super craftsmanship and her strategic approach in dealing with the problems will remain a good example in the annals of Parliamentary democracy of India.

As our Government, we only nominate an odd writing or painter to the legislatures more to recognise what he or she has done in the past. I am not aware of encouraging sycophants as you describe them".

Speaking about an alternative to the present system of democracy, she said "The only alternative to the British pattern of democracy that we have copied to the American - where real power rests in the President, rather than in the Congress or the senate".

When her attention was drawn to the vulgar display of wealth by the moneyed and the reckless spending of most states, which were in the red and enable even to pay the salaries of their employees, replied "We have lightened our procedures and cut our expenditures".

On another question that pace of development should be speeded up - and the only person, to put the nation was herself, she reacted sharply and said "I don't think I am the only one. That is a wrong mentality. No one person can do everything. This is our major weakness, that everybody depends on the Government to do things. Every group, every individual has a responsibility and must act upto it". "Another weakness is that we hesitate to search for alternatives. If there is not enough rain, we do not look for those crops that can be grown with the least water. We stick to one demand ignoring other possibilities. As some people are now doing with regard to fertilisers. The other day, a farmer from Maharashtra, whom I had met years ago, paid me a visit. At the time of our first encounter, he did not have fertilisers and had suffered from an excessive use of pesticides. Last year, he has doubled his crops by the use of earth worms. It seems that everything the earth worm does is good for the land. I told him to get me a copy of the article written on his work and I have had it distributed among all the ministries concerned".

The journalist, after asking her about religion, astrology, books etc., finally asked whether she though that she had of being a Prime Minister.

"I quite often do feel fed up with politics she exclaimed." Do you ever contemplate giving it up, "How can one give up in the midst of difficulties ?".

"But the difficulties may go on for ever and ever".

"I hope not. I sincerely hope not", she said.

"Do you believe in astrology ?".

"No". She said quite firmly.

"I do not. I don't think any one should base his actions upon it. But it arranges people. I would not come in their way".

"Don't you think we in India have gone, a bit too far in according official patronage to the creative arts has another question of the same Journalist on another occasion. In so doing we have diverted the artists attention from his real job of getting on with his work, to seeking awards".

Mrs. Gandhi turned to Sharada Prasad for elucidation of the point. He looked at the journalist to be more explicit.

"In no democratic country does the state spoon-feed the writers as we do in India. The Sahitya Academy gives them awards, you nominate them to legislatures. Give them Padmasri and Padma Bhushans. Send them out as ambassadors. It creates an unhealthy atmosphere of rivalry - not to excel in creativity but to hand round people in power".

Mrs. Gandhi replied "I don't know about other countries. But I believe in Sweden the Government does as much for its writers and artists surprised. I do spend a lot of time reading", when the question was further continued and he again asked what kind of books she reads and who the favourite authors are, she replied "I don't have favourite topics or favourite authors. I read whatever takes my fancy. I have not read much of Indian authors".

Curious to find out about her religions beliefs, he questioned her" In an interview with BBC, you said that you did need religion as a prop, could you spell that out a little more".

She pamsede. He proceeded further

"Do you believe in God"

She replied "yes, I do. But not God as some kind of be gentleman sitting"

"In front of you?"

She laughed "I was not being personal.

I suppose I believe in Vedanta".

"All of it ? Karma - transmigration of souls and the rest that goes with Vedanta".

"I don't know much about it. I believe be everyone has the right to choose the own religion - his own path".

"There is more to Vedanta than that"

"I said I have not read very much on that subject".

It was a superb performance.

When once questioned by a famous journalist "what in your opinion are our three biggest achievements during the 25 years we have been a free nation", Indiraji said "I suppose the break through in the production of food would be one ....but no, I don't like to catalogue our achievements...There is nothing tangible about such things, I would say, our greatest achievement is to have survived as a free and democratic nation. We have grown to maturity. You can include many other items in that framework".

The journalist again asked her to narrate three biggest failures. "What about our three biggest failures" hoping that she would be pinned down to one, two, three. Her reply was as vague as her reply to the first question." I would say, it is a failure in developing character of conditioning our minds to think among modern lines ....We continue, to be pre-occupied with trifling irrelevances".

When the same journalist questioned her "I don't think you got much time in reading books?, she replied "you will be.

She felt that regionalism as the basis of political action cannot have any meaningful contribution for solving the problems facing the country.

The general elections of 1971 was a sort of Indira wave. Her party could win 350 Lok Sabha seats - 120 more than before. CPM was able to get only 24 seats. All the other opposition parties were docimated. She received support from all the youngsters, who could get voting right since 1947.

• She cleverly managed to use her majority to remould her party and also the country according to her desire. She took charge of the Home and Information and Broadcasting portfolios. She pushed through a number of amendments to the Constitution. She created some new States like Himachal Pradesh, Meghalaya, Tripura and Arunachal Pradesh.

Every cause she took up, she did it with a challenge. She could successfully mobilise public opinion in her favour.

She could exhibit mastery over managing the affairs of the state. She could make Anjaiah, a coolie in the seat of the Chief Minister of Andhra Pradesh and she could successfully dispense with people whom she did not like.

Thus Indira Gandhi's objectives and institutions have been taken forward even after her demise.

Strategy of planned development initiated by Congress had laid down the foundations for self-reliant economic growth. The country had attained self-sufficiency in the production of foodgrains and India had been rated as one of the first nations in the world in the matter of industrial growth.

The gross national product, which grew by 7.5 per cent in 1980-81 had registered a further increase of 4.5 per cent in 1981-82. A resurgent and self-confident nation was emerging and making a mark in the world events too.

Of course, all the problems are not solved. But a successful attempt is being made to achieve good results.

By 1983, Congress (I) stood for a strong centre because that alone would ensure the integrity of the nation.

Congress (I) appealed to the people to be aware of the dangers ahead and to stand by the forces of integration.

PART-II

16

Indiraji's Marriage and Family Life and Her Public Life

Kamala Nehru fell seriously ill and was suffering from tuberculosis. Doctors advised her to be taken to Switzerland for treatment. In those days, in India, perhaps there was no proper medicines for treatment when she was there laying in bed, Firoze Gandhi served her and Indiraji was also by her bed side. Kamala Nehru died when Indiraji was just 17 years old, in the month of February 1936.

Indiraji developed liking for Firoze, a family friend and an active Congress worker. He was a Parsi gentleman and he stood by Indira when she was all alone and in distress. She determined to marry him. This decision was criticized by the family and also others, as Nehru was orthodox Kashmiri Brahmins. Some people even say that even Pandit Nehru did not like the idea very much.

I remember, I have read small anecdote in *Harijan* Patrika. When I stayed in Wardha Ashram in Rustum Bhavan, while writing a book on the freedom struggle of India in the year 1976, one Mr. Apte, the librarian, a freedom fighter and a very nice gentleman, helped me in locating the relevant books. He gave me old files of this *Harijan* Patrika, a fulscape paper costing one anna. Gandhiji used it as an instrument for sending a message to the people as regards our freedom struggle. In one editorial, Gandhiji wrote about his decision to give consent to the marriage of Indiraji with Firoze Gandhiji declared that Firoze was his adopted son and so Panditji's family need not have any objection on such marriage, as he is asking for the hand of Indira in marriage to his son Firoze. Since then, the Firoze has known as Firoze Gandhi, perhaps.

Her determination to marry Firoze, in spite of opposition illustrate her strength of character. They were married in 1942.

Soon after the couple are married, they were arrested and sent to prison on charges of sub-version by the Brishers. This event, Indiraji described as crucial in her life. Her first and only imprisonment lasted from September 11, 1942 to May 13, 1943 at Naini Central Jail in Allahabad. After her release, she took active part in politics. She gave birth to two sons by name Rajiv and Sanjay.

After India achieved independence in 1947, her father Pandit Jawaharlal Nehru became the first Prime Minister of India and he had none to take care of him or his official residence. Indiraji had to manage the official residence of her father and had to accompany him on his numerous foreign trips.

Firoze Gandhi, of course rose to eminence and became a parliamentarian. But some of his criticisms against his illustrious father-in-law annoyed Nehru and so they had to live separately. It was, of course, an acid test for her either to live with her father or to live with Firoze. Anyway, she could manage things intelligently, though she lived with her father officially.

Matters were moving fast and she had to associate herself with several organizations and serve the country. She became chairman of the Central Social Welfare Board (1953-57), member of the Working Committee and Central Election Committee from 1955 and the Central Parliamentary Board from 1956 and president of the All India Youth Congress from 1956 to 1960. In 1955, she was elected to the Executive body of the Congress Party and became a national political figure in her own right. Later on, in 1959, Mrs. Gandhi became the fourth woman, elected to the highest post of the president of the Indian National Congress.

Firoze passed away in 1960. So, it is to be said that Indiraji lived in the shadow of her father for many years and under his influence, she evolved as a strong personality for herself.

In 1964, the year of Pandit Nehru's death, Indiraji was elected to Parliament for the first time. During the Chinese-Indian border issue, she coordinated with civil defence activities. Lal Bahadur Shastri, appointed her as cabinet rank minister in his cabinet.

As Prime Minister, Indiraji tried to improve the lives of Indians and gave a twist to their destiny. She would be definitely remembered by the future generations for her commendable efforts in the development of science and technology, space exploration irrigation as well as policies like nationalization of banks, 20-point programme. In the international arena, she was a forceful woman to speak on behalf of the poorer nations.

She was named as the "Woman of the millennium" in a BBC Poll and she was the first Indian woman to be awarded India's highest civilian honour 'Bharat Ratna' in 1971.

17

Fine Piece of Literature—Letters to Indira Gandhi

Letters to Indira Gandhi, by her illustrious father (30 in number) were published by Oxford University Press, London and they throw light on the deep insight into several topics about Indian Culture and past. They are indeed pieces of scholarly treatment of the issues mentioned in them.

Whole writing a foreword to the first edition, Pandit Nehru wrote as follows "These letters were written to my daughter Indira in summer of 1928, when she was in the Himalayas at Mussorie and I was in the plains below. They were personal letters addressed to a little girl, ten years of age. But friends, whose advice I value, have seen some virtue in them and have suggested that I might place them before a wider audience. I don't know whether other boys and girls will appreciate them. But I hope that such of them as read these letters may gradually begin to think of this world of ours as a large family of nations. And I hope also, though with diffidence, that they may find in reading of them a fraction of the pleasure that I had in writing them.

The letters end abruptly. The long summer had come to an end and Indira had to come down from the mountains. And there was no Mussorie or other hill station for her in the summer of 1929. The last three letters begin a new period and are somewhat out of place by themselves. But, I have included them as there is little chance of my adding to them."

While writing a preface to the second edition, Pandit Nehru wrote "Emboldened by the welcome given to this little book, I had thought of adding to these letters. I had attud myself to a jealous mistress and her service left me little time or inclination to dabble in other matters. Last year, when went to Naini Prison, the thought came back to me and time was not lacking. But prison letters were not frequent and a prison does not provide books of reference. And above all, my mind was too full of making of history, as it was being made from day to day in India, for me too think of the dead past. I came out of jail and returned to it after a brief week of absence and again the months passed. On the 18th of January of this year however, I made a New Year resolve to continue these letters. I made some progress, but too soon, on January 26, I was suddenly discharged. Domestic affliction and the whirlpool of public affairs caught me in their swirl and cast me hither and thither. And I wait again for the peace and quiet of the prison cell to continue this task.

Meanwhile, Indira grows and I might not keep pace for long with her growing knowledge. (Allahabad—October, 1931—J.Nehru)

Thought it is a small book of 75 pages, speaks of many matters pertaining to India's past.

As it is very difficult to reproduce all the articles in, toto, I would like to give a glimpse of some of the articles, whom I liked.

First I will say about "The Book of Nature" "Our Earth is very-very old—millions and millions of years old. And for a long, long time, there were no men or women living in it. Before the men came, there were lonely animals and before the animals, there was a time when no kind of life existed on the earth. It is difficult to imagine this world of ours which is so full today of all kinds of animals and men, to be without them. But scientists and those who have studied and thought a great deal about these matters tell that there was a time when the earth was too hot for anything being to live on it. And if we read their books and study the rocks and the fossils, we can ourselves see that this must have been so.

You read history in books. But in ancient times, when men did not exist, surely no books could have been written. How then can we find out what happened then? We cannot 7merely sit down and imagine everything.

We have rocks and mountains and seas and stars and rivers and deserts and fossils of old animals. These and other like things are our books for the earth's early history. And the real way to understand this story is, not merely to read about it in other peoples books but to go to the great Book of Nature itself. Imagine how fascinating it is!

How then, did the pebble become so round and smooth and shiny? It will tell you its story if you have good eyes to see and ears to hear it.

In another letter entitled "How early history was written", Nehru wrote "From the Book of Nature, we could learn something those far-off days when no man or animal lived on the earth of ours......The power of thought will make them really different from the animals....As cities grew, people learnt many beautiful arts....They also learn how to write....To learn the story of these early, days of cities and countries, we sometimes get old books... The kings and emperors of old times used to have accounts of their reigns written on stone tablets and pillars.... We shall learn also of the great days of India when *Ramayana* and *Mahabharata* were written and India was a rich and powerful country. Today our country is poor and foreign people govern us."

Further speaking about *Ramayana* and *Mahabharata* in the last articles Nehru said "In *Ramayana*, we are told that Rama was helped by monkeys...It may be that the story of the *Ramayana* is really a story of the fights of the Aryans against the people of the south, whose leader was Ravana. Probably the monkeys were the dark people living in Southern India. The Ramayana is full of beautiful stories....

The icame long after Ramayana. It is a much bigger book. It tells of a great fight between Aryans and Aryans. But apart from fight, it is a wonderful book, full of great ideas and noble stories. Above all, it is dear to all of us because of that jewel of a poem which it contains *–The Bhagavat Gita.*

These were the books written in India, thousands of years ago, who but the greatest of men could have written them? Though they were written so long ago, they live today in India and every child knows of them and every grown up is influenced by them."

In between, there are letters on kings and temples and priests, fossils and ruins, language, writing and numerals, China and India, the great cities of the ancient world, the early civilizations, and the changes brought about agriculture.

And these letters make an interesting study and every child will be highly influenced by reading them.

Indira Gandhi would have been proud to be the daughter of such a great man and it was this sort of strong foundation that made her a strong and determined person.

She was born as the famous daughter of Pandit Jawaharlal Nehru. She achieved greatness by her deeds.

In just five years, after her becoming the Prime Minister, Mrs. Gandhi had given the nation a new status in the international affairs.

She could attract the attention of world media. She became a world figure and a world leader. She personified India.

18

Some Attributes to Indiraji's Contribution

While writing a foreword to a book, Zail Singh, Chief Minister of Punjab wrote "I shall not be exaggerating if I say that she is the greatest woman that the world has produced so far... we are fully confident that with all her wisdom and determination she will come out successful from all the tests of history. She has also scored a great victory in the field of diplomacy by holding the Simla Summit, and entering into a treaty of friendship with Pakistan."

When an Italian Journalist asked Indira, to name the most beautiful moment of her life. She replied "my life has been so full of excitement that it is difficult to highlight any special occasion. But I would say that perhaps the most wonderful moment was when I hold my first child in my arms."

When some people asked for her feelings as a woman prime minister, she replied "I do not regard myself as a woman in regard to the job. Even my becoming a prime minister, women have held very responsible positions in India as ministers, and governors. There are villages where elected local councils consist entirely of woman". Her attitude towards a woman during a man's job is not a delicate issue. What is right and respectful can be done by any individual, she felt. Her letter on the subject of a hand shake, indicates, how meticulous she was in her dealings with people and also in correspondence. She personally replied as many as she could. 'Answering an American interviewer, she said, preferred, the Indian style of greeting with folded hands. "It is so graceful. Besides, it is more hygienic" she said.

She was a tireless worker, rarely retiring before midnight, often working till the early hours of the morning. Once she took a plane to London after working non-stop for 20 hours.

She had to have meetings with visiting dignitaries, sittings of Parliament and its important committees, official conferences, public meetings and political confrontations.

She had remarkable patience to listen to others. She avoided philosophical discourses and she liked to stick to the point under discussion always.

Her heavy schedule left for her very little time for favourable pursuits like reading, gardening, liking in mountains or being close to nature. But she used to say "relaxations is an attitude of mind".

A Born Leader

Everyone, who observed her from close quaters during the last 6 years of her life, would certainly observe that she was a born leader. When more difficulties worried her, her self-confidence grew marvellously almost in direct proportion.

She was a powerful unifying force. Her capacity to deal with state leaders was remarkable. She always tried to keep up political stability states. Her role, of course, was not fully appreciated sometimes or realized. But she never budged an inch. She stuck to her method of working and never allowed anyone to distort her sense of balance. She always kept up her pre-eminent position. Even her success did not make her lose her balance. Her massive victory in the election was not considered by her as a triumph. She took it only as an opportunity to some people.

Her Outstanding Quality Her Courage

Pandit Nehru used to tell her it seems, "one little test, I shall ask you to apply, whenever you are in doubt. Never do anything in secret or anything that you would wish to hide. For the desire that you want to hide anything means that you are afraid and fear of a bad thing and worthy of you. Be brave and turn all the rest follows."

This lesson had a tremendous impact on her and so freedom from fear and stoic courage have been all along her outstanding qualities.

Her Loneliness—Her Plus Point

As a child, Indira led a life of loneliness because her parents and grand parents were in the political upheaval and were in and out prison frequently.

She attended her first political meeting as a restless spectator in the arms of her grandfather, Shri Motilal Nehru, a stawart of the freedom movement. At the age of three she was delivering her lectures to her pet dolls. At twelve, she organized a monkey-brigade of children, unable to move freely because of surveillance and to cook food or to give first aid to the victims of frequent cane-charges by the police.

At 24, she was in jail by herself, so was her husband, Firoze whom she married only a few months earlier. She was locked up in an ordinary prison cell along with 22 other inmates, many of whom were common criminals. She was not allowed any visitor, until she was released several months later.

She had no formal degrees or diplomas. But judging from what she has achieved, her achievements were noteworthy.

Sri M. Chalapathi Rao, Editor, *National Herald* in his "Indira—a portrait in outline" says,

"There is always freshness about what Indira Gandhi thinks or says or writes. "Her utterances are always clear. She never wobbles, she consults as many people as possible, but she makes up her mind. In whatever she had tried to be, her strength of character emerges. Then there is her awareness, her capacity in spite of silences, to come to the point, of outrageous candour. She is basically a political being, with no prevention to being a blue-stocking even among blue stockings, with no intellectual pose or of any kind. She has immense political understanding and a wide experience of men and affairs and of the worlds continents and countries. And all these and other qualities, may not be enough to make a successful prime minister. Luck is necessary.

"What is my inheritance? What am I heir to" asked Jawaharlal Nehru. To talk of Indira's inheritance as only part of a paternity is rather a petty views. She is also heir to the ages through which Indira has passed; and she will never dishonour herself or her country."

Lina Parasher wrote

"The infant Indira was brought up in a princely manner. Her Pram was specially ordered by her grandfather from a famous firm Calcutta. "I am always thinking of Indira" he wrote "The very thought of a personification of innocence is soothing. By a very easy slip, it justifies idol worship." Everyone adored her. She seemed the fully conscious of her position. "You were the proudest looking baby I had ever seen" told Sarojini Naidu endearingly to her years later she was six months old then and had come in the arms of her grand mother to receive the celebrated poetess on the steps of Ananda Bhavan.

She possesses elegance, grace and great charm. She is a person of transparent honesty and begets trust. She has legendary reputation for sincerity. She is a natural and she is consistently true to herself. She has, what is impossible in politics to keep only one face. She has lived up to the advice of Gandhi. "Indira, there are two kinds of people, those who do the work and those who take the credit. Belong to the first category."

Indira's election to the high office marks a change in the temper and mood of the nation. She is a bridge between two generations, one which fought the independence struggle and the other which is anxious to make the best use of it. She may be able to evolve a new harmony based on science and custom and give a useful lead to the younger generation distrustful of old values and apt to lose itself in the twists of a fast rhythm possessed of the lofty idealism of Nehru, and the unerring instinct of a woman for the practical she may yet prove to be the fundamental statesman of our era."

Power "Jawaharlal Nehru said brings responsibility and responsibility brings constraint and mellowness. And it goes without saying, that more than anything else, Indira Gandhi's paramount objective... to preserve the national unity to which she has become a shining symbol.

"Indira Gandhi has maintained in her handling international affairs, a style which is a cross between those of her two predecessors.

She has moved away from Shastri's "little India" posture but she has scrupulously refrained from following in her father's footsteps and getting entangled in intricate international issues. Vietnam is an eloquent example." Krishan Bhatia wrote;

"Indira Gandhi is a child of destiny. Few people in recent history have been so disinterested in power and yet have had so much responsibility and authority placed on their shoulders as Indira Gandhi.

For one who walked into office with such lack of personal ambition, Indira has always attended to her responsibilities with tremendous gusto.

Her emergence as the leader has marked the beginning of a new phase in the history of modern Indian politics. It means the end of the generation which had directed and fought the battle of independence and the transfer of power to the next generation. Indira Gandhi is apparently conscious of it. That explains her appeals to the Youth of India. K. M. Aggarwal said,

"On the occasion of Indira's taking over, Nehru said her election was an indication that the doors of the Congress were open to Youth, women and everyone who desired to serve the country. He also added that he was proud of her temperament, energy, affection and integrity—qualities which she inherited from her mother.

Indira Gandhi reacts quickly to things and takes prompt decisions. Her utterances on vital issues are unambiguous. She is firm about our policy of democracy and socialism and also in our policy of peaceful coexistence and non-alignment, one may expect her to adopt and adjust herself to new situations.

Indira does occasionally produce Sarojinis and Indiras. The wife of the American ambassador Chester Boules said "Traditionally Indian women have progressed politically and are far ahead. They went to jail along with men in the country's freedom struggle."

Courtesy (1) Indira Gandhi-A political biography by S. S. Sahota

(2) Indira Priyadarsini By Popular Book Services, New Delhi.

(Last-as a reference the chapter.)

Indira Gandhi was caricatured as "The Saviour of democracy" by B.K. Ahluwalia

"Smt. Indira Gandhi symbolizes the resurgent India of today and the aspirations of the people. Now more than ever, the Congress and the nation need her leadership and guidance."

"The nation is certainly passing through a crisis. But every crisis is also a turning point. Let us make this one of those turning points in our history heralding a big leap forward in pursuit of our national objective of a dynamic, self-reliant socialist society."

"Mrs. Gandhi is most anxious to bridge the gap between the rich and the poor and is against all privileges of all kinds. Our constitution provides equality of status and opportunity.

Indira made repaid advances in the field of science and technology as well. The underground nuclear test explosion in Pokharan in Rajasthan in May 1974 and launching of Aryabhata, the unmanned space satellite in April 1975 are the results of long years of study and research by the Atomic Energy Commission and the Space Commission respectively.

Another outstanding achievement of Indira Gandhi is the successful drilling operations in Bombay High. "Sagar Samraat", the mobile drilling platform, which arrived in Bombay waters in May 1973, started drilling operations in October 1973. Oil has been found in all the five wells drilled."

"She has great love for the masses which is heartily reciprocated by the masses. She draws the largest crowds.

Child welfare is a work nearest to her heart.

John Grigg write, "Nature and experience have made her a secret person, very good at concealing her intention, always much readier to listen than to talk. But she knows how to take the decisions and when to take them."

It is her consideration for others, sensitivity to the needs of others, social consciousness and her constant endeavour to work with a singleness of purpose to make life worth living for the people that has endeared her today to the masses and has made her the "Soul of New India"

Rafiq Zakaria wrotes,

"Her greatness lies in the fact that she has done single handed against the heaviest odds that any leader had to face, both internally and externally.

There are two distinct Indiras that merges broadly out of any study of her, the Pre-1969 Indira and the Post-1969 Indira.

The impact of her personality on men and events in the two periods has been so different and decisive that a distinctive evaluation of each period becomes inevitable.

What happened to her after the Bangalore Session in 1969?

"Mrs. Gandhi is not easy to dissect I doubt whether even those who have been close to her know her fully. She has always maintained a dignified aloofness from the closest of them.

Dr. Shankar Dayal Sharma in his article on "Indira Gandhi and the Congress heritage and pledge" says, "An inheritor of the Gandhi—an age and a child of political revolution, Smt. Gandhi started in right earnest an economic and social revolution to lend real content and substance to the ideologies and programmes that the Congress had set before the people during the struggle for Independence. In her broadcast to the nation within two days after assuming office, declared her commitment to the objectives laid down by her illustrious faiths and proclaimed "we have promises to keep to our people—of work, food, clothing and shelter, health and education."

Smt. Gandhi felt that the troubles of the country were not due to any shortcomings in basic policy or ideology, but in the economic development, as in other fields of national activity. To bridge this gap she was determined to adopt whatever changes were found necessary in the administration, in the organization and in the field of legislation.

The tasks set before the country and the party is a challenging and exciting one.

The Congress was reborn to recapture its hold among the masses to rouse new hopes and aspirations among the people and to redeem its pledges to the people.

Why Smt. Gandhi has chosen to be the torch bearer of the reorganized and resurgent Congress became meaningful when one takes into consideration the guidelines that had been handed over to her by her father and the role that he had envisaged of Congress for national reconstruction.

When the political turmoils of this age became part of history, the rule of Smt. Indira Gandhi will stand out as a unique contribution not only to India but to the whole world. Few persons in history have been able to do such yeoman service for the welfare of people in a short time as Smt. Gandhi.

If Pandit Nehru "discovered" India, Indiraji has "rediscovered" the spirit of her people.

K.P.S. Menon says,

"Mrs. Gandhi has become a world figure. There has not been a sudden debut on the world's stage but a process of gradual evolution.

The Russian Government made elaborate arrangement when Indira was on a private visit in 1953 to visit Leningrad, Tibilisi, Yalta and Tashkent, where ever she went she left the most pleasant impressions.

How right Edmund Burke was when he said "Great empires (or republics) and little minds ill together."

D. Devaraj Urs discribing her as the "greatest woman", said "Born to a great father and a brave mother, she is bravery personified. Being the product of a highly cultured and aristocratic family, she is at once a combination of the common and the sublime."

Smt. Indira Gandhi is born to fulfil a purpose and with the qualities of head and heart, she is endowed with and the remarkable toughness and fortitude, which she has exhibited in the days of the great split, at the time of the Indo-Pakistan war and during the great famine, I am sure she will be able to hold the country together and carry the people towards. The goal of an India, strong, self-reliant and unafraid."

Speaking on the foreign policy under Indira Gandhi, Dr. V.P. Dutt MP said "India's foreign policy during the decade under Smt. Indira Gandhi's stewardship had to weather many crises. Some of the crises and threats that came from outside were potentially so dangerous that they could have delivered fatal blows to the very existence to this country as an independent state. Indira Gandhi face them with a skill which some of the more mature nations in the world could have envied. In foreign relations also, the ship of state was steered through stormy waters by the prime minister through a combination of firmness, flexibility and realism.

This decade also saw the development of close cordial and fruitful relations with a large number of countries of the world, particularly the Asian and African countries, the non-alinged nations and the Socialist world. India also played a significant role in world affairs during this period. With Latin America and Africa, new links were forged.

Jawaharlal Nehru laid the foundations of India's foreign policy. The framework set up by him today, had been accepted by a large majority of the countries of the world. This has not made for continuity in India's foreign policy and the last decade has seen further development and maturity of these principles under Smt. Indira Gandhi's leadership, with the independence of the emergent countries for a more just world order.

During this period, the country was suddenly confronted with unusual and unique challenges, which required all the resilience and resourcefulness, which the country's leadership could bring into play, for at stake was the unity and integrity of India.

Millions of refugees poured into India. By the autumn of 1971, nearly 10 million crossed into this country. India was burdened with the stupendous task of feeding, clothing and providing shelter to the mass of humanity.

The liberation of Bangladesh was a victory of the forces of democracy and secularism.

One significant development in India's foreign policy had been the thrust on the development of relations with Sri Lanka, Nepal, Burma and Afghanistan. Another crucial problem requiring determined leadership was the handling of Sikkim issue. Non-aligned movement-Smt. Gandhi attended both the Lusaka summit in 1970 and in 1973 in Algiers also.

Indo-Soviet relations: with the socialist countries, India developed extensive economic and cultural relations.

India raised its voice against the war in Vietnam and supported the people's struggle for freedom and unity in India-China.

India stretched the hand of friendship to all countries of the world and Indira Gandhi's leadership could successfully meet the difficulties and challenges.

Gopal Singh said, "Nehru was the architect and Indira the builder of socialist India."

Dr. Henry Austin said, "probably no woman in history has assumed a heavier burden of responsibility and certainly, no country of India's importance has before entrusted so much power to a woman under democratic conditions. She has a sharp mind, a strong will and a dedicated spirit."

The secret of her success based on the affection of the masses of India, lies in her being the best representative of the land. She was not a day dreamer.

Marion Woolfson, Mrs. Indira Gandhi, 50-year-old prime minister, straight and slim with delicate features on a visit to Japan, looked down upon awe and amazement there, for the thought of a woman premier especially in Eastern Region-is remarkable.

Indira Gandhi gets annoyed when journalists talk of "frail health" because her health is excellent.

Because of India's huge population, the poverty that exists... no prime minister in the world has a less enviable task than Indira Gandhi.

But, knowing the kind of woman she is, I believe she will do her utmost—as she has done all her life—for the welfare of the country.

19

Indiraji's Years of Hard Endeavour– Some Selected Speeches

Address at Moscow University*

Four years ago I had the privilege of participating in the fiftieth anniversary celebrations of the historic October Revolution. Today, you have accorded me another high honour, I value it greatly, knowing that through this gesture you are demonstrating your esteem and affection for India and her people. I accept this honour on behalf of the 550 million people of India whose good wishes I bring to you and to the people of the Soviet Union.

Moscow has been the symbol of the history and spirit of your country even as Delhi is the symbol of India's endurance and continuity. Moscow is a great city, not merely because of its size, not merely because it is the capital of the world's largest country, but because it has been the home of scholars and artists, many of whom have come from this great University, and who fulfilling the hopes of your great founder, Lomonosov have enriched the world's treasure of knowledge. Specially in the last fifty years, the Moscow State University has played a notable role in the great educational processes by which the arts and the science has become the common possession of the whole people. When I was a teenager, my father wrote to me of the significance of this planned extension of knowledge to all classes. Twenty years later, when I first visited the Soviet Union I was deeply impressed by the vigour and sweep of your educational system.

We achieved independence a little over 25 years ago. These two-and-a half decades have seen major game; the doubling of food production and the trebling of industrial output. The foundations of

* September 29, 1971.

basic industry have been firmly laid. The economy has become more diversified and the absorption of modern technology has made it more resilient.

Eighty million children are now in schools, and every year 75,000 engineers are trained. In simple human terms; an index of the improvement which has taken place is that the life expectation figure, which was around 30 in 1947, has now gone up to 54. But we have still to make up for the ground we lost when under colonial rule progress by-passed us. Even if its progress had been faster, India would still have a long and hard road to travel before being able to provide basic needs to all her people.

The struggle which was led by Mahatma Gandhi and Jawarharlal Nehru released us from colonial rule and ushered in an era of peaceful endeavour devoted towards transforming our society. We now have political freedom, but vestiges of the old order—of feudalism and the tyranny of traditional social custom—still persist, and our struggle against them must continue. But the forces of progress are decisively stronger and they must prevail.

Our path has been strewn with-formidable obstructions but we have struggled and toiled and we move forward. The effort has largely been our own, as indeed it should be. But help in crucial areas has come from friendly nations to enable us to acquire modern technology. The Soviet Union is among the nations which have shown understanding of our problems. The Soviet Union has given us co-operation and has helped in the building of our industrial structure. Our people are, appreciative of this fraternal help.

A few weeks ago, the Soviet Union and India signed a Treaty of Peace, Friendship and Co-operation. The people of both countries have widely acclaimed it as an act of political sagacity. Our friendship is rooted in shared and unshakable faith in peace and progress.

The efforts of the Indian people are often thwarted by forces beyond our control. Earlier this year in our General Elections, the people of India gave us a mandate for progress. We were about to embark upon a new programme of economic advance, when from across our frontiers we had a new kind of invasion: not of armed men, but of a vast influx of helpless terror-stricken men, women and all children from East Bengal—some wounded, some ill and all hungry. More than 9 million people have come in the last six months, and they continue to pour in. Has there been a greater migration in history?

When millions of people are pushed into another's territory, jeopardizing its normal life, its plans for the future, and its very

.security, it is obvious that peace is in peril. We have shown the greatest forbearance, but it is essential that the basic cause of the crisis be immediately removed by a political solution acceptable to the people concerned. Unfortunately, there is no sign that this is being attempted. It is the word's responsibility to create without further delay conditions to enable the refugees to return to their homes in safety and dignity.

While there is hardly any area of the earth yet undiscovered, each year reveals some new aspect of knowledge and the need for deeper exploration. The journey of your valiant cosmonauts into space opened the way to new worlds—not to conquer but to comprehend.

How much has knowledge grown and man's capacity to do! What seems wonderful to us is taken for granted by today's children. The young, far more knowledgeable and competent than before, are also more restless. For, each generation tends to be bound by its own experience, and the young are impatient of all that constricts them. There is a groping in the realm of ideas whose shapes have not yet emerged in all clarity, but whose outlines are vaguely perceived. These are the ideas which will grow in the tomorrows to come. More and more people feel that narrow or dogmatic formulations cannot help much. We need the capacity to discover new concepts and to amend, to enlarge and to discard them, if necessary, in the light of new experience and growing knowledge.

The conviction that we can and must shape the future has been the motive force of political revolutions and of scientific break-throughs. We can best prepare for the future by developing minds which are free of prejudice and which override divisive bounds of creed, of race and of nation; minds, capable of understanding the forces which affect man as an individuals and as a social being. No man should feel alienated from nature or from his fellow men.

May I thank you again for the honour which you have done to me and to the people of India, by conferring upon me a degree at this great centre of learning?

Speech at Institute of International Relations*

It is indeed a privilege to address the Royal Institute of International Affairs, and this gives me the opportunity to tell you something about my country and the thinking of the one-seventh of mankind who live there. Each country is so involved in its own

* Brussels, October 25, 1971.

problems that it can seldom keep up with trends and events thousands of miles away.

The world is one but each of us sees it from a different angle. There is the national point of view, which depends upon its geographical position and its historical evolution. There is the personal point of view, largely determined by one's political philosophy and economic status. For two centuries or more, Europe dominated the world. In the present century, the United States and later the Soviet Union came to share this influence. Only after World War II did Asia become a factor in European thinking. Africa appeared on the world scene a little later.

Until the countries of Asia and Africa had struggled for and won their freedom, their problems and even their rich treasure of civilisation and culture were of concern to only a few scholars and specialists. Now there is better communication and little more knowledge, but developments in Asia are still measured by the standards and way of living of the affluent countries.

It is 24 years since our Independence. Until then we could have no foreign or for that matter, any other policy since decisions were taken for us, not by us.

My father's interest in freedom and justice was not limited to our own struggle. He came to the meeting of the League Against Imperialism here in Brussels in 1926 and met the leaders of other Independence movements. Thus, he had personal contacts with what was happening in other countries and he was a true citizen of the world. He gave our nationalist movement clear ideas about the kind of political institutions we wanted in the future and the manner in which we would conduct our relations with other countries. It is this that enabled us to see our problems not as exclusive Indian ones but in the perspective of the world's problems.

An organic world view unites our internal and external policies. Politically, we have established institutions which, in the worlds of our own Constitution, are informed by a passion "for political, economic and social justice". Our democratic impulse owes its origin not so much to the legislative institutions, introduced during colonial rule as to the entire spirit of people's sovereignty which our nationalist movement had evoked. Economically, our endeavour is to overcome, as early as possible, our crippling poverty and to lessen the inequalities which were bred by colonialism, feudalism and the delay in adopting modern technology. We are modernising our agriculture, and expanding and diversifying our industrial base so as to become self-reliant.

Since Independence the economic and social transformation of the country represents a vast qualitative advance during the first half of this century. Under colonial subjugation, India's per capita income remained stagnant. The availability of goods and services per person in the middle 1940's was roughly the same as at the turn of the century. Our sustained efforts in the years after Independence have enabled the growth of national income to be maintained at a rate of about 3.5 per cent per annum. In recent years the economy has tended to grow at an even faster pace. The country is now self-sufficient in food. With increasing expansion in irrigation facilities and fertiliser output, major breakthroughs are expected in other farm products as well. Starting from a flimsy base of consumer goods, industrial production has attained a range of depth and sophistication during the last two decades, the dramatic decline in the death rate and the perceptible increase in the longevity of our people reflects the state of progress. Disparities do remain but the standard of living has risen substantially for all sections of the community even for those who continue to be under diverse social disabilities. The rigidity of traditional Indian society is weakening. Education and the political system have given confidence to our people. Women are participating actively in all fields of life.

India lags behind the industrially advanced countries of the West in terms of material comforts, but it has a pervasive social coherence which provides a firm foundation for accelerated economic growth in the coming years. During the nationalist movement our greatest emphasis was on non-violence, tolerance and on diversity within unity. The leadership of Mahatma Gandhi conditioned us to choose the path of settling disputes through peaceful methods. This explains why, from the very moment of our freedom, we have stood for world peace, for non-alignment with military blocs, and for friendship with all nations, irrespective of their political systems.

We have never equated 'non-alignment' with neutrality or unconcern with world problems or disassociation with countries belonging to power blocs. To us, the word has meant independence of judgment and action in international affairs, according to the merits of particular issues as they affect our own national interests and world peace. In the bipolar world of the early fifties, the very word 'non-alignment' irritated some. But the years have seen a blurring of the rigidity of alignment. Those who swore by alliances are making overtures to members of the opposite camp and to the non-aligned. In the conditions of India, the principal problem of mankind is not the contest for power but the stark facts of poverty. The majority of the world's peoples are poor. They could be helped to a better life if their energy and resources which are today directed towards war were invested in their welfare. Problems on our own doorstep naturally tend to loom large.

A new crisis which has arisen surpasses in its magnitude all the earlier crises which have confronted us. Over nine million people of East Bengal—practically equal to the population of Belgium—have been terrorised and persecuted by the military rulers of Pakistan, and have been pushed inside our territory, jeopardising our normal life and our plans for the future. Should the world not take note of this new kind of aggression? This is not a civil war in the conventional sense. It is a genocidal programme of civilians merely because they voted democratically. It is cynical use of helpless human beings as a weapon against a neighbour nation. We in India have shown the greatest self-restraint but there is no doubt that our stability and security are gravely threatened. Indeed, we feel the threat is to the peace of the entire region. This basic cause of this crisis must be remedied. A political solution must be found to this problem and to be effective it must be acceptable to the elected representatives of the peoples of Bangladesh. To hold elections for seats which are not vacant in the present conditions of repression and chaos has no meaning or purpose. It is the responsibility of all those who are interested in peace to create conditions to stop the further influx of refugees and to enable those who are already in India to return to their homes in safety and dignity and without further delay.

Belgium has been the centre-piece of West European unity which is rightly the most cherished and urgent of your present objectives. Europe, so long rent by discord, is now pooling its resources for the solution of common problems. The European Economic Community is a great experiment in the voluntary coordination of national policies for larger regional purposes—not of war but of peace and development. An alliance for war provokes counteraction. But an alliance for peace has deeper ramifications. We welcome the relaxation of tensions in Europe and the treaties signed between the Federal Republic of Germany and U.S.S.R. and Poland. We hope that steps to further reduce tension will be taken.

We welcome European unity but we hope that it will not be aimed against any region, and that economic arrangements amongst advanced countries will not impose new hardships on those who like us, are making super-human efforts to stand on their feet. Belgium has adopted enlightened policies of international aid to developing countries. However, the terms of international trade have been steadily worsening for the suppliers of primary materials. A positive trade policy designed to help and not frustrate the efforts of developing countries would be worthy of the vision for which Belgium has been known.

Speech at Vienna Banquet*

It was a happy coincidence that I arrived here on your national day and was thus enabled to see a large number of your people in a happy mood. I have had the pleasure of being in Vienna several times and once in 1955 with my father. You had just signed the historic State Treaty and the last of the foreign troops were due to leave your territory. You were also giving final touches to the Opera House which was built with the help and the goodwill of all the people of your country. It was a memorable insight into the rebirth of a people after a dark period of suffering. I think it was a good time to be here and so is this for we were all delighted at your return to this high office. May I take this opportunity of offering once again my personal congratulations and those of the government and the people of India?

Vienna is beautiful in any season. Its ethos vibrates with the music of great masters and the thought impulses of authors and philosophers. It is a city of the mind in a special sense, for here it was that men at the frontiers of knowledge delved deep into the human mind to discover insights that were to revolutionise the patterns of modern thought.

Mr. Chancellor, you have referred to my father. We in India have grown up under the influence of Mahatma Gandhi and my father whose ideas raised us above the pettiness of the daily grind and the manoeuvring associated with politics. Our aim was liberation not only from foreign rule but equally from all that was evil within our own society. Even at the height of our struggle we did not allow bitterness or hatred to creep in. We made a distinction between colonialism and the British people. My father had always taken an

* October 27, 1971.

active interest in international affairs and contemporary thinking on economic and other matters. He wanted India to be rational and self-reliant. He laid the foundations of modern industrial India and of an independent foreign policy. It is my endeavour to follow the path laid down by him and to translate his dreams into reality and this is not because he happened to be my father but because that direction and those policies were based on a realistic assessment of the Indian scene and formulated in the perspective of our long-term progress.

India's journey has not been easy but step by difficult step we have gone ahead, belying the prophets of doom. Today our other and not inconsiderable problems are overshadowed by events on our borders. In Austria you have the experience of dealing with refugees. So you can perhaps imagine the burden of looking after an influx which is of the size of Austria's own population. But the problem of refugees is an incidental one. It can be solved only be going into the reasons which have compelled these helpless millions to leave their homes, to seek inadequate shelter and live in the greatest discomfort in overcrowded camps on our territory. Many of them, even during the heavy rains of the monsoon, were forced to sit under trees for days. The Indian tradition has always been to offer shelter to the persecuted. However, we cannot accept this charge as a permanent one.

At this moment our main concern is not merely looking after a large number of people but the very real threat to our security and stability which this holds, which these developments have imposed on us. The people of India value the sympathy and understanding which we have received from Austria and are grateful for the support which you have extended to us. It is our sincere wish that Austro-Indian friendship will grow steadily over the coming years. Whether in international affairs or in domestic affairs, there are bound to be problems. Our own experience has been that no sooner do we solve one problem than ten new ones come to take its place. But we think this is part of life and we think that solving each problem itself gives us the strength to face the others.

There is something written in an old Sanskrit book, "The History of Kashmir", which I should like to quote to you. It really talks about life but of course it is as true of the life of the individual as the life of the nation. "Shadow is itself unrestrained in its path while sunshine as an incidence of its very nature is pursued a hundredfold by nuances. Thus is sorrow from happiness a thing apart. The scope of happiness, however, is hampered by the aches and hurts of endless sorrow."

I thank you once again for your gracious invitation to me, for the wonderful hospitality and friendship that you and the people of Austria have given to me and my party and for the welcome which you mentioned and, if I may add, which extended even to the very good weather which you have provided for us. May I ask you all to drink to the health of the Chancellor and Madame Kreisky, to the welfare and prosperity of the people of Austria and to lasting friendship between our two countries?

Speech at Austrian Society for Foreign Policy and International Relations*

May I say first that I regard this as a great privilege to be allowed to come here and say a few words before such a very distinguished audience?

Usually, when people think of India they either think of the bejewelled fabulous maharajas, or of the abject poverty of the people. Or they think that we are idealists whose philosophy has not much relevance to the realities of the day. Perhaps all this is true but it is only a very small part of the picture of a very vast country. It is a country which has its problems, but it is not all problems. It is a country which along with the problems has music and dancing. It has its art and culture and even amongst the poorest people you will find laughter and joy in life.

I did not really want to go into the details of Indian problems, but I think it is important that people in Austria should know something about my country, because it is a importance what happens there. It is of importance not only to Asia, but, I think, to Europe as well.

India is a land of many contradictions, existing in different centuries, people strongly asserting themselves yet fearful of any fundamental change. There is a constant clash between tolerance and dogma, between the basic Indian values and the superficial habits of

Speech at Royal Institute of International Affairs**

I am glad of this opportunity of addressing such a distinguished gathering which includes many specialists on India. I am confining my remarks to only one theme, that is, democracy in India, but, I

* Vienna, October 28, 1971.

** London, October 29, 1971.

believe, there will be a question period after this. Presumably we shall be able to cover other matters then.

During our struggle for Independence, it seemed that freedom itself would be fulfilment. But, when we achieved it we knew that every completion was a beginning. For us, this was a start of a great experiment in the creation of democracy in an ancient, complex and vast country.

The story of Indian development is not without significance for the rest of the world. How could it be otherwise when it encompasses the aspirations and struggles of over 550,000,000 human beings? Political theorists with their neatly labelled indices have sometimes spoken of democracy in India as a futile quest. To them, democracy could only be a two-party system worked by those who were educated in a particular way. Perhaps as advanced people of the West a generation ago prompted that the colonial countries were not ready for freedom, so it was said that the underdeveloped societies of Asia and Africa were not ready for democracy, and could achieve order only under dictatorship of some kind or, at most, a controlled or guided democracy. Can democracy be guided any more than freedom? Is not a guided democracy a contradicting? Perhaps these questions are irrelevant. For it now seems that in some countries the word "democracy" was used as a shield for reaction and the subversion of freedom. But we did take democracy seriously. To us it conveyed the equality of all people to participate at every level in the development of their country and the functioning of government.

In the choice of political institutions, it is not inevitably the past that is decisive, but the changing condition of the lives and attitudes of people and the capacity of those who are in positions of leadership to involve the largest number of people in the political process.

The British ruled over us for two hundred years. Little did those early colonisers realise that along with their flag they brought the seeds which would destroy their rule. Macaulay, who pleaded so passionately for Western education, did not quite realise that he was undermining the edifice he was so anxious to perpetuate. The nineteenth and twentieth centuries brought ancient India face to face with the imperatives of the contemporary world. And we quickly absorbed all that was relevant and significant in Bentham and Mill, in Rousseau and Voltaire down to Marx and Weber. And all this was grafted on to the Indian sub-continent. And we then had Tagore, Gandhi and Nehru to mention only a few.

Our democracy is dedicated to planned economic development, the peaceful transformation of an old social order and the uplifting of millions of people from conditions of social, economic and technological under-development. Thus, what we are attempting in India is not mere imitation of the Westminster system but a creative application of a meaningful democracy to the vastly different economic and social problems of India.

Democracy waft not entirely new to us for its roots could be to land also in our old panchayat system. This system probably, came into being because the village and the people were too distant from the centres of political power. Today the ancient institution has been transformed into a new organ of self-government at district and what we call block level as a link between the government's programme and the people.

The concept of the rule of law and the British pattern of administration may have helped to keep order in the country but much in these institutions has remained static and without changes they are becoming stumbling blocks to progress and democracy.

There are forces in our society as in others which pull in opposite directions. The competitiveness of democracy and of contemporary living seems superficially sometimes to have strengthened the hold of caste, religion and region, for these are now exploited for social and economic gain. But this is a passing phase and these differences cannot weaken India's fundamental unity nor the basic sense of Indianness which is a powerful binding factor. Paradoxical though it may sound, we believe that the functioning of democracy itself can remove these obstacles on the democratic path.

Education has expanded tremendously. Today there are 2.5 million students in colleges. The number of children in schools has gone up from 23.4 million in 1951 to 83,000,000 in 1971. But I am sorry to say that we have not done as well as we should in our programme for adult literacy. Without being able to read, a person's world is a limited one for he cannot share the knowledge and companionship that comes with books. We must do and we are doing more for primary education, for strengthening secondary education and for adult literacy programmes. At the same time, I cannot agree with the common belief in the West that literacy by itself gives greater wisdom or understanding. Our people, illiterate though they may sometimes be, are the inheritors of an ancient culture and philosophy which has sustained them through the vicissitudes of their long history.

Indian voters have shown extraordinary insight and understanding of what goes on around them. If some are misled by false propaganda or diverted by irrelevant factors, their number is not larger than those of their literate—even educated—counterparts in other countries. The Indian voter knows where his interests lie and has exercised his right to vote with great political sophistication in spite of the competitive political platforms of numerous parties, even in the face of threat and violence. It is because of this basic soundness of our people that democracy has taken root in India.

Since long before Independence, the Congress Party had committed itself to certain programmes. Indeed, our leaders had made it clear that we were fighting not only against foreign rule but against all that was evil in our society, against injustice and poverty and social inequality. Our system must therefore cater to the genuine needs of ordinary people without neglecting the long-term development of the country. Development adds a new dimension to the challenge of democracy.

Three distinct streams of thought have combined to produce what might vaguely be called the Indian approach to democracy. There is the stream of liberalism and parliamentary democracy, which emerged out of the British system—parliamentary institutions, political parties, free elections, fundamental rights and freedom, the rule of law, which formed the political core of our democratic system. Parliament is the commanding centre of our political system, and government's responsibility to the legislature at the centre and in the states is beyond dispute.

In modem society, freedom cannot be the unrestricted play of individualism nor the apotheosis of private interests and private enterprise as against social interest and the public good. Freedom lies in a delicate and continuous balancing of the rights of the individual with the rights of society. Our Constitution and our actual political practice provide a larger degree of freedom than is obtained anywhere else in the world. We stand for the freedom of the Press, but we do not accept the proposition that freedom of the Press means the freedom of industrialists to own the Press, or that the right to property should stand in the way of progressive and necessary social legislation to lessen glaring inequalities of wealth and bring the reality of economic freedom to larger sections of the population. We have taken action to eliminate these anomalies. We have sought to amend the Constitution in order to give substance to democracy.

The second major stream is that of socialist thought with emphasis on social democracy and economic planning and developments. Indeed the entire structure of democracy is geared to social and economic development. In Europe, democracy as we know it followed the Industrial Revolution, but in India, democracy with its freedom and pressing popular demand came first, and the process of industrialisation, economic development and major welfare schemes have to be operated in the face of diverse and contradictory pressures.

This baffling combination makes our task more difficult and because of the absence of organised propaganda our achievements appear less spectacular than the accomplishments of others be different methods. But we think that we have gained something is the longer run-not so much in glittering material terms but in terms of human values gained, in terms of human suffering avoided and in terms of the enduring and harmonious development of the individual and society. I do believe that real and lasting social transformation encompassing attitudes of mind and the ways of millions of people can be effective only by peaceful means.

The third stream has emanated from Mahatma Gandhi and his philosophy of non-violence revolution. The impact of Gandhian thought and method of democracy in India is indirect, impalpable, yet subtly pervasive. It has supported and enriched India. This whole experiment, this endeavour to combine freedom, socialism and the methods of peace in an immensely complex situation, is taking place in India, not in isolating from the rest of the world, but in the midst of international cooperation and in the glare of world-wide publicity. International co-operation is a constituent element of India's effort in building a progressive economy and a democratic society. This is shy, ever since our independence we have put forward the idea of world peace and world co-operation, as an enlightened self-interest of India.

We believe in and have strictly adhered to the principle of non-interference. But can this be one-sided? Today, there is interference in or affairs and the stability and progress of our country are gravely threatened. As a result of the tragic events in East Bengal, 9,000,000 people have poured into our territory, creating a situation which seems to surpass the convulsions of partition. The crisis in Pakistan is a deep one and the spectre which haunts that unhappy country cannot be exercised by the usual recourse to blaming India. Two questions arise, first, whether religion by itself can form the basis of a nation state, especially when the state machinery is impervious to the ordinary laws of political development and cultural aspirations, and secondly, whether some action other than that of the bayonet is not necessary to win loyalty. We in India are restrained and calm in the face of provocation but we are bound to protect the interests of our country.

No country, least of all one as daring and as large as India, can be classified under one label, or another. It seems to me that even those who claim expert knowledge of our country are often wide of the mark in their assessment of India's defence. Many specialists tend to fit facts into a preconceived framework of theory about caste and models of development which have no relevance to reality. Even in Britain which has such close historical ties with us, there is a wide gap in the understanding of the forces which have shaped our great history and which are influencing us today. To have a worthwhile dialogue such an understanding is vital. Britain and India must both replace old myths by a more rational approach. Given the necessary intellectual efforts on both sides, I am confident that India and Britain can have creative and purposeful relations. It is the hope of bringing about such relations that bring me to London and to this Institute. Thank you for giving me this opportunity.

Speaking on "Tradition and change" Indiraji said "I am not a political person in the narrow sense in which politics is generally understood. The present is the road between the past and the future... To pinpoint this and to give a correct perspective should be one of the functions of the universities.

All that is born must dies and all that dies must be reborn. So, we are told in our old Philosophy.... Some people oppose change consciously. Others resist it because they feel safer with the familiar and all change implies the unfamiliar... Thus there is a constant struggle between the votaries of continuity and the forces of change... Even more than other countries, India is undergoing a revolution at all levels of its being-economic technological and social as well as intellectual, psychological and aesthetic. We are a society being forced into new dimensions of thought, perception and action by the pressures of new relationships, new tools and techniques and new avenues of the communication"..... Though the centuries, a way of seeing and thinking a way of living has survived in this country."

Thus while speaking about the sign of our great Indian philosophy, Indiraji invited modernity.

Amidst the din and dust of electionerring, she had good opportunity to meet young men and women whole addressing the convocation of Bangalore University on 8th January 1967. Encouraging them and cajoling them that they are the "bridge between today and tomorrow" and "between continuity and change" and between "tradition and modernity" she spoke in clear terms about our Indian philosophy and its basic points.

She described herself not as a pobheat person in the narrow sense, who are obsessed with "now" only. She tried to give a broad perspective to many of the problems of India.

In the true sense of the term, she tried to be "a friend", "guide" and "philosopher" to the young generation and gave them a new line of thinking. World wide view of our people, should be a plus point of our thinking, she felt and tried to inculcate some new ideas in the minds of youngsters.

After Indira achieved independence, Nation had achieved many points to its credit like agrarian reforms, abolition of Zamindari system, mass education, substantial expansion of university and technical education, some major social reforms, some more advance in the spheres of science and technology. In spite of all the progress many problems still await solution. Justice which is the basis of our Constitution is yet a goal to be fought for and achieved. Our people are resistant to change and some entertain this change with open heart.

Thus we are at the cross roads of life and we have the clear about our direction to achieve a better life. Our people have a desire to conserve all that is old and familiar. This is a most unfortunate thing.

The step that we have to take up should be in the direction of democratisation of society. Our society broken up by caste and creed, further fragmented by concepts of hierarchy and graded privileges, should be changed. Of course we cannot achieve any change by magic. We must be able to bring about the necessary change by changing the mind-set of people through proper reasoning and building up awareness, she said.

Function of Journalism

Her speech on the occasion of the Golden Jubilee function of the *Ananda Bazar Patrika*, Calcutta on 20th May 1972 was one of her masterpieces. Recalling that it was founded by her grandfather in U.P. at the time of freedom struggle, to carry the message of freedom and Satyagraha, she said that the purpose of the papers was to keep up the spirit of the people by emphasising that they had "nothing to fear but fear itself."

Of course the press was divided into two clear camps—The British owned on one side, and the nationalist papers on the other. The Anglo-Indian press enjoyed the patronage of the government. from Viceroy to the district collector, in addition to the commercial Nawabs. They had all the advantages. But the plight of the nationalist papers was different. They lived under constant threat. Their presses were liable for seal without any notice and securities were demanded. Each newspaper became an open school of sedition which was the moral law of any colonial people. The editors and managers of nationalist papers were in and out of jail frequently. They said their families had to suffer all kinds of hardships. But the profession of journalism was held in high esteem by people.

Bal Gangadhar Tilak wrote that the goal of his paper was to make people realize the value of freedom and to challenge the might of the foreign rulers. This became the motto of all Nationalist Newspapers. In between 1922 and 1947, *Ananda Bazar Patrika* had to face action by the government on 19 occasions. But the journal earned the trust and support of the people of Bengal.

"The newspaper is more than a medium. It has an attitude, a point of view, and a system of judgment and value. It is the quality of mind. The quest for knowledge, the ability to analyse and to evaluate and the need to reflect which is the source of the power of the press." Indira felt.

But unfortunately the journalists began to feel that they reached the top and so, this is no longer the reformist zeal of the best journalist of olden days. "Our Newspapers are content to devote only 5 to 6 per cent of their space to social change" she felt.

There is a complaint that there is too much politics in the country whether this is desirable or not depends on what one means by politics. How can democracy prevail, without political consciousness, she questioned "we want the press to serve the people and be the voice of the people" instead of being new centres of big business, she thought.

"If publishing houses can come up with workable solutions to basic problems", nothing like that "we welcome them with sympathy" she said.

"The climate in the newspaper industry should be such that public spirited editors and correspondents are able to fight injustice in humanity, superstition and misinterpretation. The difference between an ordinary and a good newspaper and a great one is in the extent to which, it identifies itself with the larger purposes of society." She concluded, commenting on *Ananda Bezar Patrika* on the service it has rendered to a noble cause and for the enrichment of rich and beautiful Bengali language. She also praised it as one of the leading institutions of Calcutta and Bengal especially.

Homage by Heads of Foreign Countries and Newspapers

Tributes and homages started pouring in from abroad.

Secretary General of the United Nations, Javier Perez De Cuellar, in a condolence message said : "It is with the deepest sense of shock and personal sorrow that I have learned of the tragic death of Prime Minister Indira Gandhi. Throughout her long and distinguished career, Mrs. Gandhi was a highly respected figure worldwide and at the United Nations, which she supported staunchly. Following in the tradition of her illustrious father, Pandit Nehru, she represented on the international scene the spirit of moderation, tolerance and understanding, which is so vitally needed in the world today.

"The untimely passing of Mrs. Gandhi is a great loss to India, to the United Nations and to me personally."

The Commonwealth Secretary General, Dr. Shridath S. Ramphal, sent the following condolence message to the President of India :

"I send to you, President, both on behalf of the Commonwealth and in a very personal sense on my own behalf, the most profound expressions of grief and sorrow on the cruel passing of Smt. Indira Gandhi.

"India has lost a great leader but so, too, has the world, and the Commonwealth to a very special degree. As we awakened today to the news of Mrs. Gandhi's assassination there would have been in every corner of the world and among political leaders of countries everywhere a deep sense of loss— in many cases of personal loss. Mrs. Gandhi died not just as the Prime Minister of India but as the leader of the non-aligned movement and the Chairman of the Commonwealth's last summit. Not only because of India's greatness but because of her personal qualities which combined so uniquely compassion and courage, grace and determination, humility and pride, a passion for India but a soul for a wider humanity, leaders and people the world over will mourn with India.

"For me her passing away is a very personal matter. I have known and worked with her for most of her public life. In my own early years in the non-aligned movement but more recently for nearly 10 years in the Commonwealth. India through Mrs. Gandhi's great father, Jawaharlal Nehru, had made the modern Commonwealth possible. Indira Gandhi gave the Commonwealth connection relevance and validity. Her invitation to the Commonwealth to come to New Delhi last November—just under a year ago—was both a compliment to the Commonwealth and a service to it. Many Commonwealth leaders will today be recalling that occasion. It was one of the Commonwealth's best summits and the leadership Mrs. Gandhi gave to that occasion, which was not without issues of contrcversy and division, was symbol of the vision who brought to the affairs of a world that will miss her sorely.

"I am leaving immediately for New Delhi so that I may join with the nation and many other nations in paying respect to Mrs. Gandhi's memory".

The President of the United States, Ronald Reagan, sent the following condolence message to the Prime Minister, Rajiv Gandhi, on the death of Indira Gandhi:

"I want to express my shock, grief and regret at the assassination of Prime Minister Indira Gandhi. The people of the United States and Nancy join me in extending our deepest sympathy and condolences to you and your family at this sad time.

"As a true nationalist, she embodied the strengths and values that are India. As Prime Minister of the world's largest democracy, she understood the importance of freedom as she sought to ensure a better life for all Indians. As Chairman of the Non-aligned Movement, she worked relentlessly to promote peace, security, and economic development in the world.

"Ever since her visit to Washington in 1982, the Prime Minister and I had remained in touch. Our correspondence covered a variety of areas. In all of them, she displayed her personal commitment to her people and her desire to sustained good relations between India and the United States. She welcomed Vice President Bush to India in May with the hospitality for which your family and country are famous.

"As you move into office as the next Prime Minister of India, please accept our prayers and wishes for strength necessary to carry you through these terrible days. We mourn with you through these terrible days. We mourn with you the passing of a great leader."

Soviet President and party chief Konstantin Chernenko said "the name of Indira Gandhi will remain forever in the grateful memory of the Soviet people".

In a telegram to Rajiv Gandhi, Konstantin Chernenko as general secretary of the Communist Party of the Soviet Union recalled that Mrs. Gandhi attached much importance to strengthening friendship and developing comprehensive cooperation between the USSR and India.

The presidium of the USSR Supreme Soviet and the USSR Council of Ministers sent a separate telegram jointly to the President Zail Singh, 'wrathfully" condemning the criminals and their patrons" who dared to raise their hand against "the outstanding leader of India who enjoyed well-deserved prestige and deep respect all over the world."

Erich Honecker, General Secretary of the Central Committee of the Socialist Unity Party of Germany and Chairman of the Council of State of the German Democratic Republic, conveyed his condolences to the President of India:

"It is with great shock and deep grief that I received the sad news of the insidious assassination of India's Prime Minister, Indira Gandhi. We join the people of India and all progressive mankind in their sorrow at the irreplaceable loss India has suffered through the death of Indira Gandhi.

"As the Prime Minister of the Republic of India and Chairman of the Movement of Non-aligned countries, lasting credit is due to Indira Gandhi in the striving for peace, disarmament, understanding among nations and international cooperation. In the German Democratic Republic she will always be remembered as an outstanding personality in the struggle for India's national independence, the unity of the country and its social progress.

"On behalf of the Central Committee of the Socialist Unity Party of Germany, the Council of State, the Council of Ministers and the people of the German Democratic Republic, I convey to you, the friendly people and the government of India my sincere sympathy and heartfelt condolences."

In a separate message to Rajiv Gandhi, Prime Minister of India, Erich Honecker of German Democratic Republic said :

"The insidious assassination of your mother, Indira Gandhi the Prime Minister of India, has caused deep shock in the German

Democratic Republic. On behalf of the Central Committee of the Socialist Unity Party of Germany, the Council of State and the Council of Ministers of German Democratic Republic, I extend to you and your family our heartfelt sympathy."

Prime Minister Rajiv Gandhi received the following message from Her Majesty the Queen of Britain:

"I was appalled to hear the terrible news about your mother, and Prince Philip and I send our heartfelt sympathy to you and your family in your tragic loss. Mrs. Gandhi will always be remembered for her outstanding service to India and the Commonwealth."

The British Prime Minister, Mrs. Margaret Thatcher, sent the following message to the Prime Minister, Rajiv Gandhi, on the sad demise of Indira Gandhi.

"I was appalled to hear early this morning of the murderous attack on Mrs. Gandhi and grieved by the subsequent news of her death. India has been robbed of a leader of incomparable courage, vision and humanity. And the Commonwealth has lost one of its most formidable and vital personalities.

"For my part, I shall feel greatly the loss of a wise colleague and a personal friend. I always looked forward to our talks together. They had some special quality and understanding.

"The British Government and people utterly condemn this barbaric and treacherous deed. It is a tragedy for India, for the Commonwealth and for the wider world. "We share your deep sorrow."

The Prime Minister, Rajiv Gandhi, has received the following condolence message from President Karmal of Afghanistan:

"I am grieved to hear about the assassination and death of your mother, the great Prime Minister of India Indira Gandhi. She was not only a leader of India but the leader of all Asian peoples who are marching on the path of progress and development. Her loss is not just the loss of India but of Afghanistan and Afghan people also. I personally share your grief at this shocking event. Please accept deep condolences and sympathies from our very heart on the passing away of your distinguished mother who contributed so much to the resurgence and strength not only of India but people all over Asia. Her sacrifice in the cause of the good of her people and the people of poor and Non-aligned countries like Afghanistan is incomparable. Please rest assured that the leadership, the party, the Government and the people of Afghanistan will stand by the people of India and with you in this hour of deep sorrow and grief."

In his homage, the President Mitterrand of France said: "The tragic loss of Mrs. Indira Gandhi inspires in me as well as the French people a very deep sorrow. The Third World loses a champion of its rights, of its independence and of its dignity. The community of nations loses with her an important personality to whom one used to refer.

"My country will keep the memory of a courageous and faithful friend, always attentive to the culture and to the friendly voices from friends to the reinforcement of the Franco-Indian cooperation."

The Prime Minister of Turkey, Turgut Ozel, in a statement on the sad demise of the Prime Minister, Indira Gandhi said :

"As has given many victims to the International terrorism, the Turkish Nation is deeply grieved by the passing of the Prime Minister of India, Mrs. Indira Gandhi, as a result of a despicable assassination.

"Mrs. Gandhi has not only successfully governed her country as a Prime Minister, but she was one of the eminent world leaders who served the cause of world peace and distinguished herself with her valuable contributions for the stability in her country and in the region.

"We are now expressing our sincere condolences to the friendly Indian people which have lost their great leader and wish them patience forbearance.

"As I state on every appropriate occasion, this assassination that took the life of Prime Minister, Mrs. Gandhi, is a very shocking event which indicates clearly that it is high time to realize that effective struggle against terrorism could only be assured through the close cooperation among nations."

In a condolence message to the President, Giani Zail Singh, the President of Uganda, Dr. A. Milton Obote said :

"The outrageous assassination of the distinguished Indian Prime Minister, Mrs. Indira Gandhi, is a loss which the people of Uganda, my Government, myself and my family share with you and the entire people of India. This is a very sad event of world proportions. Indira Gandhi was not only the leader of the largest democracy in the world, but was also the elected leader of the struggling people in the Non-aligned Movement.

"I join you in mourning a most outstanding lady who was one of the greatest leaders in modern times. She made her mark on the Indian political scene through the support of the people. She has left that scene at the hands of gunmen. I pray that the Indian democracy will survive this violent tragedy and that the people of India will rally in unison against political violence, both in memory of the first lady Prime Minister of India and for the good of all the people of India and in the member-countries of the Non-aligned Movement."

The President, Giani Zail Singh, and the Prime Minister. Rajiv Gandhi, received the following messages of condolences from the King of Malaysia, Sultan Iskandar Yang Di-Pertuan Agong, and the Prime Minister, Dr. Mahathir Mohamad.

Following is the text of King's message to President:

"We are extremely grieved at the tragic passing away of Prime Minister, Mrs. Indira Gandhi. The untimely demise of the distinguished leader who has contributed much to international cooperation and understanding is not only a great loss to India but also the international community particularly the third world and the Non-aligned Movement.

On behalf of the Government and people of Malaysia, we wish to extend to your excellency and through you to the bereaved family and the people of India our heartfelt condolences."

Following is the text of King's message to Rajiv Gandhi : "We are deeply grieved at the untimely demise of your beloved mother. Her passing away is a great loss to you and your family as well as to the Indian nation and the international community. In this moment of grief, we share with you the profound sorrow and extend to you our sympathies and heartfelt condolence. We pray that you and your family will find the courage and fortitude to bear this irreparable loss."

Following is the text of PM's message to Rajiv Gandhi :

"I am deeply grieved and shocked at the untimely demise of your beloved mother. The world has lost one of its most distinguished leaders and we mourn her death.

On behalf of the Government and the people of Malaysia and on my own behalf I wish to extend our heartfelt sympathies and condolence to your excellency and members of your family. In this moment of grief, I pray that your excellency and members of your family will find the courage and fortitude to bear this irreparable loss.

The unenviable and heavy responsibilities of leading the nation has been entrusted to you. I have every faith that India under your able leadership will overcome all challenges and trials and that the close friendly relations existing between our two countries will continue and further strengthen."

The Foreign Minister of Federal Republic of Germany, Hans Dietrich Genscher, contributing an article in the journal. Anzeiger under the title 'Hopefully peace would be preserved in India' has said that Mrs. Gandhi has continued the work of her great father, he writes :

"Mrs. Indira Gandhi has fallen victim to a criminal assassination. On the occasion of this shocking news the German people express their cordial sympathy to the people of India. Mrs. Gandhi has continued, as a politician, the work of her great father. She has served her mother country with energy and utmost personal engagement. She ensured the unity of the country. Simultaneously she worked for the peace in the world and for a real Non-alignment in a manner which has earned her the repute of a significant statesman like personality of an international standard.

"Germans are greatly indebted to India. We have never forgotten that it was !ndia of Nehru which extended first of all the hand to the young democracy in the year 1950. At that time we and India stood before a new beginning. Since then we esteem India as the biggest democracy of the world. We admire her performance in the development we recognise the role which India is to play as a leading power of the Non-aligned Movement. This role is aimed at maintaining a real Non-alliance and to make her internationally a stablising factor. We are deeply impressed by it that India has succeeded in feeding her population over 700 million people and in addition to it she has performed economic and scientific achievements. We are happy that we have a functional cooperation with India which bears an examplary character also in the North-South relationship. India's cultural and civilisation achievement as well as her spiritual radiating power have not lost anything of her fascination for the German people. The great performances of India are inseparable from the names Nehru and Indira Gandhi.

"All Governments of the Federal Republic of Germany have seen, esteemed and assessed India's significance and her high position indiscriminately for our external relations. All political parties represented in the 'Bundestag' (Lower House of the German Parliament) have always attached great importance to further development of Indo-German relations. This applies to the economic exchange as well as to the close consultations and cooperation in the political field and to common projects of future in the field of culture, science and transfer of technology.

"We have sought the exchange of opinion with India's leadership in respect of all problems which move us concerning safeguarding of freedom and peace. We had a close exchange of ideas for the shaping of North-South relations.

"The contribution made by Mrs. Gandhi in pursuit of her policy aimed at achieving compromise and moderation in the North-South summit conference of Cancun remains unforgotten. She helped in organising the North-South summit conference with the power of her personality.

"It is to be hoped that peace would be preserved in the subcontinent. We wish to the people of India the internal compromise and stability which she required for the development and progress. We rely on it that also in this difficult hour and in view of the serious test which she is making at present, she would demonstrate the political maturity as she has already shown so far."

King Birendra of Nepal conveyed his condolences through his brother Prince Gyanendra to the Prime Minister, Rajiv Gandhi. He said :

"Excellency, I am sending my brother H.R.H. Prince Bir Bikram Shah with letter only to tell you how grieved we are at the sudden bereavement of Madam Indira Gandhi. Indeed it was with deep distress and shock that we in Nepal heard the news of the sinister attempt made on her life. No sooner that I sent a personal message wishing her well then I was told, to my profound grief the news about her demise. These sad events have taken place so rapidly that we have been at a loss to find words to explain our feelings of sorrow and grief on the loss of a leader who certainly had been held in high esteem / in Nepal. Bereft of the love and care of a mother who meant so much for you, I can well imagine how much you would miss her. But these harrowing times, call for our patience and forbearance.

"This is not the time to touch upon bilateral matters but I certainly wish to emphasise that our hearts and sympathies and with your family. If you feel that, I on my part, can contribute in any way, please do let me know. May God, Almighty grant Madam Gandhi eternal rest and may peace prevail in India may God ever guide you with wisdom as you bear up on your shoulders, the great responsibility towards your country and people."

Julius Nyerera, President of Tanzania, in great grief at her death said "you in India know how dedicated she was to the unity of your country to the progress of its people, and in particular, to the welfare of the poor. We in Tanzania recognized and respected her as a friend of Africa as well as a supporter of the liberation of this continent from the colonialism and racism... we know also how important was her contribution to the struggle of the third world for justice and peace. Her chairmanship of the non-aligned movement was a recognition of her great abilities and the world's need of them. The cause of world peace and justice was being dealt a heavy blow by this assassination comments by Foreign Press.

Indira's assassination occupied a dominant place in the German Democratic Republic. The "News Denutshland" said Indira's death has brought moorning, dismay and indignation in India and the entire world. The newspaper described her as "The great leader of the Indian people, champion of world peace and independence."

The cuban daily "Granma" held back its edition to put the news of the death on its front page.

News papers in Asia have widely commented over Indira Gandhi's assassination expressing concern over what they described as "growing violence and terrorism against world leaders."

Pakistan Newspapers said that the death of Indira Gandhi has brutally cut short an illustrations career of one of India's most eminent politicians and the third world's outstanding personality. The Karachi based *DAWN* said that Indiraji provided the country with a decisive leadership at a time when it needed it and this was her greatest asset as leader.

Pakistan Times said "one cannot but feel sad at the turn of events whatever its motive, and from whatever source it may emanate, violence cannot be countenanced."

The *Urdu* daily *JUNG* said "felt that it was unfortunate Indira Gandhi fell victim to violence."

The Chinese press while giving extensive coverage to the death refrained from carrying its own comments. "*China Daily*", the only English language newspaper ran a 3-column headline lead story and a large portrait of Indira Gandhi. The *People's Daily* organ of the risking communist party also carried on the front page two stories, quoting the official Xinhua News Agency.

The *Washington Post* in a lead editorial devoted to the assassinated leader praised the immediate appointment of Rajiv Gandhi as the new prime minister.

Australian Newspapers described Indira Gandhi's death as a "Tragic blow of the world's largest democracy."

Manil a *Daily Express* said "The murder of Indira Gandhi will surely be deplored by the International community as a despicable butal attack."

The Singapore *Monitor* said, "The gunfire that ended the life of the prime minister, Indira Gandhi may have critically wounded the nation as it has existed all these decades."

Newspapers in Sri Lanka, praised Indira Gandhi as a "World Leader" and condemned the killing as a despicable act. In an editorial entitled "A loss of humanity," *The Daily News* said, Indira Gandhi was a sobering influence, a stabilising factor in South Asia.

The *sun* in its editorial said "Farewell Indira" India has lost its noblest daughter, the non-aligned movement a good steward and the world a great stateswoman."

The African press paid fulsome tribute, saying that her association was a shot in the heart of the third world.

The *Kenya Times*, official organ bf the ruling Kenya Africa National as Party, said in an editorial that the intransigence and fanaticism of those who have opted for violent means to achieve their sectional ends pose one of the greatest dangers to the various forms of democratic political systems world wide."

The *Nation* said "Mrs. Gandhi's courage was indisputed and even her political enemies admired her administrative skills."

Malaysian television showed recent pictures of Indira Gandhi, while giving detail of the cowardly act that ended her life.

Rajeev Gandhi has apthy remarked "Indira Gandhi is no more but her soul loves India loves India is immortal. The spirit of India is immortal."

She loved and died for her country. She paid the highest price for safe guarding the unity of India.

Her magnificient love came to an abrupt end. But her soul loves for ever.

The leading editorial in the *States Man* revealed to which extent public life in India was effected. The editorial said "The fatal attack in the Prime Minister revels extent to which public life has degenerated."

The *Hindu* its editorial entitled "a colossal Tragedy" rightly observed that the tragedy has not the common people as a personal loss.

The editorial said:

"The void created in national life by the brutal assassination of the Prime Minister, Mrs. Indira Gandhi, by her own security guards in her own official residence is one that of Indians are going to find it extremely difficult to accept or adjust to across the nation that is in reality a subject..."

Indian Express voiced that sentiments of the people when it stated in its editiorial entitled "Indira and India", that an attack on Indira was an attack on India. The editorial read "An assassins bullet has tragically ended the life of Indira Gandhi, who dominated the Indian stage for a generation 16 years as Prime Minister. She was a strong personality, charismatic and not removed from fierce political controversy. But her murder is an utterly foul and dastardly act horrified and deeply stired the democratic conscience of the nation."

20

Her Speeches about India's Problems

"The time has come to rise above pettiness and to breakdown meaningless barriers, to join together not just for better things but to reach out for the values which could make no better beings, each one of us adding something no matter how small, to the total of the world's dignity and courage, its happiness and goodness, its beauty and wisdom".—Indira Gandhi.

Her speeches at International forums are exemplary and very deep-rooted with lots of sentiment and broad vision. They speak of her ideas on the role of India in world affairs and her noble contribution.

Now I would like to include some of her bright speeches at UNO, some of her bright speeches at UNO, Belgium, in the League of Nations and at the Commonwealth conference.

The future of any society, its development and direction depends on the activities taken up by its leaders.

Of course India is an ancient country, trying to build up its future. It is in the midst of several transformations. A social order based on agriculture, authoritarian feudalism is being reshaped into a new progressive economy and to achieve progress on democratic lines.

Poverty, illiteracy as unemployment or mal-employment, feelings based on religion, caste or regional differences are some of the problems standing on the way. At the same time, an atmosphere of confident and creative thoughts should be created to help us towards solutions.

So Smt. Indira Gandhi recognizing that many of India's problems need solution in the broader perspective, and so she took up whirl wind tours to the foreign countries and made the foreigners aware of our dire problems.

She spoke on several occasions in several forums and tried to impress on the foreign audiences about India's problems. I will now give some glimpses of her speeches.

'Man and His World'

Address to the United Nations Conference on Human Environment, Stockholm, 14 June 1972

It is indeed an honour to address this Conference. In itself, it is a fresh expression of the spirit which created the United Nations, namely, concern for the present and future welfare of humanity. It does not aim merely at securing limited agreements, but at establishing peace and harmony in life—among all races and with nature. This gathering represents man's earnest endeavour to understand his own condition and to prolong his tenancy of this planet. A vast amount of detailed preparatory work has gone into the convening of this Conference, guided by the dynamic personality of Mr. Maurice Strong, Secretary-General of the Conference.

I have had the good fortune of growing up with a sense of kinship with nature in all its manifestations. Birds, plants and stones were companions and, sleeping under the star-strewn sky, I became familiar with the names and movements of the constellations. But my deep interest in this, our 'only earth', was not for itself but as a fit home for man.

One cannot be truly human and civilised unless one looks upon, not only all fellow men, but all creation with the eyes of a friend. Throughout India, edicts carved on rocks and iron pillars are reminders that twenty-two centuries ago the Emperor Ashoka defined a king's duty as not merely to protect citizens and punish wrong-doers, but also to preserve wild life and the trees of the forest. Ashoka was the first, and perhaps the only monarch until very recently, to forbid the killing of a large number of species of animals for sport or food, foreshadowing some of the concerns of this conference. He went further, he regretted essence from circumstances; to accept joy and sorrow with some degree of equanimity. Perception and compassion are the marks of true spirituality.

I am reminded of an incident in one of our tribal areas. The vociferous demand of elder tribal chiefs, that their customs should be left undisturbed, found support from noted anthropologists. In its anxiety that the majority should not submerge the many ethnical, racial and cultural groups in our country, the Government of India largely accepted this advice. I was amongst those who entirely approved. A visit to a remote part of our north-east frontier, however, brought me in touch with a different point of view the protest of the younger elements that while the rest of India was on its way to modernisation, they were being preserved as museum pieces. Could not we say the same to the affluent nations?

For the last quarter of a century, we have been engaged in an enterprise unparalleled in human history - the provision of basic needs for one-sixth of mankind within the span of one or two generations. When we launched into that endeavour our early planners had more than the usual gaps to fill. There was not enough data and there were no helpful books. No guidance could be sought from the experience of other countries because their conditions political, economic, social and technological were altogether different. Planning of the kind which we were innovating, had never been used in the context of a mixed economy. But we could not wait. The need to improve conditions for our people was pressing. Planning and action, the amassing of data for improved planning and the action to implement it, was a continuous and overlapping process. Our industrialisation tended to follow the paths which the more advanced countries had traversed earlier. Throughout the '60s, and particularly during the last five years, we encountered a bewildering variety of problems, some due to our own shortcomings, but many inherent in the process, and in existing attitudes. The feeling is growing that we should re-order our priorities and move away from the single-dimensional model, in which growth is viewed from a narrow angle and which seems to accord a higher place to things rather than to people. Such an approach increases our needs but not our enjoyment of life. We should have a more comprehensive approach, centred on man, not as a statistic but as an individual, with many sides to his personality. These problems cannot be treated in isolation but must be regarded as an integral part of the unfolding of the very process of development.

The extreme forms, in which questions of population, or environmental pollution, are posed, obscure the total view of political, economic and social situations. The government of India is one of the few which has an officially sponsored programme of family planning. This programme is making some progress.

We believe that planned families will make for a healthier and more conscious population. But we know also that no programme of population control can be effective without education and without a visible rise in the standard of living. Our own programmes have succeeded in the urban or semi-urban areas. To the very poor, every child is an earner and a helper. We are experimenting with other methods of approach; the family planning programme is being combined with those of maternity and child welfare, nutrition and development in general.

It is an over-simplification to blame all the world's problems on increasing population. Countries with but a small fraction of the world population consume the bulk of the world's production of minerals, fossil fuels and so on. Thus we see that when it comes to the depletion of natural resources and environmental pollution, the increase of one inhabitant in an affluent country, at his level of living, is equivalent to an increase of many Asians, Africans or Latin Americans at their levels of living.

The inherent conflict is not between conservation and development, but between environment and reckless exploitation in the name of efficiency. Historians tell us that the modern age began with the will to freedom of the individual. And the individual came to believe that he had rights with no corresponding obligations. The man who got ahead was the one who commanded admiration. No questions were asked as to the methods employed, or the price which others had had to pay. Industrial civilisation has promoted the concept of the efficient man, he whose entire energies are concentrated on producing as much as possible in a given unit of time and from a given unit of manpower. Groups or individuals who are less competitive and, according to this test, less efficient, are regarded as lesser breeds - for example, the older civilisations, the black and brown peoples, women and certain professions. Obsolescence is built into production, and efficiency is based on the creation of goods which are not really needed and which cannot be disposed of, when discarded. What price such efficiency now, and is not the word reckless a more appropriate term for such behaviour?

All the 'isms' of the modern age—even those which in theory disown the private profit principle—assume that man's cardinal interest is in acquisition. The profit motive, individual or collective, seems to the expectation that this Conference can achieve miracles, or solve all the world's difficulties, but in the hope that the opinions of each nation will be kept in focus, that these problems will be viewed in perspective and each project devised as a part of the whole.

On a previous occasion I have spoken of the unfinished revolution in our countries. I am now convinced that this can only be taken to its culmination if it is accompanied by a revolution in social thinking. In 1968, at the Fourteenth General Conference of UNESCO, the Indian delegation, along with others, proposed a new and major programme entitled 'a design for living'. It is essential to grasp the full implications of technical advance and its impact on different sections and groups. We do not want to put the clock back or resign ourselves to a simplistic natural state. We want new directions in the wiser use of the knowledge and the tools with which science equips us. And this cannot be just one upsurge but a continuous search into cause and effect, an unending effort to match technology with higher levels of thinking. We must concern ourselves, not only with the kind of world we want, but also with the kind of man who should inhabit it. Surely we do not desire a society divided into those who condition and those who are conditioned. We want thinking people, capable of spontaneous, self-directed activity, who are interested and interesting and who are imbued with compassion and concern for others.

It will not be easy for large societies to change their style of living. They cannot be coerced to do so, nor can governmental action suffice. People can be motivated, can be urged to participate in better alternatives.

It has been my experience that people who are at cross purposes with nature are cynical about mankind and ill at ease with themselves. Modern man must re-establish an unbroken link with nature and with life. He must again learn to invoke the energy of growing things and to recognise, as did the ancients in India centuries ago, that one can take from the earth and the atmosphere only so much as one puts back into them. In their 'Hymn to Earth', the sages of the *Atharva Veda* chanted:

What of thee I dig out, let that quickly grow over,
Let me not hit they vitals, or the heart.

So can man himself be vital and of good heart and conscious of his own responsibility.

Interest in the accelerated progress of the less developed world? Or will it confine itself to one narrow concern, that of exclusive self-sufficiency?

The first essays, in and technological disparities, failed because the policies of aid were made to subserve the equations of power. We hope that the renewed emphasis on self-reliance, brought about by the change in the climate of aid, will also promote a search for new criteria regarding human satisfaction. In the meantime, the ecological crisis should not add to the burdens of the weaker nations by introducing new considerations in the political and trade policies of rich nations. It would be ironic if the fight against pollution were to be converted into another business, out of which a few companies, corporations, or nations, would make profits at the cost of the many. Here is a branch of experimentation and discovery in which scientists of all nations should take an interest. They should ensure that their findings are available to all nations, unrestricted by patents. I am glad that the Conference has given thought to this aspect of the problem.

Life is one and the world is one, and all these questions are interlinked. The population explosion, poverty, ignorance and disease, the pollution of our surroundings, the stockpiling of nuclear weapons and biological and chemical agents of destruction, are all part of a vicious circle. Each is important and urgent but dealing with them one by one would be wasted effort.

It serves little purpose to dwell on the past or to apportion blame, for none of us is blameless. If some are able to dominate others, this is at least partially due to the weakness, the lack of unity, and the temptation to gain some advantage on the part of those who submit. If the prosperous have been exploiting the needy, can we honestly claim that in our own societies, people do not take advantage of the weak?

We must re-evaluate the fundamentals in which our respective civic societies are based, and the ideals by which they are sustained. If there is to be change of heart, a change of direction and methods of functioning, no organisation or country-no matter how well intentioned an achieve it. While each country must deal with that aspect of the problem which is most relevant to it, it is obvious that all countries must unite in an overall endeavour. There is no alternative to a co-operative approach, on a global scale, to the entire spectrum of our problems.

I have referred to some problems which seem to me to be the underlying causes of the present crises in our civilisation. This is not in the carnage of his military conquests and enjoined his successors to find 'their only pleasure in the peace that comes through righteousness'.

Along with the rest of mankind, we in India - in spite of Ashoka —have been guilty of wanton disregard for the sources of our sustenance. We share your concern at the rapid deterioration of flora and fauna. Some of our own wild life has been wiped out. Vast areas of forest, full of beautiful old trees, mute witnesses of history, have been destroyed. Even though our industrial development is in its infancy, and at its most difficult stage, we are taking various steps to deal with incipient environmental imbalances. The more so because of our concern for the human being—a species which is also imperiled. In poverty, he is threatened by malnutrition and disease; in weakness, by war; in wealth, by the pollution brought about by his own prosperity.

It is sad that in country after country, progress should have become synonymous with an assault on nature. We, who are part of nature, and dependent on her for every need, speak constantly about 'exploiting' nature. When the highest mountain in the world was climbed in 1953, Jawaharlal Nehru objected to the phrase 'conquest of Everest', which he thought arrogant. Is it surprising that this lack of consideration and the constant need to prove one's superiority, should be projected into our treatment of our fellow men? I remember Edward Thompson, a British writer and a good friend of India, once telling Mahatma Gandhi that its wild life was fast disappearing. Remarked the Mahatma: 'It is decreasing in the jungles but it is increasing in the towns!'

We are gathered here under the aegis of the United Nations. We are supposed to belong to the same family, sharing common traits and impelled by the same basic desires; yet we inhabit a divided world.

How can it be otherwise? There is still no recognition of the equality of man, or respect for him as an individual. In matters of colour and race, religion and custom, society is governed by prejudice. Tensions arise because of man's aggressiveness and his notions of superiority. The power of the big stick prevails and it is used not in favour of fair play or beauty, but to chase imaginary windmills—to assume the right to interfere in the affairs of others, and to arrogate authority for actions that would not normally be allowed. Many of the advanced countries of today have reached their present affluence through domination of other races and countries, and exploitation of their own masses and their own natural resources. Their sheer ruthlessness, undisturbed by feelings of compassion or by abstract theories of freedom, equality or justice, gave them a head start. The first stirrings for political rights for the citizen, and economic rights for the toiler, came after considerable 'advance has been made. The riches and the labour of the colonised countries played no small part in the industralisation and prosperity of the West. Now, as we struggle to create a better life for our people, it is in vastly different circumstances, for obviously with the eagle-eyed watchfulness of today, we cannot indulge in such practices even for a worthwhile purpose. We are bound by our own ideals. We owe allegiance to the principles of the rights of workers and the norms enshrined in the charters of international organisations. Above all, we are answerable to the millions of politically awakened citizens in our own countries. All these make progress costlier and more complicated.

On the one hand the rich look askance at our continuing poverty, on the other they warn us against their own methods. We do not wish to impoverish the environment any further and yet we cannot for a moment forget the grim poverty of large numbers of people. Are not poverty and need the greatest polluters? For instance, unless we are in a position to provide employment and purchasing power for the daily necessities of the tribal people, and those who live in or around our jungles, we cannot prevent them from combing the forests for their livelihood, from poaching and despoiling the vegetation. When they themselves feel deprived, how can we urge the preservation of animals? How can we speak to those who live in villages and in slums about keeping the oceans, the rivers and the air clean, when their own lives are contaminated at the source? The environment cannot be improved in conditions of poverty. Nor can poverty be eradicated without the use of science and technology.

Must there be a conflict between technology and a truly better world, or between enlightenment of the spirit and a higher standard of living? Foreigners sometimes ask what to us seems a very strange question, whether progress in India would not mean a diminution of her spirituality or her values. Is spiritual quality so superficial as to be dependent upon the lack of material comfort? As a country, we are no more or less spiritual than any other, but traditionally our people have respected the spirit of detachment and renunciation. Historically, our great spiritual discoveries were made during periods of comparative affluence. The doctrines of detachment from possessions were developed not as a rationalisation of deprivation, but to prevent comfort and ease from dulling the senses. Spirituality means the enrichment of the spirit, the strengthening of one's inner resources and the stretching of one's range of experience. It is the ability to be still in the midst of activity and vibrantly alive in moments of calm; to separate the overshadow all else. This overriding concern with self and today is the basic cause of the ecological crisis.

Pollution is not a technical problem. The fault lies not in science and technology as such, but in the sense of values of the contemporary world which ignores the rights of others and is oblivious to the longer perspective.

There are grave misgivings that the discussion of ecology may be designed to distract attention from the problems of war and poverty. We have to prove to the disinherited majority of the world that ecology and conservation will not work against their interest but will bring an improvement in their lives. To withhold technology from them would be to deprive them of vast resources of energy and knowledge. This is no longer feasible, nor will it be acceptable.

The environmental problems of developing countries are not the side effects of excessive industrialisation. Rather they reflect the inadequacy of development. The rich countries may look upon development as the cause of environmental destruction, but to use it is the primary means of improving the environment, for living, for providing food, water, sanitation and shelter; and also of making the deserts green and the mountains habitable. The research and perseverance of dedicated people have given us an insight which is likely to play an important part in the shaping of our future plans. We see that however much man hankers after material goods, they can never give him full satisfaction! Thus higher standards of living must be achieved without alienating the people from their heritage or despoiling nature of the beauty, freshness and purity so essential to our lives.

The most urgent and basic question is that of peace. Nothing is so pointless as modern warfare. Nothing destroys so instantly, so completely, as the diabolical weapons which not only kill but maim and deform the living and the yet to be born, which poison the land, and leave long trails of ugliness, barrenness and hopeless desolation. What ecological project can survive a war? The Prime Minister of Sweden, Mr. Olof Palme, has already drawn the attention of the Conference to this in powerful words.

It is clear that the environmental crisis which is confronting the world will profoundly alter the future destiny of our planet. No one among us, whatever his status, strength or circumstance, can remain unaffected. The process of change challenges present international policies. Will the growing awareness of 'one earth' and 'one environment' guide us to the concept of one humanity'? Will there be a more equitable sharing of environmental costs and greater international

***The Modern World**, Keynote address to Commonwealth Heads of Government Conference, Kingston, Jamaica, 30 April 1975*

Mr. Chairman, this is such a vast subject that it is a little difficult for me to know how to cover the entire ground in such a short time. I hope that the distinguished Presidents and Prime Ministers will forgive me if I merely touch on some points.

The most important factor since we last met is the emergence of the Arab people as a political force through their economic power. I am not going to dilate on this subject, because we all know how this has happened, and we know the reasons. It has also helped some sort of a Pan-Islamic movement in what most people call the Middle East, and we call West Asia, because we know that geographically it is a more correct expression. There is now far greater realism in the area itself, and in the approach of others, towards the problem. Many set positions have changed, largely under the pressure of the oil situation, and because of the Arab peoples' unity. There is also far greater African unity today despite certain problems and despite set-backs in some areas.

The other very significant factor is the collapse of Portuguese rule in Africa. We welcome the changes in Portugal which have made this development possible and which in turn were due to the national struggles of the people of these African countries. As you, Mr Chairman, so aptly described it, Africa has liberated Portugal. We welcome and greet the emergence of Mozambique and Guinea Bissau and, soon, of Angola. In this context, I should like to express our appreciation of the significant role played by President Kaunda and President Nyerere and other distinguished Heads of OAU.

The Commonwealth is essentially an association of small and medium nations. My father's vision of the Commonwealth was one of an interdependent world, and he had hoped that this would be a beginning which would gradually influence other countries in the same direction.

We, the member countries of the Commonwealth, are also members of the United Nations and of other world agencies. So the Commonwealth should work to strengthen the United Nations, although the big powers, it seems to us, have become less enthusiastic about it, because they feel that they cannot use it in the same manner as before. Of course, they now say that it is the poorer nations who are using it to their ends.

In international affairs, as in others, there has to be a spirit of compromise. Sometimes, by pushing too hard and making claims that are too large, we may jeopardise or delay the achievement of our objective. If I say this, it is not because we want to slow down, it is merely that we take a more practical approach. In showing a sense of responsibility in this respect, we do not wish to provide alibis for others who want to avoid taking such decisions or such action.

As far as India is concerned, there are many misconceptions. I referred to one a little earlier. Some may be genuine misunderstandings. Some, we feel, are deliberate. Our poverty is not new, it is a legacy of feudalism and colonialism and we have been struggling these last years against tremendous odds to lessen it and to remove the disparity which exists between different sections of our people. Great changes have taken place. I travel constantly, not only in the cities, but to remote tribal areas and villages. And I see a great change in the way the people look, in the way they dress, in what they eat, and in fact in what they demand, because today our major problem is that everybody wants more of everything. Just before coming here, I visited one of the worst drought-affected areas in the west of India. Here we organise what we call test-relief works, that is, we give work to people to provide them with purchasing power to buy grain and we have fair-price shops. Now, obviously, it is the poorest people who come to work and dig in the terrible heat, but of the thousands of people I saw, not one looked hungry or was unduly thin or was in any way pathetic looking; only two had torn clothes. So this shows that although we do have poverty, especially in the hilly tribal areas and so on, the change in these areas is quite significant.

We have laid special stress on agriculture. Our food production has risen from fifty-one million tons to one hundred and seven million tons. But vestiges of colonialism continue in such parts of Southern Africa as Namibia and Zimbabwe. In spite of all the declarations that have been made, racialism still persists. There is no evidence of any sincere change in the domestic policy of the Union of South Africa. As this question is going to be discussed almost immediately afterwards, I shall not say more at this stage, except to add that dialogue with South Africa can have meaning only if it is accompanied by steps to assure the dignity and the democratic rights of its own people.

There is growing African solidarity on this question. Not only among Africans, but also among the non-aligned and other groups, there is a much greater feeling of togetherness on this question, which is bound to have an effect. While this struggle is on, we notice new forms of racialism, such as discrimination on a colour basis, in Europe, and in other parts of the world. I mention the non-aligned countries. But just as unity and greater cohesion amongst them were gaining strength, a cleavage has appeared between the oil-rich and the others; and I should also like to contrast the unity of African nations with the inability of Asian countries to co-ordinate their interests.

Another significant factor has been the change in South East Asia. I have seen, in the newspapers, that the Saigon Government has finally surrendered. It was a long and bitter struggle. I am sure that we should all like to send our greetings to the PRG.

This event indicates the failure of a policy, which was based on misconception and false assessment, and which led to intervention and the propping up of unrepresentative governments in these countries. This policy showed also a failure to appreciate the meaning of post-colonial nationalism. I say 'post-colonial' because in the USA there certainly was an earlier appreciation of nationalist movements. Before the war, especially, we in India received understanding from them, but after the war there was a change of attitude. They completely misjudged the calibre of a man like Ho Chi Minh and his fierce desire to mould the future of Vietnam in consonance with the genius of its people, and underestimated the determination and capacity of the Vietnamese people to withstand any pressure—even the mightiest military onslaught—in defence of their freedom.

Such assumptions are made far too easily and superficially in international affairs, and we find that we ourselves are victims of them. For example, almost every time that I am met by various foreign dignitaries or members of the foreign press, they ask me if we are being influenced by the Soviet Union. I would like to say that it is absolutely ridiculous to suggest that we are under Soviet, or any other, influence. The USSR came to our support at the right time, at no cost to themselves, and it may have been the policy pursued by the USA which enabled them to do so.

Recent developments in Cambodia have similarly, illustrated that the will of a nation cannot be thwarted by outside military intervention. In Laos, one hopes that a dialogue between the two sides will lead to reconciliation and the formation of a national government representing the wishes of the Laotian people.

It is interesting to note that the Soviet Union has hesitated to take advantage of the situation in South East Asia, as indeed of the economic crisis in Europe, as one might have expected it to do.

Now to the trends which emerge. The fear of a nuclear conflict has receded; there is a lessening of tension in many areas, and this has led to increased economic and scientific, exchange and co-operation, but the hope of steady progress, which many of us who supported detente had wished for, has been deferred. We in India, as I think most of us around this table, welcome every step towards detente, but the overall detente and the compulsion to maintain open conflict leaves room to manoeuvre for positions of advantage, and this may not be in the interests of the smaller countries. Competitiveness and strategic rivalries have spread to other areas and have taken new forms. Although open confrontation has often been avoided, local conflict and tension have often been intensified.

Arms supplies to various nations fuel tensions. In Europe, the detente was partly a product of deterrence, a precarious mixture of fear and trust. The level of deterrence as well as its cost is getting higher. Vertical proliferation of conventional and nuclear arms is continuing; and this points to the need for an agreement upon lower levels of deterrence.

It was believed by my father that detente would be conducive to greater arms control, and to disarmament, and that the funds thus released would be made available for the uplifting of the poorer countries of the world. But the arms-control measures so far undertaken by the great powers are meant to preserve their overwhelming superiority in arms, whilst reducing the risk, as I said earlier, of certain types of confrontation. The economic aspect of disarmament, therefore, remains a distant dream.

In all this, however, medium and small powers do have a contribution to make. For their voices to carry greater weight, they must strengthen their own independence and self-reliance. Whatever the pressures they face, it is essential for them to assert their own interests.

Parts of the world. The idea that four, five, or six great powers, interacting amongst themselves, can preserve peace in the world, is an extension of the ideas developed in Europe in the nineteenth century. Such ideas have little relevance today for various reasons. For one, the world has become extremely complex due to the emergence of a large number of new states. Although, in orthodox power terms, these states are weak, they do have the capacity to upset any scheme of things which is imposed against their will. It seems to us that any approach to peace and stability, and any concept of a world order of the future, must be based on an understanding of the complex realities of the contemporary world, rather than on a nostalgic preference for the kind of stability which Europe enjoyed a century ago.

There is some speculation about the revival of an isolationist attitude in the United States. I do not think this is valid. The United States has deep-rooted conceptions of its own global responsibilities and has the instruments of policy for their implementation. The pressure on unacceptable regimes has not diminished, new bases are coming up. In this context, I would like to mention the resolution which Sri Lanka put forward in the United Nations with regard to peace and co-operation in the Indian Ocean, one that had the warm support of all the littoral states. It is not a question of what any one power does, but of the counter-moves it invites by doing it. We in India are against all foreign bases.

On the economic scene there has been a collapse of the post-war Bretton Woods System; there has been rapid inflation in almost every country; there were sharp rises in the price of food and fertiliser, which we discussed yesterday, and of course, later on, there was the rise in oil prices. All of this has had a great impact on the poorer countries, especially countries like India, which is somewhat in the middle. That is, we do need a certain amount of oil and fertiliser and we are not developed enough to be able to produce our own. We have found some off-shore oil but it is expensive to exploit, and this will take time and enormous resources. There is also a great shortage in the world of the equipment which is needed for this purpose.

Earlier it was said by the Communist countries that they were not affected by this inflation, but now they are acknowledging that European inflation has had an impact on their own economies; and it is going to hit them much harder because they fixed their prices for a number of years and so the change will not be gradual. What again is interesting is that one would have expected them to say 'This is the collapse of the system, this economic crisis has been caused by capitalism.' But in point of fact, they have not done so. Their criticism has been in a very low key for obvious reasons. They realise that instability in Europe is bound to have an effect on their own economies.

So far as the developing countries are concerned, in Africa as well as in Asia to some extent, this period of inflation, and higher prices, and shortage of essential commodities, has coincided with a period of severe drought over large areas. This has affected our whole planning process and it has certainly slowed down our development. In India, from about 1972, when we had a very bad drought throughout most of the country, up to 1974, the graph of prices was rising like the Himalayas. It was just a straight line going up and up and up. There were moments when we did not know how the country would survive. However, we took courage, and in July and August we adopted certain measures. At that time my own party and a lot of people felt that though these measures were necessary, the government could not possibly survive them and would have to go. But we felt that it was better for the government to do something that was necessary for the economy than to say 'Let us win the next elections and face whatever the future brings.' So we did take very, very, strong measures, thereby annoying every section of the people the big industrialists, the big businessmen, the industrial workers, the farmers, housewives, every possible section. But we did it. I am sorry to say they continued to be annoyed but we did manage to curb inflation. These measures were taken in July and August and by September the upward curve had already stopped and from then on it came down, although not substantially. But the very fact that prices are not rising, but are coming down, is a very welcome sign and people appreciate it. Of course, it meant taking a very stiff line with industrial workers and dealing with strikes in a manner which has brought us a great deal of criticism from the ILO and other such international bodies; and we have been visited by delegations from Japan and other countries. However, except for saying that the strike was not in the national interest, we did not do anything that was illegal. Some of the accusations made against us, of torture and so on, are completely without foundation. But we had to suspend a number of workers during the railway strike. This strike took place at the worst period of the food shortage. Food could not reach the areas where grain was needed. Coal could not reach the industrial areas; there was tremendous hardship on the travelling public; we had no way out.

The situation all over the world has been greatly aggravated by the oil crisis. We fully sympathise with our Arab friends, because we know that raw materials have been purchased very cheaply for many years, and the profits have been made by the big oil companies and other such organisations, to the detriment of the producing countries. We fully understand, therefore, the position of the oil producing countries, but the fact remains that most of the money that they have made has flowed back to the highly industrialised countries in the form of investments, and in purchases of machinery and so on. Only a very, very, minute portion of it has come back to the developing countries. In spite of the hue-and-cry raised by the advanced countries, it is the poorer countries which have suffered most. The countries least affected by these adverse developments were the United States and the Soviet Union, with their continental, and largely self-sufficient, economies.

There have been some attempts at trying to find ways and means to help those countries which have been most affected. There have been excellent declarations by UNCTAD, and in Dakar, and elsewhere, but the gap between the perception of problems and the will to do anything about them has not in any way been bridged.

As Mr. Manley said yesterday, most of these are global problems whether the) concern the environment, or population or food. We do need a global response. We are going to have discussions on economic matters and on the EEC later. All I want to say now is that when the idea of the UK joining the EEC was first broached, we did not want in any way to discourage the UK because we felt that they should do what was in their best interests. But we did fear that the EEC would become another rich man's club. Fortunately, it is a little more outward-looking now. We have entered into commercial agreements with the EEC and we also have bilateral relations with member countries and I think that man other countries are doing the same.

We welcome the decisions of the Lome Convention in which the points of view of a number of Commonwealth countries have received some understanding. We would like to regard the Lome Convention as a precursor to similar arrangements with other regions.

Finally, I would like to say that the need today, more than ever before, is for co-operation. We now need interdependence between the advanced, the financially affluent and the developing countries. The Commonwealth can be not only a model for co-operation but a positive factor for new economic initiatives for the welfare of individual members of the Commonwealth. Political problems are important, but we find that they too are being more and more influenced by economic trends and economic demands and economic needs.

'The Unfinished Revolution'

Address to the Non-Aligned Summit Conference, Lusaka, 9 September 1970

Mr. Chairman, distinguished delegates, I welcome this opportunity to give the greetings of the people of India to the Government and people of Zambia, and to the Heads and Representatives of the nations who have gathered here. President Tito deserves our special thanks. But for his unremitting efforts, this meeting would not perhaps have taken place. We are glad that this Non-aligned Conference is meeting for the first time in southern Africa, close to the spirit, the mood, and the very heart-beat of Africa.

Here, in Lusaka, we can feel the ebb and flow of the continuing battle against the remnants of colonialism in Angola and Mozambique. We can feel the vibrations of the struggle against the minority Government in Zimbabwe, and the apartheid policies of the racist regime in the Union of South Africa, and of the stirrings of the national movements in Namibia and in Guinea Bissau. These freedom fighters are engaged in the same battle as we ourselves were but recently. They are risking their lives for the same principles that we hold dear. We extend our support to these brave men and women.

As I said, yesterday, the revolution of our times is unfinished; the purpose of this conference is to draw up a clear programme of action to carry it forward. This is the challenge that the decade of the seventies places before the non-aligned countries.

Only a short while ago, the issues of war and peace, of the disposal of human beings and their destinies, were decided in a few capitals of the world. It is no longer so, because millions of people in the resurgent continents of Asia, of Africa, of Latin America and the Caribbean, have the situation in south-east Asia has further deteriorated. We are deeply concerned about the spreading of the conflict to Cambodia. All foreign forces should withdraw from the various countries of Indo-China, the lead being taken by the USA. Our assessment, based on talks with the various parties concerned, has led us to believe that a broad-based government, comprising every element in South Vietnam, would pave the way for the success of the Paris talks. Recent developments in Laos indicate the possibility of talks between the two sides there. As Member and Chairman of the International Commission, we have offered our good offices to both the concerned parties for this purpose. To preserve peace and to provide for the reconstruction of this war-torn area, some kind of international convention or agreement should be signed by all the parties to ensure respect for the neutrality, independence, territorial integrity and sovereignty of all the Indo-China states.

We have been deeply disturbed by the reported intention of the United Kingdom and other Governments to supply arms to the government of South Africa. This dangerous and retrograde step will threaten the neighbours of South Africa, and the area of the Indian Ocean. Any accretion to South Africa's military capability will abet its policy of apartheid and racial discrimination, and may encourage it to annex other territories. The argument, that this is being done to protect the so-called security of sea routes, is untenable. We would like the Indian Ocean to be an area of peace and co-operation. Foreign military bases will create tension and great-power rivalry.

The spirit of freedom goes hand in hand with the spirit of equality. Beyond the political problems of the Unfinished Revolution, there are complex and difficult economic tasks. A realistic appraisal, however, of our natural resources, our capacities, and our competence, reveals the possibility of our working together to reduce our dependence on those who do not respect our sovereignty, so that economic leverage, for thinly disguised political purposes, cannot be used against us. Neocolonialism has no sympathy with our efforts to achieve self-reliance. It seeks to perpetuate our position of disadvantage. International markets are so manipulated that primary producing countries have a permanent handicap. The levers of technology are also operated against us by means of agreements and collaboration that is not on an equal footing.

Hence we have to redouble our effort to gain for each nation the opportunity to develop to its full stature. The primary responsibility rests upon each developing country, but we also owe a duty to one another. The fallacy, that there is no complementarity between our come into their own. This is because we determined that decisions involving us-whether concerning war and peace, or the direction and pace of our social, economic and political development, could be made only by us, in our own way, and in our own countries. That is how non-alignment was born. It expressed our individual and collective sovereignty, our devotion to freedom and peace, and our urgent need to give to our people a better life and the opportunity to live in freedom, in dignity and in peace. At no time was there any intention to set up a third world.

This is our endeavour. The odds are tremendous. Each step has met with criticism and opposition. But we have carried on. Let us not be deterred by cynics and the hostile propaganda of the powerful media of communication. From the beginning, there has been no lack of inquisitors who looked upon non-alignment as heresy, and distorted its meaning. They said it would not work. But, we can answer back in the famous words of Galilee. 'And yet—it moves'.

The criticism of non-alignment has shifted on two counts. Those who now concede that non-alignment had some utility in the days of the cold war confrontation now maintain that this is no longer so. They no longer revile the basis and the principle, but only the practice.

Have the non-aligned states lost their relevance? The answer is an emphatic no. Twenty-five years after the last holocaust, the world is not yet on the brink of peace. The nuclear balance of terror still confronts us. The war in Vietnam is said to be waged with 'conventional' weapons, yet these include chemical contamination of food and plant life. The only way to have a clean war is not to have a war at all. Hence India stands and works for total disarmament.

The Great Powers certainly have the major responsibility for international peace and security. We welcome all initiatives towards the resolution of differences through negotiation, but even if the Great Powers reach accord on their common interests, and decide upon a mutually acceptable limitation of their strategic arsenals, the rest of the world, of which we form a considerable part, can hardly remain mere onlookers. We have an equal stake in peace, but the quality of that peace should be such as will ensure our own sovereignty' and security.

Not only national honour, but national interest, demands that we do not mortgage our right of decision in domestic and international affairs to foreign powers. This is one element of our policy of non-alignment. As the logical corollary, we reject the enmities of our erstwhile rulers. As my father declared: 'We are in no camp - and in no military alliance. The only camp we should like to be in, is the camp of peace, which should include as many countries as possible.' May I thank the Conference for its gracious gesture in memory of my father, and the many distinguished delegates for their kind references to him?

We decided that our respective territories should not be used for the subjugation of other people, for subversion, or for the carving out of spheres of influence. Indian manpower and resources were once used for imperialist purposes. When we gained our freedom, we declared that this would no longer be permitted.

We have all been subjected to domination, exploitation and the humiliation of racial discrimination. We cannot compromise with racialism in any form. The pernicious theory that one man is superior to another, merely on the grounds of race or birth, has been proved to be false, yet it continues to dominate the thinking of many people.

Today's world is a single entity. We are deeply convinced that by staying out of military pacts, the non-aligned countries can use their collective wisdom and influence to tip the balance of power in favour of peace and international co-operation.

These have been the positive achievements of non-alignment. If today belief in the efficacy of military pacts has weakened, if historic animosities are giving way to essays in friendship and co-operation, if a breath of realism is influencing international policies towards detente, the nations assembled here can claim some credit. This should not, however, lull us into complacency.

The big powers have never accepted the validity of non-alignment. Neither colonialism, nor racialism has vanished. They have returned in a new guise. There are subtle intrigues to undermine our self-confidence and to sow dissension and mutual distrust amongst us. Powerful vested interests, domestic and foreign, are combining to erect new structures of neo-colonialism. These dangers can only be forestalled by our being united in our adherence to the basic tenets of non-alignment.

I have touched upon certain general points, but on such an occasion one cannot ignore some of the explosive situations which confront the world.

I should like to take this opportunity to convey our admiration and best wishes to President Nasser for his statesmanship and courage in accepting the ceasefire. We disapprove of Israel's intransigence. Israel should be prevailed upon to comply fully with the UN Security Council Resolution of November 1967. We cannot deny to the people of Palestine their inalienable right to the homeland from which they were exiled economies, has so far made it difficult to realise the undoubted potential of mutual co-operation. There is greater complementarily amongst our economies than there is between the economies of developed nations. Advanced nations have been more successful in forming instruments operation amongst themselves. Our own effort in this direction has not even begun. The potential for trade and economic co-operation amongst us has been left virtually unexplored. By meeting each other's needs, we could diversify our trade, safeguard it against the caprices of international commerce, and reduce our dependence on middlemen and brokers.

This conference should formulate means for strengthening one another, and design methods for giving due priority, in our national policies, to positive measures for mutual co-operation. Such cooperation will help each of us achieve the capability of inducing these changes in the economic system at global level.

Through the United Nations' Conference on Trade and Development, we have tried to persuade the international community to make changes which are overdue in the economic system. This is now well understood all over the world. Although some have been accepted in principle, their implementation has been tardy. In a few weeks, the Second Development Decade will be launched by the UN General Assembly. So far, there has been little progress in evolving guidelines for international co-operation. Many nations which have the capacity, and if I may say so, the duty, to make a decisive contribution, hedge their statements with reservations. For too long has international co-operation been viewed as a one way traffic from the richer to the poorer nations.

As the Prime Minister of Guyana said yesterday, between ourselves, we possess the major part of the world's natural resources. Our manpower resources are no less plentiful. It should not be beyond our ingenuity to develop these resources, and employ our manpower for the production of wealth for our peoples. Through historical circumstance, economic relations between ourselves have not been developed, only relations between each of us and the erstwhile metropolitan powers. We can now make the first attempts to discover areas of co-operation in many fields of development—generation of power, agriculture, road, rail and telecommunications, the expansion of higher education and the development of training in science and technology. If we decide and I hope we shall to make a beginning with this study, India will be glad to play her modest part. We all recognise the malaise afflicting the development process. We know of the growing gap between developed and developing countries, between the northern and southern hemispheres, of the indifference of the affluent, the disappointments of the First Development Decade, and the failure of the affluent countries to transfer even one per cent of their gross national product. We are painfully familiar with the pitfalls of 'aid', in which most credits are tied to purchases from donor countries, and with the fact that a large portion of new credits always goes to the repayment of old loans. But the question is: must we endlessly wait in the hope that some day the developed countries will undergo a change of heart and acknowledge that disparities in the world are not in their own interest? It would be unrealistic to expect miracles of magnanimity. Even if this should happen, I am afraid that it would be to no avail if the right conditions in our own countries are absent. We must determine to help ourselves, to sacrifice, to pool our resources of knowledge and initiative. We must work together on a bilaterial, regional and multilateral basis.

I know from my own experience, that willpower, unceasing endeavour and the capacity for sacrifice, sustained and strengthened us during our struggle for political independence. These same qualities will help us towards economic freedom.

The power to question is the basis of all human progress. We are free because we questioned the right of others to rule over us. But intellectual and cultural emancipation is just beginning. We are rediscovering ourselves, and the fact is that a country sees things in terms of its own geography and history. Those who dominated the world's political affairs, and manned its economic controls, also held the monopoly of ideas. For years we accepted their values, their image of the world and, strangely enough, even of ourselves. Whether we like it or not, we have been pushed into postures of imitation. We have now to break away from borrowed models of development and evolve models of the worthwhile life, which are more relevant to our own conditions not necessarily as a group, but as individual countries with distinctive personalities.

The world today is united in peril, the peril from nuclear destruction, but more insidious is the daily pollution of our environment. We should be united in prosperity, and in the blossoming of the spirit of man. The non-aligned countries must be in the vanguard of the movement to create the world of tomorrow and to enrich the content of human life. The Unfinished Revolution can reach fulfilment if we have faith and confidence in ourselves and the assurance that, however long and arduous the journey ahead, we shall reach our destination.

'Indo-Belgian Friendship'

Speech at the Royal Institute of International Affairs, Brussels, 25 October 1971

It is indeed a privilege to address the Royal Institute of International Affairs, and this gives me the opportunity to tell you something about my country and the thinking of the one-seventh of mankind who live there. Each country is so involved in its own problems that it can seldom keep up with trends and events thousands of miles away.

The world is one but each of us sees it from a different angle. There is the national point of view, which depends upon geographical position and historical evolution. There is the personal point of view, largely determined by one's political philosophy and economic status. For two centuries or more, Europe dominated the world. In the present century, the United States and later the Soviet Union came to share this influence. Only after World War II did Asia become a factor in European thinking. Africa appeared on the world scene a little later.

Until the countries of Asia and Africa had struggled for, and won, their freedom, their problems, and even their rich treasure of civilisation and culture, were of concern only to a few scholars and specialists. Now there is better communication and a little more knowledge, but developments in Asia are still measured by the standards and way of living of the affluent countries.

It is twenty-four years since our Independence. Up till then we could have had no foreign or, for that matter, any other policy, since decisions were taken for us, not by us.

My father's interest in freedom and justice was not limited to our own struggle. He came to the meeting of the League Against Imperialism here, in Brussels, in 1926 and met the leaders of other conditions to stop the further influx of refugees, and to enable those who are already in India to return to their homes in safety and dignity and without further delay.

Belgium has been the centre piece of West European unity, that unity which is rightly the most cherished and urgent of your present objectives. Europe, so long rent by discord, is now pooling its resources for the solution of common problems. The European Economic Community is a great experiment in the voluntary co-ordination of national policies for larger regional purposes - not of war, but of peace and development. An alliance for war provokes counteraction. But an alliance for peace has deeper ramifications. We welcome the relaxation of tension in Europe and the treaties signed between the Federal Republic of Germany and the USSR and Poland. We hope that steps to further reduce tension will be taken. We welcome European unity but we hope that it will not be aimed against any region, and that economic arrangements amongst advanced countries will not impose new hardships on those who, like us, are making superhuman efforts to stand on their own feet. Belgium has adopted enlightened policies of international aid to developing countries. The terms of international trade, however, have been steadily worsening for the supplier of primary materials. A positive trade policy designed to help, and not frustrate, the efforts of developing countries would be worthy of the vision for which Belgium is well known.

independence movements. Thus he had personal contacts with what was happening in other countries, and he was a true citizen of the world. He gave our nationalist movement clear ideas about the kinds of political institution we wanted in the future, and the manner in which we would conduct our relations with other countries. It is this that enabled us to see our problems not as exclusively Indian, but in the perspective of world problems.

An organic world view unites our internal and external policies. Politically, we have established institutions which, in the words of our own constitution, are informed by a passion 'for political, economic and social justice'. Our democratic impulse owes its origin not so much to legislative institutions, introduced during colonial rule, as to the entire spirit of people's sovereignty' which our nationalist movement evoked. Economically, our endeavour is to overcome, as early as possible, our crippling poverty and to lessen the inequalities which were bred by colonialism, feudalism and the delay in adopting modern technology. We are modernising our agriculture, and expanding and diversifying our industrial base, so as to become self-reliant.

Since independence, the economic and social transformation of the country represents a vast qualitative advance. During the first half of this century, under colonial subjugation, India's per capita income remained stagnant. The availability of goods and services per person, in the mid-1940s, was roughly the same as at the turn of the century. Our sustained efforts in the years after Independence have enabled the growth of national income to be maintained at a rate of about 3.5 per cent per annum. In recent years the economy has tended to grow at an even faster pace. The country is now self-sufficient in food. With increasing expansion in irrigation facilities and fertiliser output, major breakthroughs are expected in other farm products as well. Starting from a flimsy base of consumer goods, industrial production has attained a wide range and depth of sophistication during the last two decades; the dramatic decline in the death rate, and the perceptible increase in the longevity of our people, reflects the degree of progress. Disparities do remain but the standard of living has risen substantially for all sections of the community, even for those who continue to be under diverse social disabilities. The rigidity of traditional Indian society is weakening. Education, and the political system, have given confidence to our people. Women are participating actively in all fields of life.

India lags behind the industrially advanced countries of the West in terms of material comforts, but it has a pervasive social coherence which provides a firm foundation for accelerated economic growth in the coming years. During the nationalist movement our greatest emphasis was on non-violence, tolerance and diversity within, unity. The leadership of Mahatma Gandhi conditioned us to choose the path of settling disputes by peaceful methods. This explain why, from the very moment of our freedom, we have stood for world peace, for non-alignment with military blocs, and for friendship with all nations, irrespective of their political systems.

We have never equated 'non-alignment' with neutrality, or unconcern with world problems, or disassociation from countries belonging to power blocs. To us, the word has meant independence of judgment and action in international affairs, according to the merits of particular issues as they affect our own national interests and world peace. In the bipolar world of the early 'fifties, the very word 'non-alignment' irritated some. But the years have seen a blurring of the rigidity of alignment. Those who swore by alliances are making overtures to members of the opposite camp and to the non-aligned. In the conditions of India, it is not the contest for power that creates the principal problem, it is the stark fact of poverty. The majority of the world's peoples are poor. They could be helped to a better life if their energy and resources, which are today directed towards war, were invested in their own welfare. Problems on our own doorstep naturally tend to loom large.

One new crisis surpasses in its magnitude all the earlier crises which have confronted us. The more than nine million people of East Bengal—practically equal to the population of Belgium— have been terrorised and persecuted by the military rulers of Pakistan, and have been pushed inside our own territory, jeopardising our normal life and our plans for the future. Should the world not take note of this new kind of aggression? This is not a civil war in the conventional sense. It is a genocidal pogrom of civilians merely because they voted democratically. It is the cynical use of helpless human beings as a weapon against a neighbour nation. We, in India, have shown the greatest self-restraint, but there is no doubt that our stability and security are gravely threatened. Indeed, we feel the threat is to the peace of the entire region. The basic cause of this crisis must be remedied. A political solution must be found to this problem and, to be effective, it must be acceptable to the elected representatives of the people of Bangladesh. To hold elections for seats which are not vacant, in the present conditions of repressions and chaos, has no meaning or purpose. It is the responsibility of all those who are interested in peace to create

When we carefully follows her speeches, we notice one salient point.

That the removal of economic disparties is one of the paramount solution. Another problem which we have to take care of is building up an atmosphere of unity.

Of course, India faces many challenges, we have to find solutions for all of them. We have to keep wider issues in view and surmount all the difficulties that come on the way.

Holding elections is one way of ascertaining the views of the millions on several of our issues. People of India are also able to carry many burdens and will continue to do so. The inner strength and the wisdom that citizens possess are worth commenting, though they are illustrate, they are wise enough.

Each and every country is having its own problems and they are being by their people in their own way, which suits their situations. All said and done,

The foreigners are hundred of years ahead of us. They have achieved technological advancement in the 19th century itself. They could increase their quality of life by the industrial revolution. There is no comparison between their conditions and the conditions of India.

In India, there is a peculiar situation. All sections of people cannot raise their voice and fight for their rights. Because of the colonial rule and suppression, some sections are very backward. So, we have to see that we should defend not only our rights but the rights of those who are not able to raise their voice. This obviously, is not government's responsibility but a responsibility of every citizen. Age-old inequalities of such nature weaken our country. So, the responsibility of building up unity and strengthening it lies with every citizen.

This sort of awareness comes only because of political awakening.

But, many of them who work in the fields or factories also, would like to know what is happening around them and how far the country has moved and how far the country is backward and in what respects.

This is, no doubt, a healthy sign.

An inner revolution is also needed, in an individual, in addition to outer revolution or outward development. When new depths or wants are unfolded and when a new defined good is expected, some principles need the modified. A spirit of sacrifice also should work. Hope and trust in each other should be inculcated.

Within a democratic framework some processes which are of social, political and economic nature should be started and their main aim should be removal of all kinds of inequalities. The vested interests make a hue and cry when their interests are damaged.

Without any prejudice against any section, sense of participation in the process should be build up among all. Our intention as per the democratic norms is not to remove right to property. The social principles preached by the revolutionaries in Socialists

Republic of Russia failed miserably and the system it created did not live for long. It failed before a hundred years people lost their innovative to work when facilities were given in plenty but human incentive or healthy competition was not there. They are trying out HMT watches, because there was no production in their factories.

This is a glaring example of how human effort fails in producing goods when there is no incentives.

The situation in India is entirely different.

After all democracy is not work much if it does not involve all the people or give them incentives.

Poverty is a terrible condition which makes people frustrated and makes them lose faith in humanity. So, the benefits of affluence should, which some people enjoy, should also accrue to those, who have nothing. So, we must be determined to implement our programmes one after another with determination and courage.

So as to inculcate confidence in the people, who work for the people, some significant steps should be taken to amoliarate the conditions in the country.

As we see today, a wave of change is sweeping the country like our India and many such countries in the world. No one can remain unaffected by this new wave. We need not any fear about it because we are swimming with it—with the current. We are giving a direction to this current and we are ready to face whatever future brings to us.

There have been floods in some areas of the country and drought was there in some parts. Despite all this havoc, enough food was produced in the country.

Indian people believe in a great philosophy of human existence. One would try to live in spite of several odds, as life is considered to be a gift given by God. It is this philosophy that enriches an Indian mind.

'Live and let live' is our great philosophy and people believe in the doctrine "Ahimsa Parama Dharmah".

It is with this slogan that Gandhiji fought with the mighty British Empire, and millions and millions of people joined his movement and fought the Britishers.

It is this Gandhian philosophy that made people bold to face *lathi* charges and imprisonments.

That inner strength and moral courage are the two essential characterstics of humanity, that are greatly respected in India.

At the moment of independence, our energies turned from the tension of struggle to immediate problems.

Our quest had been friendship with all but submission to no one.

Our freedom will be complete only when we are able to create good living conditions for our people.

Toleration of others views had been out tradition. We must maintain and strengthen this glorious tradition so that the entire mankind benefits from it. Quality of mind implies strength of morality not wealth nor affluence. Quality is not to be judged by wealth, rank or efficiency but by its depth of compassion, by a sense of responsibility or maturity.

Indira Gandhi, sincerely believed in the centuries old centre of learning. She hoped that this great centre would send into the wide world, men and women with a spirit of humanism dedicated to quest for knowledge and understanding.

She visited many countries and spoke on several platforms about our cultural ethos and our commitment to certain values.

She also expressed her views on several issues confronting humanity.

She expressed that "The Story of Indian development is not without significance for the rest of the world." How can be otherwise when it encompasses the aspirations and struggles of over 550 millions human beings while defining Indian democracy in such clear terms she also said "In the cause of political institutions, it is not inevitably the past that is decisive, but the changing conditions of the lives and attitudes of people and the capacity of those who are in positions of leadership to involve the largest number of people in the political process.

Democracy was not entirely new to India, for its roots could be found in our old panchayat system. This system probably came into being because the village and the people were too distant from the centres of political power. Today, this ancient system has been transformed into a new organ of self-government at district and block level as a link between the governments programmes and its people."

Let us know about some of her opinions about some issues.

While defining democracy, she said "democracy could only be a two-party system worked by those who were educated in a particular way, perhaps as advanced people of the west of a generation ago protested that the colonial countries were not ready for freedom. So, it was said that the under-developed countries societies of Asia and Africa were not read, for democracy and could achieve or guided democracy? Can democracy be guided any more than freedom? Is not guided democracy a contradiction? Perhaps these questions are irrelevant for it now seems that in some countries the word 'democracy' was used as a shield for reaction and the subversion of freedom."

She announced boldly that "we did take democracy seriously. To us it conveyed the equality of all people to participate at every level in the functioning of government

21

Indira Gandhi's Opinions on Some World Forums

Indira Gandhi, as a towering personality spoke at several international forums. Speaking at Columbia University she said, "Although we have great diversity of languages of religion, even of races, of customs, we do not think it is a weakening factor. In fact, it is a surprise to me when I come abroad and at almost every place, I am asked this question, "Will Indian unity hold? How do you manage these different languages?" Each state has its language and the people study their language. But it does not prevent their working in other states, travelling in other states. It does not upset the basic feeling of Indianness which binds us all together.

Indian unity is an established fact. It is not dependent on the political party or a person. It is something which exists in Indian and I do not think it can be easily diminished or weakened. There are many tendencies which could weaken unity. I think, in the whole world, there is always constant conflict between things that divide and weaken and others which cemant together. It is for us to work towards the cementing, uniting, strengthening factors rather than others."

Wherever she went, she had to answer several questions. In India, can democracy survive? Can unity survive? Can the government feed the growing population? She boldly answered all of them saying 'Yes': democracy had been strengthened, unity is stronger than before. We are fully self-sufficient in the production of cereals like rice or wheat. We face the future with confidence. She gave confidence to the masses in clear words and told the world population also, how matters were moving in India.

She also gave a picture of India. "We had reached a point in economic growth, in social stability and it was not an easy task. It was achieved against very great odds."

Speaking about a question time and again "how is it that a woman lead a government or a country". She firmly said "This question is never in India. Not in the smallest village because our society and philosophy are based on the importance of the individual. We are not concerned whether that individual is a man or woman or the person is a Christian, a Hindu or Muslim. We only say this is a human being. What has he to contribute to the society. Society would make use of such contribution.

In her speech at Paris Lunchon, she said "the achievement of Indian civilization is its persistence over thirty centuries. This survival has been possible because of tolerance, the power of assimilation and the belief that the values of life are more important than power and position. After many vicissitudes we are once again in the mainstream of history. We are engaged in overcoming the stagnancy perpetuated by years of feudalism and colonial rule when we were deprived of industrial, technological and social change."

Speaking about technological advancement, we would certainly like society to benefit from technology but we do not want to be imprisoned by technological structures. We have no wish to reinact. the experiences of the west. Our national personality must evolve in its own way. Increasing material affluence does not seem to have satisfied man's deepest yearnings. Society must be imbued with the values which will enable man to find fulfillment. She also emphasized that 'this is the principle which has been guiding our endeavours. It is not easy to transform the older order revolution or to mould a diverse people into a modern nation. In a rational basis without recourse to compulsion.

Thus she tried to evolve a definite personality of India, in the larger perspective of international peace. Of course, the task is too vast and the result does not come out of any fanatic appeal.

In a speech at Bonn Banquet, she said "between Germany and India, there is old bond of friendship and goodwill which was fashioned first by poets and scholars. In recent years, it has widened into friendship between the two peoples. We have always admired Germany's tremendous energy and ....we have watched the miraculous manner in which the Federal Republic has recovered from the ravages of war and has been working for the establishment of a new temper in Europe and in the world.

In the midst of your preoccupations, you have not forgotten the struggles of the peoples of Asia and Africa to build a better life......

The changes taking place in this part of the world have aroused interest. It is important for us to keep in touch with these developments....

"It does seem a little ironic to us in India and Europe, which was a scene of conflict not so long ago, should have an earsing of tensions which in Asia too conflicts are continuing and a third is threatening. Dr. Radhakrishnan used to say that to be an Indian is not merely to have an Indian nationality but it is in the way you think in the things in which you believe that the quality of Indianness exists. And one of the things about which we have thought through the ages is peace. And we have defined peace not merely as the absence of conflict, but a positive approach and effort to promote cooperation. How well the lemon-groves grow depends upon how well the gardeners work. Peace is a call for never-ending extertion to achieve the good, not of a limited area, but of all human beings in deed of all that is in creation ... The Indian Upanishads say "man may roll up his skill, roll up the sky, yet these will be no end to this suffering unless he finds the Luminous one within.." The area of argument can grow and the area of peace can also grow".

Courtesy: Publications Division
Govt. of India, New Delhi (1971)
B.K. Ahluwalia

Moulding Intellectual Climate

I am glad that you have called me here. But I do not really have very much to say at this stage because, I think, it is more important if we hear what ideas our young people would like to suggest.

Dr. Rao ended his speech by referring to, I think, my larger loyalty to the country or some such words. I think that fundamentally all of us feel that way. I do not think that it would be fair for any Indian to say that he does not have the welfare of the entire country at heart. What does happen is that for a particular reason or for a particular period one likes to exploit a smaller loyalty. Sometimes, politicians, labour leaders and many others do this. And this is perhaps inevitable. What we have to see is that these smaller loyalties do not come in conflict with the larger loyalties. What we have to see is how to develop this loyalty, which already exists in people, into more of a kind of passionate involvement in the welfare and the future of the country. And that is why unity is so important.

That is why we talk of integration—emotional, intellectual and otherwise. I am one of those who believe that underlying all our diversity and our differences, and our quarrels, there is a very fundamental and basic unity, which has kept India together.

There is no doubt that there are trends and forces which would try to introduce ideas that would crack this unity or weaken it and herein lies the importance of young people, and especially people of the Universities, gathering together and trying to see how these forces or this type of ideology can be countered.

We all talk of our rich cultural heritage. But there is a consistent effort to show as if there is only one strain in the cultural heritage. There is a consistent effort to deny all the other strains and influences which have made us what we are and we are no less mixed than perhaps any other people in the world. There has been a great deal of interchange of ideas between North and South India, between Dravidian culture and the North Indian culture. Similarly, in science, in music, in architecture, to name only a few, we have been influenced from Turkey, Persia, Afghanistan, from the Arab countries and from Central Asia also. Amongst our own many of the things, which are common today, are things which have been invented or brought to us by people of different religions or different languages in the country. For instance, in U.P., Amir Khusro has perhaps made the greatest influence on the contemporary language which is spoken by the ordinary people. I must say that this has changed somewhat since the great onslaught of high-flown Hindi.

I think that teachers and students can be and should be the moulders of the intellectual climate of the country because now our quarrel, our fight is with certain ideas which have flowed and ideas can only for fought with other ideas and we hope they are better ideas.

Dr. Rao mentioned a scheme of having maps and studying other areas or other States. I was reminded when many years ago I visited a pioneer palace in the Soviet Union. One of the schemes they had was just like we have—a student from one State going to another State. But there they do not go just on a visit. Before they go, they divide up into groups which would study the mineralogy, the plant life, and the animal life. So, when they came back, between them they had a full picture of the whole area. Also, in doing so they had got involved with the people of that area who were interested in that subject. This always gives greater purpose to what one is doing. It gives a greater meaning if one does it with some purpose.

When we talk of being an Indian, I do not know what each person probably means. But I have been alarmed to see lately that many people confuse being Indian with being Victorian. This is, I remember, what our grandparents were, but the younger people today may not be so. When I was a very small girl, women of our family wore very short sleeves. But there were other people who said this was very un-Indian. But if you go inside Indian villages, you will find that nobody ever heard of long sleeves in their long history. Many of the ideas which came to us from the British, from Queen Victoria, King Edward or whoever it was, were very much mixed up in what people today think is being Indian. So that being Indian is something which is not at all superficial—as to what one wears, or how one does one's hair and what sort of beard one has or something like that. But it is something which is very much deeper. And here we are rather more fortunate, I think, that people in other countries, because the roots of our culture are so broad-based that basically they are quite modern also—not all of it, but much of it. The basic search for truth is timeless and will fit into any period.

Dr. Rao also mentioned textbooks. This is a very-very important item because it is through textbooks that one forms the minds of young children. I must confess I saw textbooks two years ago; since then I have not seen any. I am told that, firstly, the standard is not always what it should be. Secondly, a lot of misinformation is given about other peoples, sometimes about other States and by other people—I mean even within our own country. There has also been an effort, right here in Delhi, I think, at re-writing some of our history. These are dangerous tendencies which we must look into. Without wishing to gag anybody, we must see that trends and tendencies which will weaken our unity, which will weaken our growing together, should not be allowed to gain strength.

Of course, unity at no time means regimentation because richness of India is in its great diversity. And, I think, we should not keep false diversity. But if it is natural, it should be allowed to flower and grow in its own way.

There is another dangerous doctrine being preached that some people to be Indianised. Actually, I did deal with this in the beginning in rather a general way. But I am just putting forth some ideas which need to be thought out. I must confess that I have no clear idea myself as to how people are going to meet this situation. I think it is only the people, who can give a lead out of their experiences in their colleges—how they feel, whether they feel there is integration between them and their colleagues speaking other languages, or from other States or of other religions, and even of the same religion if they belong to different castes. It is horrifying to know that even now in spite of our Constitution and so on, there is still a distinction made between Scheduled Castes and other Hindus. This is as important a part of integration as Hindu-Muslim or Hindu-Christian or Hindu-Sikh unity.

Writers as Crusaders

It is always a privilege to meet writers, and you are all welcome to our capital city. Writers are gifted with insight and more intense feeling than their fellowmen. The written word has powerfully influenced the mind of man and has enhanced its awareness and sensitivity. Writers and poets give voice to the innermost urges of the people. They affirm a nation's basic beliefs and ideals.

Writers have often been pioneers of protest. They have raised their voice against foreign rule and domestic social injustice. In India, many leaders of our freedom movement, as also of social reform, have themselves been outstanding writers. Others have had close relationship with writers and thinkers. This is but natural, for there can be no political or social transformation without a corresponding intellectual effort. Thought and action must arise out of a searching analysis of social forces. It is this search which produced in France the leaders of Revolution. In Russia, it produced, Lenin and Gorky; in India, Tagore, Gandhi and Nehru.

At the most significant and creative phases of history, the man of action and the man of ideas do not live in isolation. They work together and take the people with them. They lead revolutions. Or if their effort is allied to sensibility, as poets and writers, they become powerful instruments of change. If writers choose to be unmoved by the situation around them, they become irrelevant and might even be impediments to progress.

The writers' purpose is to communicate to the people their search for truth and beauty. In the colonial age, everything was politics, because every person of integrity could have only one objective, that is, freedom. Love of freedom acted as the focus of all creative effort. Most nations of Africa and Asia have now achieved freedom. We have overcome the humiliation of being regarded as interlopers in .our own land. But in our two continents, there still are people who are struggling for independence and equality. Our sympathy and salutations naturally go out to all those valiant soldiers of freedom who fight for national honour.

Even though we are politically independent and sovereign, the battle of freedom is not completely over. Social transformation is still to be completed. Forces are at work within our country to limit true freedom. Some are interested in keeping the newly free nations weak and divided. Unfortunately, some writers sometimes allow themselves to be exploited by these forces.

In India, our political system gives the fullest freedom to every person to express his point of view. We are confident that the people have the wisdom to weight and to decide the validity of contending theories, and that they will reject false doctrines and choose the right one. If writers propound narrow and harmful theories, the people will ultimately disown them.

One of the great struggles which we in the newly free countries have to wage is against the forces of superstition. Seeds of dissension, whether in the name of religion, caste or language, threaten national integrity and freedom. Our experience during our struggle for Independence has taught us that it is our inner division which makes us vulnerable, that whenever we have been united, our strength has been enormous, and that this does count, regardless of military forces. In our country, despite the great figures of history—Buddha, Ashoka and Akbar, despite Mahatma Gandhi and Jawaharlal Nehru, religious fanaticism and feelings of caste superiority do persist. In fact, after my father's death they seem to be on the increase. Thus writers have a very great role to play in our society. Their writings should propagate the larger freedom which is based on social equality, secularism and rational thinking.

Every now and they the question is asked: Must writers be in politics? It is for them to choose, not for politicians to decree. Whether or not writers enter politics, they cannot ignore life's challenge and adventure. They cannot ignore the joys and sorrows of the people. Else, what literature would they create.? Should they not add to the human content of life through their poetry and essays, their plays and their novels?

The technology of printing and broadcasting has not always been used for human welfare or for the good of the people. Countless books and journals advocate prejudice, hatred and violence. In nations where literacy is not yet universal, the printed word is apt to command more veneration than it does in advanced societies. Exaggerated claims or baseless accusations are given credence. Hence, what might be described as eccentricity elsewhere, could create misunderstanding and tension here.

Although all nations have become politically independent, we continue, to some extent, to view the rest of the world from the angle of our erstwhile rulers. In some Afro-Asian countries, books especially of advanced study, are largely those of British and American authors. In others, there may predominantly be books by French authors. Certainly there are liberal and open-minded scholars both in English and in French. But can national bias be kept out? It is urgent that we should establish direct nation-to-nation relationship amongst ourselves. We should encourage more scholars and authors to study one another's language and write authoritative books on one another's culture and society. Two months ago, I found in Zambia that messages from Lusaka could come to Delhi only through London. Mechanical help is understandable, but sometimes we have allowed third-country filtration of our ideas and attitudes. Translation almost invariably travels through a European language. This conference might initiate a major programme of direct literary exchange and translation.

In India, writers are not accountable to Government. They are answerable to their own conscience and to the judgment of the people. Their responsibility is to society as a whole. They must advocate all that makes life more free, more just, more humane and more beautiful. Their guiding principle should be that of the early seers of our country: Lead me from untruth to truth, from darkness to light, from death to immortality.

Immortality, in spite of all the new medical miracles, does not mean of physical immortality, but the survival and continuity of great ideas, I ideas which liberate man from aggressiveness and narrowness of mind, from hatred and from fear.

Literature does not lay down moral precepts. It creates an atmosphere where values are cherished. It strengthens moral fibre and judgment, and fashions attitudes.

A conference such as this can help to enlarge awareness amongst writers of their own role and responsibility not only within their national but in the international community also. So fast is the development of technology and communications that formal institutions of governance, of education and of social organisation will become obsolete everywhere if they are not reformed to meet the needs of the contemporary and the future world.

The most significant development in the last two decades has been the explosion of human consciousness, the consciousness that we are becoming one human family, one world. National frontiers are bound to remain, but these are no longer impenetrable to the flow of ideas land thoughts. The newly free countries of Asia and Africa naturally find greater kinship with one another. I hope this conference will strengthen mutual understanding and friendship.

I should like to congratulate those of our friends who have received awards. We know that they and many who are not present with us have been deeply involved in what is happening around them or deeply concerned with the problems of poverty, of social injustice and inequality. We know that peace and justice can only come if these problems are solved. We must solve them in partnership with one another.

Conferences like yours, and this conference I hope, will be a step forward in this direction of creating understanding leading to friendship and peace.

Eternal Values

Swamiji and friends, I am glad to be associated with this function because of my admiration and respect for you, Swamiji, and for the great order of Shri Ramakrishna which you so ably represent. Our country is rich in its thought, in its philosophy, in its culture. But somehow we have not been able to project these outside, or even to all of our own people, perhaps because many of us look at these matters rather superficially. But Swami Vivekananda and Swami Ranganathananda have been notable exceptions. The excellent work-done by the various branches of the Ramakrishna Mission all over the world has helped to fill the gap to some extent. The two books being released today will give an insight to people into our ancient teachings and will deepen the understanding of those who already have some knowledge.

There has been some interest in philosophy and the basic religious teaching. But today it is not merely the grey-haired who search for reality or the meaning of being. Questions are being asked by millions of young people everywhere.

I often talk of progress and modernity. Progress to me means the blossoming and deepening of the human personality, of the individuals and also of the nation. Obviously the evils of poverty and of a stratified society are obstacles and must be removed. However, at every step we must ensure that this process of attaining a higher material standard of living does not impinge on man's personality, does not give him a feeling of alienation from his society and his environment, but, on the other hand, helps him to be a participant in development and enriches his spirit.

Does modernity consist merely in using modern amenities or in following certain fashions or aping the more affluent nations, or should we look for a more profound meaning? Swamiji himself has given the answer in one of these books. He says, "That man is modern who is inquisitive, who has a passion for truth and the power of rational investigation, who never takes things for granted but always strives to get at the heart of things, and constantly asks what next, what next."

When I received Swamiji's books late last evening I picked up the one entitled *Eternal Values* and-by chance it opened with a quotation from the Upanishad : "Men may roll up the sky like a piece of leather. Still there will be no end of sorrow for them without realising the luminous One within." On the same page follows another quotation, this time from Europe, from Schopenauer: "All men who are secure from want and care, now that at last they have thrown off all other burdens, become a burden to themselves." How true this is, and should we not seek the reason why it should be so?

Human beings are quick to find somebody or something to blame. Seeing the world's present predicament people find fault with science and with technology. The problem is not in the nature of technology but in the nature of man itself and the value systems which he has made for himself. The habit of generations becomes entwined in a sort of network of integrated circuits which resist any change. Is it not time now to disentangle ourselves from all these wires?

In contemporary life, in most countries the accent is on competition, not co-operation. This naturally leads to aggressive and suspicious attitudes within the nation as well as in the international sphere. A man's love for his family does not diminish because he cares deeply for his country, nor does a man become less of a patriot because while cherishing his country and its culture he feels concerned for the welfare of humanity as a whole. Man can utilise the vast riches of the earth without despoiling or denuding it.

The question before us here in India is how we, can make the best use of knowledge and of resources, how we can create an atmosphere of co-operation and harmony. Can we do this unless we consciously attempt to modify the value systems which encourage selfishness or acquisitiveness and to replace them with others which would seek to advance the interest of the individual along with those of his fellowmen rather than at their cost? We must build our social institutions along principles which will enhance the dignity, the security and the potential of human life.

Since our Minister for Planning is present, I cannot resist this opportunity of saying to him that the criterion for all planning should be not only maximum production but optimum human development. In achieving this we have much to learn from our ancient thought which is so beautifully rendered into understandable modern idiom by Swamiji in these two books which I have great pleasure in releasing.

The Cult of Violence

The Home Minister touches many spheres of national activity. So, this debate naturally is an important one and ranges over many areas.

Hon. Members have touched on many points. They have drawn attention to many defects and shortcomings.

Sir, no one is more conscious than I, that in our country of this size and diversity, and with our background of feudalism and colonialism, our problems are bound to be of immense magnitude. With development, some problems are solved and others are created. Even societies which are regarded as affluent and stable are not immune from trouble, from unrest and even the growth of violence.

So, none of these questions is peculiar to our country. We know that rapid urbanisation has increased crime and violence in other countries.

I hope Hon. Members will not think that I am trying to minimise our own duties or responsibilities, of which I am deeply conscious. But, I should like the Hon. House to see our problems in perspective and lot to forget that these are not normal times for us.

Our programmes and the recent elections to which many Hon. members have referred, aroused expectations of change. But, just when we were poised for rapid advance in many directions, we have been overtaken by the tragic events on our Eastern border which have imposed it very severe strain on our entire administration.

Therefore, areas of hope and despair do exist side by side; and, when despair is exploited to propagate violence, this is bound to be a matter of concern.

I know that violence has many aspects and emerges from different roots. As I have said, the problem is not peculiar to India. Also, we are a developing society and development produces its own tensions and other difficulties.

Nevertheless, the problem that their coming has created does threaten the security of our country and the stability of our country. Amongst them aee people who are not genuine refugees. So, from all these points of view, they are threatening our security and, therefore, it is now, we have remained restrained. But we have silenced some Pakistani guns, we have dealt with their tanks and we have brought down some of their intruding aircraft. But we have not posed a counter-threat in any sense of the word. But we cannot allow the annihilation of the people next door to us. I mean, this is what has to be very clearly understood by the world and which I did speak to them. It is not like two equal armies fighting there, the Mukti Bahini and the West Pakistan troops. It is a fully equipped army fighting with the people, some of whom have been trained in the East Pakistan Rifles and the East Bengal Regiment, some of whom have been trained very quickly in the various camps run by the leaders of these two para-military forces. But nevertheless, they are not equal in that way to the army, and it is not in our national interest that an entire people, not just the Mukti Bahini, but the entire unarmed population of Bangladesh should be annihilated. Although the threat is already great, anything like this happening or even happening partially would increase the threat to our security immediately and also for the future.

On the western side, our armed forces were deployed some time after the Pakistani troops moved up to our borders. We have not taken any initiative there. But, as I said, we shall meet any threat to our freedom or our security and, of course, we feel that the present threat just is not merely a threat but a threat to the very foundation on which India is built and on which India is surviving.

Now, there are suggestions you have heard about the withdrawal of troops. I have already explained in the other forum why we cannot withdraw our troops in the west because our lines of communication, the cantonments and so on are so placed that Pakistan has a very great advantage, and having twice been taken unawares by Pakistan in this very area, in Kashmir and so on, we cannot afford that risk. But I would certainly welcome the withdrawal of troops and I think the troops that should be withdrawn straightway are the Pakistani troops in Bangladesh. They, are far from their homes, they are also suffering and I think that they should be taken back to rejoin their families and friends in West Pakistan. And this would be a positive response from Pakistan to show that they do want a solution in Bangladesh. It would be a gesture for peace. And I do feel that in today's circumstances, the very presence of Pakistani troops in Bangladesh, as ! said earlier, is a threat to our own security.

I think that I have answered most of the points. So far as the present situation is concerned, as you know, the Mukti Bahini is facing very courageously; it is a very difficult fight but they are fighting very bravely, and they have our good wishes, and they have our support also. Nobody can predict what the future will bring but, as I have said on an earlier occasion, nothing is going to ease the situation immediately. No matter what happens, what steps we take, the next month will be of very great difficulty to us and also to the people of Bangladesh. I mean we have to know there is no solution, which is a magic solution, which will end the suffering of the refugees or end the burdens on us. This just cannot happen with the best will in the world. I am glad that this unity has been shown. Shri Chatterjee spoke something about our singling out his party and so on. I can assure him that it is not at all our intention. But certain things had happened in West Bengal. I am glad that the situation has improved greatly and once there is peace there will be no cause for anybody to be poised against anybody else, and this is the time when all parties should unite, because, as I said, the burden on the Indian people is very great and the challenge and the difficulties we face are extremely difficult, and they will need all the strength we have, all the resources we have and all the unity and determination which we can bring to bear upon. I have full confidence that all parties will respond to this challenge and together, we will be able to come out of what is a dark period for us and for the people of Bangladesh. We will come out of it and they will be able to make a new life for themselves.

We Shall Succeed

You are all aware that we are facing a new crisis. The people of Bengal and the rest of the country had stood by us and returned us to power in the last general election. We had imagined that all obstacles in the way of our progress had been removed and we shall work hard .to build up a strong country. But soon after, a tragic event happened which cast a big burden on our people, although we were in no way involved in it. In the beginning, it was purely an economic burden. The large influx of refugees from East Bengal seriously affected the lives of the people in West Bengal, Assam, Meghalaya and Tripura and increased their hardships. We imagined that we shall have to bear this burden for only a few days and we shall be able to do so easily with the help of other countries. But the help we received was meagre compared to what was necessary. If some people offered help, they were not in the least worried about the causes of the crisis— why a huge mass of people were quitting their homes and coming to us like a river in flood. No disease can be cured unless it is correctly diagnosed. What is to be done if, without caring to find out the cause of the influx, we try to stop it? We told the truth and others agreed with us, but nobody did anything in the matter.

To understand the present crisis, we have to go into its historical background and find out how Pakistan was formed. The battle for freedom was fought in the whole country—also in the region now called Pakistan. Khan Abdul Ghaffar Khan, better known as Frontier Gandhi, and Abdul Samad Khan, who was called Baluch Gandhi, took part in the fight for freedom. But when Pakistan was formed, it was not these leaders of the people who came to power. In India, the freedom fighters won the elections and set up their Government. But in Pakistan, they remained behind prison walls and those who were co-operating with the British set up their Government. They held positions in the Army or other offices. There was a basic difference in our ideologies. We were anxious then and are so even now that we should have the best of friendly relations with our new neighbour—now that Pakistan had come into being. It is not good for any country to be always quarrelling with a neighbour. But whenever we extended our hand of friendship, we were faced with a closed fist on the other side and also an atmosphere of tension. We believe that the reason for this was that several countries were encouraging Pakistan to do so. If the big powers, which were friendly to Pakistan, had advised it in the very beginning not to fight with India, Pakistan would not have taken up the posture of war. Pakistan had neither the strength nor the courage to go to war with us. But they did so because they were getting help and war materials from abroad. Even when they went to war with us, they got all encouragement from their friends. They were not branded as aggressors with the result that they did not change their ways. The result of all this was that despite its friendship with Big Powers of Pakistan could not become a strong power. It grew weaker.

We are all Indians though we speak different languages and profess different faiths. To whatever State we belong, we are all citizens of this country engaged in the common endeavour of taking it forward towards progress. What binds men of different religions, habits, dress and languages are some high ideals. Religion and language cannot bind any people in the world of today. We have to get over these. Religion is good and everyone must adhere to his religion. But you cannot build up a nation and keep the people united, on the basis of religion. We said this at the time of the formation of Pakistan but neither the British nor others listened to us then and Pakistan came into being. But we saw from the very beginning that in Pakistan, the people of one religion committed atrocities on the minorities belonging to a different religion.

Another thing that was happening in Pakistan and which the world overlooked was that even those who were in a religious majority in the country were being oppressed. We knew it but we could not interfere in the affairs of another country. But the situation could not last long and in the end this has weakened Pakistan. If Pakistan has, become weak, it is not because we wanted it. It has become weak because other nations helped it in pursuing wrong policies, which were probably in their own interest and not in the interest of Pakistan. We also were pressurised to follow their policies but it was our good fortune that we had leaders who followed policies which were in the national interest and stuck to them firmly.

Our development plans are in progress but, in the meanwhile, a big burden' has been cast on us. The burden is economic because the number of refugees is very large. The influx has also created social, administrative and political problems. But the most important thing is the danger it poses to our security. If might develop into a big danger.

You are aware that we have rehabilitated all the refugees who came to us so far. We did so although we are a poor country and received meagre help from outside. We became worried as the danger to our security slowly increased. Across the border between West Bengal and East Bengal, there was the Border Security Force on our side and East Bengal or the East Pakistan Rifles on the other side but they had changed their name and called themselves the Mukti Bahini.

At this stage, Pakistan moved its forces towards our borders; in the west they moved further towards Kashmir, Punjab, Rajasthan and Gujarat. When their forces reached the Kashmir border, we drew the attention of the U.N. observers towards this. They told us that the Pakistani forces were carrying out training exercises. Who could believe it? Could a country, which had been the victim of Pakistani aggression thrice, believe it ? The danger to our security increased but we took no steps for ten days. After ten days, we also moved our forcas forward. As long as we had not moved our forces towards pur borders, no country in the world, big or small, took note of the presence of Pakistani forces on our borders. They were not worried about the danger posed to our security and that they should do something. No opinions were expressed about it. But when our forces moved forward, not on another's territory but on our own, some world powers raised a furore that peace was in peril and they began saying that both the countries should withdraw their forces. How could we agree to this ? No Government with any sense of responsibility, no minister or any officer could endanger the security of the country and its borders. We asked why the Pakistani forces had been moved to our borders and whether it did not involve a risk to our security. If we withdrew our forces, they had to be moved far from the borders where our cantonments and other arrangements exist. But the cities and cantonments of Pakistan are quite close to their borders. If they withdraw just a little, they will still be in an advantageous position. They can reach the borders quickly whenever they want to attack us. We cannot do so. Who are there to guarantee that if we are attacked, they would help us and get us back quickly the land occupied by the aggressor? Nobody is prepared to consider this aspect of the matter. They all say that the forces must be withdrawn. We do not say "No" to this demand. We have suggestions to make. But how far is it proper that only the suggestions made by the other party should be accepted? Our suggestion is that the Pakistani forces should be withdrawn from East Bengal. It is their arrival and their stay which has resulted in a reign of terror there and the influx of refugees into this country. If they leave East Bengal, the fighting will stop immediately. But no one is prepared to think on these lines.

We were also told to agree to have U.N. observers on our

eastern border as well. As far as I am aware, a few of them were there. Possibly they are still there. But the question is why should they be posted there? Will their presence ensure the return of the refugees? The refugees say they will not go back unless there is complete peace in Bangladesh. How can we ask them to go when we see there is a war in progress there, people are being massacred, women are being tortured and one village after another is being set on fire? How can we ask them to return under these conditions? The first duty of the world community as well as our own is to try to establish peace there. We waited for many days, waited to see if other countries could help in the matter and stop the reign of terror.

I visited some countries in Europe and the United States. I was assured everywhere that they agreed with me on the need of a political solution to restore peace in Bangladesh and to ensure the return of the refugees. They said they were stressing this aspect of the problem. But nothing came out of it. We do not threaten, nor do we raise a hue and cry. But we know what is in our national interest and we are not going to give it up. The people of East Bengal are shedding their blood to achieve freedom. This has happened in the past in our country as well. A large number of farmers, intellectuals and members of the Bar sacrificed their lives for freedom. Now if some countries want that we should not defend our freedom and allow them to carry out their own evil designs, we cannot be the victims of their evil designs.

Every citizen of this country has to share this burden, be he young or old, man or woman. We have to share all hardships and meet the danger. Although the whole country has to bear the burden, you in Bengal have to bear a little more of it. We should be prepared for whatever happened.

I assure you that I do not want war. I earnestly desire peace. I know what is and how it affects the people, specially the weaker sections of the community. I detest war. It is my sincere wish that I should not be instrumental in bringing about war. Nehru talked much about peace and wanted peace but even he said that if we have to meet any attack on our freedom, we must do so with all our might.

Some foreign papers have described me as stubborn. I am stubborn in matters affecting our security and, in my opinion, the massacre going on in Bangladesh must stop and peace restored. The annihilation of the 75 million people of Bangladesh is not in our national interest. Therefore, we have to ensure that the terrible atrocities going on there must stop. This is not being stubborn. There is no alternative to this if we consider our own national interests. You are aware that we have taken some steps only after calm consideration. We have done nothing in haste. We are doing only what is proper and in our interest. Whenever some foreign power talked to us, it was only after careful deliberation that we refused to accept any suggestion made and we accepted what we could. We are faced with a crisis and there must be enthusiasm among the people. We have also to see how to utilise this enthusiasm to meet the challenge before us. An army must fight to be victorious. This will not be possible if our industries and schools are closed down and the working of our hospitals is affected. If we want to be truly victorious, the citizens of Calcutta must ensure that the work in towns and villages is carried on more efficiently and with greater vigour.

It is a testing time for our country but I am confident that we shall succeed. Whatever the nature of the fight, we shall deal with it firmly and with a cool head so that the promises we have made to the people are fulfilled and we continue our march towards progress. However great the danger, however great the pressure, we have to move forward even if we are alone. The people who live near our borders know that the Pakistanis have been firing, on Agartala and other places. Our hospitals are full of injured people. Our hearts go to them and I express gratitude to them on my behalf and on behalf of the nation. We are proud of their courage and we hope that their morale will continue to be high. Although they are now no longer in uniform, they are our soldiers. We are proud of their bravery and enthusiasm.

22
Indiraji a Martyr

A few days before her tragic death, four eminent intellectuals met Indira Gandhi to seek her opinion on some crucial problems and issues facing the country.

As Mulk Raj Anand says "In her spontaneous conversational manner, imbued with grace, Smt. Indira Gandhi spoke words which would became memorable for the new young, if only because they are the last words of a martyr."

It was decided to do film interviews by Smt. Fatima Zakaria of *Times of India*, who had done some brilliant reporting of talks with Indira Gandhi, Narinder Pal Singh, a dynamic Punjabi writer, Dr. Satish Chandra an educationist and R.K. Mishra, Editor of Patriot.

For these meetings, Indiraji gave 8 hours of her busy time and answered several questions on current national and international affairs. She spoke in a free and frank manner and answered questions, in a relaxed and easy conversational manner with utmost grace. Her answers on controversial matters revealed that she was no strong will egoist, asserting some doctrinaire formulas to solve some important issues she spoke as a devoted lover of the country and of the people, says Mulk Raj Anand.

The words used in her film-interviews are thus a legacy for the new young.

Talking in WHO Indiraji, said in the 34th WHO Assembly Geneva, 6th May, 1981 "Life is and perhaps will always be, a struggle although its nature is constantly changing. To meet it, we need vision, faith, courage and dogged perseverance. These are the qualities I admire in individuals and in organizations. These are the characteristics of the World Health Organisation that is why I have come all the way to express our appreciation of its work, and to assure 'it of my Governments' support. I give it my good wishes."

Speaking on the development of Foreign Policy, she said,

"In the early years, we had neither the resources nor the desire to become entangled in rivalries, conflicts and preparations for war of the big power blocks. Our problems were so big as to require our total attention. Only in conditions of peace, could we concentrate on development..... whatever the difficulties of self-reliance and we should not underestimate them. We cannot depend on other either, self-reliant development is not merely desirable, it is the only possible way.

....Even when the direction is clear, foreign policy needs careful steering because it is unaffected by waves and winds from within and without. She frames of policy and their executors and interpreters. The country's diplomatic service need the benefit of continous public debate."

India has to mourn for centuries the sudden demise of Indira as she strived for an India every living being in it could hold his head high.

The Soviet Newspaper *Pravda* and other daily reported in detail about the "Treacherous assassination of the worthy daughter of the Indian people. Pravda carried her portrait profile and ran three column splashes on what is termed as "Villainous assassination."

Sovietskaya Rossia, a respected Soviet Newspaper, carried a five column spread on "the glorious daughter of a great people."

In a 18-minute sequence on Soviet Television prime time, they showed her pictures.

The Guardian in an editorial entitled "The terrible challenge to India" said "The International sense of dissolation of the murder of Indira Gandhi is not merely a measure of the fact that the largest democracy has lost its elected leader to the gunmen's bullets."

She is dead. But she is alive to the ideals she cherished. We have to offer homage to her immortality.

23

End of an Era

On 30th October, 1984, Mrs. Gandhi returned from her 2-days trip to Orissa by an IAF Plane.

The British writer-actor-director Peter accompanied her. In his T.V. serial called "Peter Ustinov personalities" he included a TV documentary in Mrs. Gandhi for which, the last interview, was to be recorded the next morning.

Mrs. Gandhi was keen on giving maximum cooperation for his film. She cancelled all her morning engagements. She agreed to walk across the Road No.1 Akbar Road, just adjacent to PM's house, in which her office was situated.

Ustinov came half an hour earlier than the scheduled time and set up his cameras on the lawns where a chair and a table were placed for the use by the PM.

It was nearing the time of appointment, she emerged from her bed-room and met two of her friends waiting for her. "How is my make-up". She queried displaying her 'Gerva' saree and slightly roushed cheeks. "Is it alright for a TV camera" She asked again and both the ladies agreed. At that moment, she rang the bell and called her servant. He came and enquired for instructions.

She ordered for 3 cups of tea–two for her friends and one cup for make-up artist. Then she said "bye-bye" to her friends and emerged from the side-door to the open courtyard. Two security guards bowed to her to *namaskar* her and she nodded to acknowledge their greetings. Beant Singh was in her way. She suddenly noticed the revolver in his hands as he finished his *namaskar*.

"What are you doing with it" she wanted to shout. "Do you want to kill me" but the question remained unspoken on her lips. She heard the report of the revolver first. Then she received the hit on her breast and slumped on the lawn. Sixteen bullets entered her body. The senior of the two remarked "We have done what we had to do, now you do what you do want to do". Saying this they entered their room. The end came and she lay unconscious in a pool of blood. The news of Indira Gandhi's death spread like wild fire throughout the country.

One Dr. Tirumala Rao, a child specialist and president of a freedom fighters' association, arranged a special train to go to Delhi from Hyderabad to discuss with her about the problem and the programmes of the freedom fighters. There was a big send-off function at Secunderabad Railway station and early 500 people were prepared to go to Delhi. It was a real sight to see, with khadi-clad elders in 70s and 80s wearing Gandhi cap on their heads and with a twinkle in their eyes and a cheerful smile on their faces.

As my brother, who was a freedom fighter, also joined the group as one of the participant, I had the good fortune to attend such grand function.

When the train reached Warrangal by 9.30 AM news arrived that Indiraji was shot and All India Institute of Medical Science, New Delhi is undergoing treatment and so they were advised to return to Hyderabad.

It was a shocking news to all and by evening, TVs and radios carried her portrait all along with horrible news of her demise. It was also announced that Rajiv, her son took over as Prime Minister of India. Every one felt sorry for the passing way of a star like 'Amma'.

Common be your prayer.
Common be your purpose
Common be your deliberations
Common be your desires
Common be your end."

—A Sanskrit Prayer.

Indira Gandhi was declared dead on 31st October 1984 at about 4 O'clock by the doctors of All India Institute of Medical Science "The Iron lady of India". Indira Gandhi was a product of the freedom struggle.

After becoming a Prime Minister she met the high and low–from heads of State to simple peasants. All went back to satisfactorily. This rare quality was inherited from her father. As she grew older in age, she acquired poise and dignity. Her style of oratory also improved.

When Sonia Gandhi was carrying the body of Indira Gandhi to All India Institute of Medical Science, her husband Rajiv was making a speech in Calcutta. Later a police inspector informed him that Mrs. Gandhi had been injured. But details he did not know. When flying to Delhi, the pilot informed him that the news of the death of Indira Gandhi was confirmed.

That night, when he took over as the Prime Minister of India, he addressed the nation and combined his grief with that of the people. He mourned about the death of his mother more–because he did what the mother wanted him to do.

The son devoted himself to the nation and he also shed his life in the service of the nation, which is another tragic death.

The brave little women went about her job as if there is nobody to harm her or there is no threat to her life. She never entertained the idea that she may be in danger from anybody or from any corner of the world.

But, people who are interested in her welfare, warned her but she never felt that she was in danger.

She was travelling from place to place in the country. This involved considerable risk but she ignored.

After the Blue Star Operation, after the entry of the army in the Golden Temple of Amritsar, the intelligence reports of the chiefs warned her but she never paid heed to it. This shows with what measure of tenacity or fearlessness, she was carrying on her duties with firmness of mind. Perhaps, she never felt that her assassins would be her own security guards.

It came to light later on that she signed the file and approved the appointment of those guards saying that "Am I a Prime Minister of a secular State or not."

She never expected any harm to her, in view of her involvement with the programmes for the masses. She never disbelieved anybody no suspected anybody. She thought, perhaps, that all people born as Indians are her own people and she had love for them as brothers and sisters or her own kith and kin.

She was not a doctrinaire politician. She never believed in high sounding phrases.

She used to say that the basic tenet of our national movement lay in asserting the sovereignty of the people of India, both of British India and of the Indian States.

"As far as I am concerned, I have only one reply, that I am prepared for the people to judge. When the people say 'we do not want you, I will very gladly resign'.

On another occasion she said "It is not my concern that I shall stay in power or be the Prime Minister. Had that been my concern I should not have taken the number of risks which I have taken. But why I am taking these risks? It is because I know that one of these steps once taken will be reversible, no matter what happens and that is the important fact."

"I have said from the public platform on almost every occasion in every public meeting since our Bangalore session. It is not I who am showing a new light to the people. It is the.people who are showing a new light to us.... Everybody knows that there was a division in the thinking of the party. There was one section which wanted socialism, which wanted major changes and there was another section which thought that Independent India could grow and prosper within the old structure."

It appears that she was conscious of the serious repercussions, that arose, on account of her policies. But she dared to take the country in a particular direction and she had to finally pay a heavy price of her life itself for what all she had done.

When I went to Pawnar Ashram to have Darshan of Vinobaji a Sanskrit scholar and know from him about Manu Dharma Sastra, while writing a book on the status of Indian Women.

I was told that the previous day, Indira Gandhi left the Ashram after meeting Vinobaji. The inmates of the Ashram were telling me that she was worried about some problem and elaborate discussion with Vinobaji. Of course, I did not know what it was about.

After some months her death was announced and all felt sorry for losing a personality like her.

Indira Gandhi entirely life dedicated

Indira Gandhi epitomized the aspirations of the entire human race. She was dedicated to the ideals of the United Nations and principles of its chapter. She was one of the foremost champions of peace and total disarmament She stood for an international order in which power was tempered with compassion, knowledge and capability and at the service of humanity. She was against all forms of exploitation and considered military and all political blocs as impediments to world peace.

She was in the front rank of non-aligned movement. She was elected as chairman of the movement of the 7th summit which met in Delhi in March 1983.

In spite of her total involvement in the cause of our nation at home and peace and progress of the entire humanity she was taking interest in all that was beautiful in nature. Her magnificent life of radiance and charm was brutally and heinously cut short by a treacherous act of her own security men.

Preserving the unity and integrity of our nation was the great mission in her life. She fought boldly against communalism, and religious fundamentalism of all types. She warned the nation several times that communalism and obscurantism were the tools employed by the force of destabilization.

She laid down her life in defence of certain ideals on which the unity and integrity of the Indian Republic depended.

Her martyrdom for upholding the unity of India will never be forgotten and reverberate across the centuries.

Rarely in history, one single individual will be totally identified with the fortunes of a nation. She became the indomitable symbol of Indian's self-respect and self-confidence. Death devoured her at the peak of her career. In the death of Indira Gandhi, India lost a leader of dedication and consistent brilliance at a crucial moment of political and economic development. The nation owes a great debt of gratitude to her decisive, brilliant and compassionate personality.

Only a day before her death she said:

"Even if I die in the service of the nation; I shall be proud of it. Every drop of my blood, I am sure, will contribute to the growth of this nation, and make it strong and dynamic."

The nation grieves the untimely death of this great daughter of India and places on record its admiration and gratitude.

On one occasion she said:

"A large country like India must act with an inner conviction of its strength. I have tried to devote my life to build a tolerant India, a secular India and a peaceful India.

I wish to continue to work for it and devote all my energy for it and if necessary die for it. Let us not be bogged down in petty squabbles which diminish the nation. Let us deploy our strength to face the issues which affect the long term interests of our people."

On another occasion she said:

"Let us not shed blood, Let us shed hatred."

Once she said:

"To us Indians, the Himalayas are not just a great mountain range. They are an inseparable part of the very Indian consciousness, standing for eternal values."

Talking about friendship between nations. Indira Gandhi mentioned "To our minds, there are three causes of the present disturbing situation–the growth of armaments, the increasing disparity between the rich and the poor, both between and within nations, and the thoughtless wounding of our earth.

The world is one, yet we treat it as many giving different names to the segments. As they are politically used, the words East and West, North and South are not even geographically apt.

More than 3,000 years ago, when the world has greener, the sages of my country wrote an "Ode to the Earth." It is so pertinent today that should like to share some lines with you.

"Do not push me from the West or from the East
or From the North or the South
Be gracious to us, O earth! Let not those find us
Who waylay people on the road.
Take deadly weapons for away from us."

Brief Profile of Indira Gandhi

She was educated at various schools, and institutions like ECOLK NOUVEDLLE, BEX, Switzerland, Ecole Internationale, Geneva, pupils own school Poona and Bombay, Badminton School, Bristol, Viswa Bharti, Santinikentan and colleges like Somerville College, Oxford ; Honourary doctorate degrees conferred by various universities, Andhra, Agra, Bangalore, Punjab, Vikram, Gurukul, Nagpur, Jamia Millia, Poona, EL Salvador of Buenos Aires, Vaseda of Tokyo, Moscow State, Oxford, Charles of Prague, Mauritius, Baghdad and the USSR, Academy of Sciences, D.Litt (Honoris causa Andhra and Agra Universities)

Her literary, Artistic citation of distinction from accomplishments. Columbia University; Publications to her credit "The years of challenge" (1966-69); The years of endeavour (1969-71); India (London) Indo (Lausanne) 1979 and numerous other collections of speeches and writing.

Travels Abroad

Widely travelled all over the world and had paid official visits to the following countries. Afghanistan, Algeria, Argentina, Australia,

Austria, Bangladesh, Belgium, Bhutan, Bolivia, Brazil, Bulgaria, Burma, Canada, Chile, China, Czechoslovakia, Egypt, Federal Republic of Germany, France, German Democratic Republic, Guyana, Hungary, Indonesia, Iran, Iraq, Italy, Jamaica, Japan, Kenya, Malaysia, Mauritius, Mexico, Nepal, Netherlands, New Zealand, Algeria, Oman, Poland, Rumania, Singapore, Sri Lanka, Sweden, Switzerland, Syria, Tanzania, Thailand, Trinidad, and Tobagu, UAR, The United Kingdom, USA, USSR, *Uruguay*, Venezuela, Yugoslavia, Zambia, and United Nations Hd. Qrs.

Honours and Awards:

Mexican Academy Award for liberation of Bangladesh (1972)

2nd Annual Medal FAO 1973

Sahitya Vachaspati (Hindi) by Nagara Pracharini Sabha (1976)

Recipient of Mother's Award USA (1953)

Islbella Este Award of Italy for outstanding work in diplomacy; Yale University's Howland Memoral Prize for 2 years (1967-1968); was woman most admired by the French according to a special gallop poll survey in USA. Diploma of honour conferred by Argentina Society in 1971 for protection of animals.

Some More Relevant Information

She actively participated in the freedom struggle—worked in riot-affected areas of Delhi under Gandhiji's directions in 1947. She was Chancellor of (1) Viswa Bharati University, (2) Jawaharlal Nehru University, (3) North-Eastern University–was patron in chief Indian Council for Africa–was life patron; Indian Council for Child Welfare-was patron (1) Foreign Student's Association in India and (2) Indian–Society of International Law–was president (1) Board of Trustees of Kamala Nehru Hospital (2) Himalayan Mountaineering Institute, (3) Dakshin Bharat Hindu Prachar Sabha, (4) Nehru Memorial Museum and Library Society, (5) Jawaharlal Nehru Memorial Fund–was honorary President, Adisory Council of Education Centre, International Cooperative Alliance; was President International Council of Child Welfare; was chairman (1) Swaraj Bhavan Trust (2) Bal Bhavan Board and Children's National Museum, New Delhi (3) Citizen's Central Council and Sangeet-Natak Academy (4) New York World Fair Advisory Committee of the Ministry of International Trade, (4) Hindi Salahkar Semiti; was founder and President, Kamala Nehru Vidyalaya, Allahabad, was Founder and Chairman Bal Sahyog, New Delhi; was Vice-Chairman, Central Social Welfare Board; was Trustee (1) Gandhi

Smarka Nidhi, (2) Kasturba Gandhi Memorial Trust; was member (1) Delhi University Council, (2) Executor Board of UNESCO, (3) National Defence Council, (4) Executive Committee of National Defence Fund. (5) Nation Integraton Council, (6) Edwina Mountbatten Memorial Fund, (7) Governing Body of Tibetand Home Foundation and (8) All India Handicrafts Board. She was associated with (1) Federation of Film Societies of India, (2) India International Centre, (3) Childrens Book Trust-and (4) The Associated Journals LTD, Lucknow.

Political Positions: was chairman, National Integration of AGCC (2) was member organs of AICC (1) Working Committee, (2) Central Parliamentary Board, (3) Central Election Committee, (4) Central Disciplinary Action Committee (5) Seven Men Committee for General Elections, (6) Fund Collection Committee and, (7) Programme Sub-committee.

"Reading history is good" Nehru wrote to Indiraji once in one of his letters; "However, it is better to help make history "As far as she was concerned, the words proved prophetic. She could make history, not once but on several occasions.

She faced several adversities, which would have crushed any other person with less caliber. With great courage, deep commitment to peace and freedom, like her father, she guided the destiny of 700 million Indians for two decades almost single-handed.

Behind a delicate exterior and disarming smile, there was an unconquerable spirit and emerring instinct and rare political acumen, she used to study every aspect of a problem by consulting every one concerned but made up her mind finally. The great attribute which she in herited from her father, extraordinary sympathy with the feelings and aspirations of minority groups. She wanted and aspired for an India, in which every person living in it could hold up his head in peace and dignity.

History will be witness to the magnitude of Indira Gandhi's contribution of a vibrant India on march to modernity.

Mrs. Gandhi had given the nation, a momentum.

The green revolution initiated by Lal Bahadur Shastri was carried forward very vigorously and India was self-sufficient in food by her encouragement. She inspired and gave a new orientation not only in economic policies but also in arts. She created a new sense of new frontiers in several fronts. The army which had been humiliated in 1962 and just held in its own 1965, was converted into a support force, which won one of the most brilliant victories in 1971, in modern warfare.

Above all these achievements, her major achievement was upholding the ideals of democracy. In 1977, when she lost election, she handed over power very peacefully. Country's faith in democracy was established by this experience. Democracy again triumphed when she returned to power in 1980, with a sweeping victory. India thus proved among the masses of the third world Nations that it could hold its head high, as a symbol of freedom, integrity and civilization.

It is an interesting fact, she took a firm decision to divide Punjab and create Haryana in order to please Akaliles, after she became the Prime Minister of India.

There is no greater sacrifice that a human being can make than to give one's one life for the sake of the country. Indira Gandhi, a brave daughter of a proud tradition sacrified her life for the country she loved.

After all, she should have moments of despair also. But her achievements outweighed her failures. In 1966, when the Congress Party elected her as Prime Minster, they thought that she would be a 'Gudia' in their hands. But, she asserted herself as a big political force in her own right. She thought of several measures to ameliorate the conditions of the poor amidst opposition. For instance, bank nationalization was a big task, which she could achieve in spite of odds and bad propaganda. War of Pakistan, or the threat of the USA fleet in the Bay of Bengal during the Bangladesh Imbroglio, panic was a word that found no place in her lexicon.

Unable to counter her political decisions or pronouncements, her opponents descended to the level of casting aspersions on her principles. When she warned them about the threat to the nation's security, the propagated that it was an election propaganda. But, she could prove all of them wrong in the ultimate analysis.

Those who lived or worked with her in hard times of her period as Prime Minister, will not fail to notice her tenacity, her grit, stamina or her charismatic magnetism to handle political situations. Of course, she was not an intellectual politician like her father but she was more a practical-minded, more bold in taking important decisions and she proved her mettle on several occasions.

She was her own in critical times. Her personality had tremendous impact on her political decisions and her political skilll, beyond doubt, proved her capacity to fight. She evolved herself as a single force at times.

She did not like the people who criticized her. But her true political self was described in a poem, which her father wrote to her in a letter from prison in 1943–"Those lovely lines by Yeats on an Irish airman"—

Nor law, nor duty bade me fight,
Nor public men, nor cheering crowds,
A lonely impulse of delight
Drove to this tumult in the clouds;
I balanced all, brought all to mind,
The years to come seem wasted breath,
A waste of breath the years behinds
In balance with his life, this death.

If we try to assess her strengths and weaknesses of her political career, it appears to me that her growth to International eminance from a low-key profile in the beginning of her political career, speaks volumes of her capability, her flexible and pragmatic policies and her ability to arouse strong feelings on her democratic ideals. Her style of functioning in mid-seventies and eighties took her to a towering stature.

Out of all her qualities, what appealed to my mind, rather impressed me, was her affirnity with the masses. When she spoke of "Garibi", people use to criticize, whether she has tasted anytime 'Garibi' one need not actually experience poverty to have sympathy with the people suffering from poverty. It needs a good heart, a mother's heart to understand the difficulty of poverty or lack of basic needs of life. Her sentiments to fashion her political platforms or slogans made an appeal to the suffering millions and she could win their hearts. Her rapport with the masse-suffering in remote tribal areas was exemplary. Her emotional attachment, in a way with the grieving millions could win her laurels and even her opponents were stunned to see her love for them. Common people, one even working as a Bhangi, could feel that she was their saviour, and custodian of their interest. This was her biggest achievement in life, I suppose and her major characteristic. Any tribute to her will be less if this factor is forgotten. She was not an ordinary person or an ordinary Prime Minister. The qualities found in her, are not found in any other political leader of her times. To preside over the destiny of a country like India, as vast and diverse as India, demand higher degree of management skill and human approach, which is not an easy task for any person in a position of highest responsibility as Prime Minister.

There might have been many irritants in her functioning she was also made a target for many of the problems. But her great vision created many opportunities for realization of many issues in a proper perspective by one and all in the country.

She was dedicated to the unity of the country, to the progress of the Republic and in particular to the welfare of the people. She was regarded as the hope of the nation. This was the highest tribute paid to her by her countrymen.

In her footsteps, Sri Rajiv Gandhi, tried to keep up peace and unity in the country, after he took over the reins of Government. With respect to modernity, he laid down more stress on the development of Information Technology. Rajiv used to listen to the difficulties of people, with great patience. He used to mix up with people wherever he went.

We know the bulk of the landless are from the Scheduled Castes and Scheduled Tribes and it goes without saying that any Government should expedite measures for land reforms. Of course, this problem, is not only the concern of the Schedules Castes or Scheduled Tribes but of all the communities. The ideal of equality and social justice can only be achieved only when increasing attention and effort is put up by the Government and all the concerned sections.

Housing also in extremely important. To predicate poverty and backwardness in the country was his main purpose in life, and he worked for 20 hours a day. He derived satisfaction in working for his goal. After he won and got elected as Prime Minister in 1984 with great majority he made himself busy with several programmes and identified himself with masses.

Syam Goenka in his "Eternal Rajiv epitome of humanity" mentations about the few lines that Rajiv write as a father to Rahul. "You should not forget that the work that we take up should be in the proper direction. You must conclude it. Your should not leave it halfway. What you feel to be the first, you must do first . Even if you have to do it with great strain, don't leave it until you achieve perfection, don't leave it."

"Congress ka Haath—Garibon ke Saath"

This slogan was the plank on which the Congress Party fought elections in 2004. After Rajiv's assassination in 1984, P.V. Narasimha

Rao, became the Prime Minster and after 5 years opposition could win power and rule the country.

BJP under the leadership of Bajpai formed the National Development Alliance and with a common minimum programme ran the Government with a definite motto. There were religious upheavals here and there and their identity as a religious organization was taken note of by people.

Sonia Gandhi entered the political arena, with a purpose of reviving the Congress and to bring back a secular Government. As opposition leader, the experience she gained was useful for her, in evolving a personality of her own. She conducted road shows and people gathered in large numbers to have a glimpse of her.

She toured from place to place and moulded the sentiments of people for a better tomorrow. She mustered the support of the minorities, Schedules Castes and Schedules Tribes and especially women. People felt that the Government of "Indiramma" would come and their lives would be different. They voted for the Congress to the utter dismay and disappointment of the rulers. NDA people were confident of their wining because of their deeds and people would prefer them as better saviours.

Of course, their strategy played in some states like Madhya Pradesh and Rajasthan and they had to close in some other states. They conducted political gatherings, group discussions and made promises and propagated "feel good" programme that everything is good in the country.

People attended such gatherings in large numbers. Political surveys conducted by several organizations told much for and against the BJP and NDA Political Pandits made their own assessments.

But people were wise and voted for the Congress disproving all calculations. It was not easy for the rulers to swallow this defeat. Their one-points programme that Sonia was a foreigner, could not be appealing to the masses. Their aim and purpose was to vote for the forces that can deliver the goods and better their lot. Water and electricity–The ordinary day to day affairs gained much popularity and those, who indulged in mere theories, or slogan mongering people did not believe. They thought of practicalities and gave the Congress, the nationalist party, which fought for the freedom of the country its due respect and recognition. The strong foundations laid down by Pandit Nehru and Indira could attract the people.

A different political situation prevailed in the country and the masses became more mature in deciding men and matters. They were well aware of the crucial problems of the country and the people as well.

Sonia was dubbed a foreigner to become a Prime Minister of India. But people gave her priority and voted for Congress. It was made very clear by people that Sonia was preferred. There are instances in Indian history that from several centuries, Kushans, Macedonians and Mughuls mixed up with Indian people and the founder of Congress A.O. Hume was a Britisher and C.F. Andrews was also a Britisher; Anne Besant, who took part in Home Rule Movement was an Irish Lady and Meera Behn was the daughter of British army officer Indian people respected them. Political leaders are often talking of her foreign origin on account of political reasons. But when the time came for the Congress party to choose their leader, Sonia declined to be the Prime Minister with a generous mind and made Manmohan Singh as the leader. This shows her sacrificing spirit and her dedication to the cherished ideals of Congress party and also of Nehru family.

For the first time, she got elected as an MP from UP and spoke on 29th October 1999, for the first time. Within 5 years she could unite all Congress leaders under her leadership and bring back Congress to power and form the government at the Centre. With great strategy, she could win over Sarad Pawar, Lallu, Karunanidhi and also the leftists.

Above all, she could win over the hearts of people. Poll surveys, analysis of all political Pandits, proved false before the wisdom of people and they gave verdict in Andhra Pradesh, Sikkim, Karnataka, Orissa, in favour of Congress and its policies. "Feel good" propaganda of NDA was rejected. It was clear that Sonia will lead the nation under the influence of the great ideals of the Congress for a better life of the people.

24
Conclusion

Any party has to survive on the support and sympathy of people. When it loses its hold on the people, future of that party seems to be bleak. The Congress organisation, which won freedom for the country and which made many sacrifices during the days of freedom struggle, could not be honoured by the electorate when they felt that a "few individuals" tried to dominate the scene.

But Mrs. Gandhi was graceful in accepting the entire responsibility on her as a leader and also as the Prime Minister. She honoured democratic functioning and bowed to the electorate as a true democrat. Apparently, the electorate welcomed the Janata Party in preference to Congress. The percentage of votes that Congress got in some states were a little higher than what it secured in 1977 Lok Sabha elections but it was clear that the election results still reflected the anger of the people towards Congress.

The election results also proved that the Janata wave of March 1977 Lok Sabha elections did not subside, except in West Bengal.

Janata Party won 2/3rds majority in Haryana, Himachal Pradesh, Rajasthan, Orissa and Delhi. In Punjab, Akali Janata won absolute majority but in Tamil Nadu, DMK won majority of seats. In West Bengal, the CPI (M) and its others secured 2/3rds majority. That means that Janata's gamble in bringing elections on the states, swept it to power in March 1977. The game paid out handsomely. Barring Tamil Nadu, Pondicherry and Goa, the Janata Party came to power.

Mrs. Gandhi in her words said "when we are trying to build up India, there are problems of transition also. A feudal society is getting modernised. In fact all the societies in the world are changing. They may have their own problems. Likewise, we have our own problems inherent in a developmental process.

There was a time when men were considered to be bread winners for the family. In the lower economic sections, women earn and feed the family. While men gamble away their income.

Families still feel that the first duty of a wŏman is to keep the house and be a wife and a mother.

Entering politics is frowned upon sometimes. Such an attitude is changed to some extent. People are realising the importance of education among girls and the importance of raising income. There are many facilities provided by government for education and empowerment of women.

General male idea is that women are in different to fighting for common bettlerment. Indian women are used to live in isolation and so the same lithergy is continuing. Millions and millions of middle class women are still aloof from the mainstream of life.

What is ailing our society is our inability to arouse the necessary awareness among people and to utilise the talent and time and energy of our women. The biggest resource to us is our women and it must be used for the cause of society and the nation. Indira's life is a great lesson for all women of the country. She was considered to be the only "man" inthe cabinet with determination.

She ruled with a mothers heart. She was not mother to Rajiv only. She was mother to all.

She grew up from a shy little girl to an extraordinary person. This was on account of her self-confidence and charisma.

How far we move, where, we move, that responsibility is still with us. They do think that we have been able to push back the forces of inertia and of status quo.

Indira Gandhi, however, felt that the Congress, to some extent, stayed away from the common people. This could largely be attributed to the fact that the party's Bhuvaneswar resolution of 1964, which directly advocated the cause of socialism was not given serious consideration. The people's enthusiasm for the Congress and the government had therefore diminished. To restore people's faith, "we have to take big steps" and bank nationalisation was one of them.

She further said that Congress party should never be conceived as a party of the privileged but as a party of the masses.

Thanks, although, primarily and social measure, has become a dynamic symbol of the paramountcy of the people. This is why, it has released the latent enthusiasm of the people to such an extent. More than any other decision, that we have taken in dependent India, it proclaims that the few cannot constitute themselves into the managing agents or arbiters of destinies and fortunes of the many.

Apart from nationalising the banks, the Central Government also decided to set up a judicial commission to inquire into alleged irregularities by the Birla group of industries. In fact, the above two had been the major demands of the radicals inside the Congress. Morarji always frowned upon these demands and over these demands, Desai and the radicals open by and publicly clashed.

Pandit Nehru's untiring efforts in reshaping India are unparalleled. But the comments on his life and work by political thinkers, scholars, commentators, theoreticians, diplomats, world dignitaries are many and varied. He lived upto the high ideals of democracy, though he as branded as "popular dictator" and less of a democrat.

To him, Gandhian doctrines appeared to be declistic and far from realities prevailing in India. But Pandit Nehru and also Indira Gandhi understood the spirit of India and talked in consonance with the "Conscience of India". They believed in the dignity of the individual and had faith in democracy as a way of life and as a basis of social structure. Nehru gave a broader definition to democracy when he remarked "democracy is not only political, not only economic, but something of the mind it involves equality of opportunity to all".

Indira Gandhi's political ideas are also based on Nehru's philosophy. Defining her concept of democracy and socialism, Smt. Indira said "by socialism, we do not mean any textbook definition of socialism or any pre-conceived theory, but that we should evolve a direction suited to the needs of Indian People".

She also said that country most inexperienced in self-government and a people untrained in the processes of the functioning of democracy really need certain special defenses against dangers of disruption and disintegration.

Her Attempt to Bring About a Social Change

We have chosen a democratic system, which gives room for ventilating grievances and inequalities. It also affords opportunity for the exploitation of these grievances, if they are not dealt with properly and in time.

Several men of great vision have joined our National Liberation Movement and we achieved our Independence. Likewise social change should be brought about, with the same dedication and highest levels of quality, integrity and a spirit of public service.

Awadi Congress resolved to build up a 'socialistic pattern of society', where everyone has a voice of speech and has a right to receive recognition. No exploitation by one section over the other. This sounds ideologically alright. But, for a nation, which has to face many challenges, both socially and economically, development cannot be a slow process. The downtrodden and the underprivileged should gain attention and should have their share from the resources of the Nation. Very True ! But how ? on what lines ?

But the manner in which the schemes for their betterment, are implemented so speedy as to gain their confidence.

The scheduled castes and the scheduled tribes are gaining attention of Government and several schools are launched for their betterment. Progress is also spectacular in some areas.

There are certain curious situations. Those who could achieve some education and prestige are not able to show pity for their own people. Not only that, social and economic progress should be mingled with moral values. Sometimes, they are lacking. This may give rise to friction in some areas.

There is a big controversy over the phenomenon, as to why the upper castes intellectuals are leaving the country ? This is a colossal loss to the country. Their intellect and talent is lost to the nation and foreign countries are gaining the benefit. How can this be avoided ?

The larger interests of the nation, should not suffer on account of the interests of some sections on account of reservations of seats in colleges, and in jobs, some sections are not able to get employment in open competition and so they are flocking to other countries. As a result, the quality of performance is suffering. Only set-standard people are in the jobs. This is not a healthy trend!

What will happen to India after a decade ?

Unemployment is a matter for concern. There is strong awareness and growing impatience with inequalities. There is rampant rising of "expectations" among the poor.

The farmers need more amenities. Housewives complain of sky rocketing prices. The unemployed demand jobs and the workers in factories demand more wages. All these cannot be solved with a stroke of pen. There is a peculiar situation in the country, over which, none can be complacent. Discontent will lead to unrest and where there is unrest, there cannot be any stability or unity.

Our major interest should be to protect the hard-won freedom and to keep up the unity of the nation..We are witnessing how some governments are dislodged in neighbouring and distant countries and how their stability is being paralysed. Gandhiji used to say "To allow fresh wind to enter my mind, I keep the doors and windows of my mind open. But, the wind should not be such as to uproot me". So, we can learn from outside, but we should not forget our own issues.

"Long years ago, we made a tryst with destiny, and now the time comes when we shall redeem our pledge ...At the stroke of the midnight hour, while the world sleeps, India will awake to life and freedom. A moment comes, which comes but rarely in history, when we step out from the old to the new, when an age ends and when the soul of a nation, long supprissed, finds utterance".

Jawaharlal Nehru
to the Indian Constituent Assembly,
New Delhi, August 14, 1947.

A calm and determined nation its unarmed men and women possessing the strength of suffering are the only asset they want to live with honour and human dignity, in spite of their problems and sorrows. War against poverty, war against dogmatism and war against evil, is the only line of action, that could save the country from destruction.

"Blood, toil, tears and sweat"are the only weapons that Indians are endowed with.

We are and there is no short-cut to achieve progress. The vicious circle of poverty makes sustained economic growth impossible. Diverse and difficult problems call for a highly competent, mature, statesmanlike, patriotic, public-spirited and purposeful steward. It is none else than Indira Gandhi! She is indeed the woman of destiny! She was presiding over the fate of the nation ! The nation needs direction in these critical times.

India was proud to have a leader of her charisma, wisdom and statesmanship. She was the only hope of the millions and remains the only symbol of change with stability, peaceful social revolution in the midst of violence, around the world.

She was...in deed the "woman of destiny".

Appendix

Election Manifesto

[Adopted at the Bangalore Meeting of the All-India Congress Committee, July 1951]

The achievement of independence and the establishment of the Indian Republic concluded one phase of the Indian people's struggle for emancipation. The success of this phase of our struggle for freedom was unique in many respects. Under the leadership of Gandhiji the National Congress carried on this struggle and endeavoured to follow, to the best of its ability, the policy and methods which Gandhiji had laid down. In cooperation with vast numbers of the men and women of our country, it was the high privilege of the Congress to serve the cause of the country and of the masses of our people and lead them to success. The Father of the Nation told us to value the moral ethical basis of national life and made this the condition of political action. He emphasised that means were as important as ends and the means we adopt ultimately shape the ends which follow. In accordance with India's immemorial teaching and heritage, the performance of duty was given first place, and rights and privileges naturally flowed from them. The Congress and the people could perfectly follow this teaching, but the inspiration they drew from it, benefited them and led them towards their goal. It is necessary for all of us to keep this in mind when conflict darkens the world and dissensions and a lowering of standards threaten our public life. It is only by adhering to these first principles that real success can be achieved and India can prosper and rise to her destined heights.

2. Even during our struggle for independence, its content was not merely political freedom, but also the freedom of the masses from exploitation and want. The provision of basic material needs of food, clothing and shelter was the first essential, to

be followed by the provision for cultural growth. On the attainment of independence, exceedingly difficult problems confronted the nation and even thretened the newly won freedom. During the last four years, these great problems of ensuring the freedom an integrity of the country, of integrating the various parts into the Union of India, of attempting to rehabilitate millions of displaced persons, and of laying the foundations for future growth have absorbed the mind and energy of the country. The last great war put an end in many ways to the old world that we knew and posed entirely new problems; the partition of India left a bitter legacy behind. Our civil and Military Services had to be organised afresh and the very large foreign element in them replaced by Indians. India's relations with her neighbour country, Pakistan, have in spite of our best efforts continued to be abnormal and have raised and are still raising difficult problems.

3. Because of the multitude of the complexity of the problems the country has had to face since the achievements of independence, our economic progress has not been satisfactory. Millions in the country still lack sufficiency of food, clothing and shelter. The objectives of the Congress, which have been embodied in the Constitution of India, still remain, in a large measure, unrealised. The time has come for our struggle for emancipation to enter into its second phase of realising those objectives, without which political freedom can have little meaning for most of us. Economic progress must therefore be given first priority, subject only to the maintenance of the freedom and integrity of the country.

4. The key to the character of the future economic and social organisation of the country and its motive power is provided in the Congress Constitution, which has as its objective the establishment in India, by peaceful and legitimate means, of a Cooperative Commonwealth based on equality of opportunity and of political, economic and social rights, and aiming at world peace and fellowship. Thus, the objective as well as the method is one of cooperation and the avoidance, as far as possible, of competition and conflict. This conception of social organisation inevitably leads to the secular State in which every individual has equal rights and opportunities, and the removal of barriers

which may divide the people into opposing groups on the basis of religion, caste, class or region. The application of this principle in the national sphere would lead to social progress and peace and would strengthen the nation. Its extension to the international sphere leads to an independent foreign policy basing itself on the promotion of world peace.

5. The progress of a country with limited resources, such as India is at present, depends on the most effective utilisation of such resources for the public good. This involves a planned approach to the various aspects of national life and activity. The Congress welcomes therefore the functioning of the Planning Commission and considers that the method of planned development is essential for progress and must be continued. But such planning, in order to be effective, must have full support and cooperation from the public. Planning must include all aspects of our national life so that progress may be uniform and might not be held up by some backward sector. In India to-day, stress must inevitably be laid on the progress of the rural areas and the people who live there. Not only do they contain the vast majority of our population and are the basis of our economy, but they have suffered neglect in the past and this must be made good so that they might have full opportunities for economic and cultural advance and to live the good life which is our aim. The first and vital step has been or is being taken to free the land from the burden of old and out-of-date agrarian systems of tenure. The abolition of Zamindari, Jagirdari and the like must be rapidly completed. Security of tenure and fair rents should be assured to tenants and tillers of the soil.

6. Increased agricultural production is absolutely essential for putting our national economy on a firm basis. Small and uneconomic holdings stand in the way of rapid advance in agricultural production. The line of advance should therefore be cooperative farming with the objective of making the whole era, substantial part of a village, a unit of cooperative management.

7. The conditions of agricultural labour should be improved, especially in the lower wage pockets. Opportunities for work and employment in small scale and cottage industries should be afforded to them. They should be given preference in

allotment of land in newly reclaimed areas, which should be worked on cooperative lines. Facilities should be given to them in regard to housing sites.

8. The preservation of milch and draught cattle and upgrading of cattle breeds are important for increasing the supply of milk and improvement of agriculture. Increasing attention will have to be paid to this.

9. The burden on the land of too many people subsisting on it has to be reduced by the diversion of part of this population to other vocations. Some of these can be absorbed in large industries but, in the main, scope for absorption will come through small scale and cottage industries. These cottage industries are particularly important in India and must be developed and protected with the aid of the state and co-ordinate with other forms of industry. But it must always be borne in mind that the best techniques should be employed for small scale and cottage industries in order to make them effective and economic. For this purpose the state should encourage research. Cottage industries should be organised in industrial cooperatives, wherever possible. The main field of employrnent for the educated youth has to be found in well-organised and properly conducted industries. The handloom industry is our major cottage industry and deserve every help from government. It has suffered from lack of yarn and because of this many handloom weavers have been unemployed or only partly employed. Government should make special arrangements for the supply of adequate quantities of yarn to them.

10. It is not possible to pursue a policy of laissez-faire in industry. This has been rejected in most countries and is peculiarly unsuited to present-day conditions in India. It is incompatible with any planning. It has long been the Congress policy that basic industries should be owned or controlled by the State. This policy holds and must be progressively given effect to. State trading should be undertaken wherever the balance of advantage lies in favour of such a course. A large field for private enterprise is, however, left over. In this field the aim should be to develop cooperative enterprise on an increasing scale. Thus, our economy will have a public sector must accept the objectives of the National Plan and fit into it. The progressive

extention of the public sector in the field of what is now the private sector must depend on various factors, including the results achieved, the resources available and the capacity of the country at the moment. The test should always be what serves the social ends in view. No vested interest or inherited privilege should be allowed to come in the way of the country's economic progress, nor should we allow ourselves to be distracted by slogans and doctrine which sound attractive, but which might lead to a worsening of the condition of our people.

11. The general objective of economic progress has to be translated into concrete programmes in close relation to the needs of the people and the available means and resources. The first consideration must always be to avoid a breakdown on any point in respect of whatever is essential for the life of the community. This necessitates a system of controlled distribution in regard to commodities which are in short supply. It is also of the highest importance to keep prices from rising and to endeavour to reduce them. Many of our difficulties to-day are due to a high and rising price level and economic development has been seriously hampered because of this. If prices rise, this will not only come in the way of all progress, but will even prove detrimental to the real interests of those very sections of our people for whose supposed benefit an increase in prices is sometimes advocated. Therefore, it is of essential importance to follow firmly a price policy aiming at first, a prevention of a further rise and secondly, to reduce present prices. Steps must be taken to maintain a fair and proper structure of relative prices as between agricultural commodities *inter se*, and between them and manufactured articles.

12. If prices have to be held and reduced, some measure of controlled distribution system becomes essential. In the matter of food, the fate of millions of people is bound up with the presence of a nation-wide system of controls. But for these controls, the threat of famine might have materialised in different parts of the country. We must endeavour to create conditions of relative abundance of articles which are necessary for the masses. As this happens, these controls can be progressively dispensed with. But till we have an adequate supply, we must co-operate to make the controls function more effectively.

Hesitancy and opposition to controls themselves produce weakness in their working. It is true that controls have led to corruption. The way to deal with this is to make the controls effective and to improve their administration.

13. Considerable progress has been made in the development of scientific research and the application of science to industry. This must be continued and adequate provision made for technical education. Top priority has been given and must continue to be given to river valley schemes which are basic for the development of agriculture and power supply. In regard to heavy industry, priority should be given to those industries which are considered of basic importance, such as steel, heavy chemicals, fertilisers and machine tools.

13. Any alround development of the country on a significant sale nust strain its resources to the utmost, necessitating the need for much larger savings on, the part of the community. In order to build a better future we must be prepared to suffer hardships in the present. The necessary sacrifice in consumption has to be spread as widely as possible, but those with higher incomes have special obligations to fulfil in this respect. Corporate savings should play an increasing role in capital formation. Steps have already been made in several States to utilise the voluntary effort of the people for constructive purposes and these have to be met with considerable success. A planned effort should be made to canalise, in an organised way, the unused time, skill and other resources of the people on a voluntary basis for the economic and social betterment of the community.

15. The achievement of economic equality and social justice must proceed side by side with economic progress. Thus, alone can social peace and democracy be preserved. The post-war shift in relative prices has, to some extent, rectified the disparity between the rural and the urban sectors. The measures for economic development being undertaken by the State, particularly the large irrigation and power projects and the programmes for agricultural improvement, will lead to further levelling up of the standard of living of the masses, especially in the rural incomes, the gap has been narrowed in terms of the standard of living. Much more remains to be done.

Redirection of public expenditure in the interests of social welfare and the imposition of estate duties on succession should be fully availed of as a means for the removal of inequalities. The tax structure should be examined and other methods explored for bringing about a reasonable relationship betweeen the minimum and the maximum incomes, both in the private and the public sectors, in keeping with the economic conditions of the country. Inequalities have been accentuated during recent years largely in consequence of illegitimate gains from black-marketing, tax evasion, a certain forms of speculation and other anti-social activities. To give immediate relief to the people and to promote social justice, these evils should be curbed with a strong hand. There has been uneven economic development in various regions in the country. In our further programmes for development of irrigation, power, agriculture and industry, the claims of these regions should be given special consideration.

16. The concern of the state for safeguarding the rights and interests of labour has expressed itself in several advanced measures of legislation. There is, however, much room for improving the implementation of these laws. Housing for workers is of great importance and should be encouraged by the State to the best of its ability and resources, in cooperation with the employers and the workers. A rise in the standard of living of the workers is not only desirable in itself, but leads to greater productivity. The per capita productivity in India, when compared to some other countries, is low. This may be due to a variety of causes which must be investigated. It must be borne in mind, however, that without higher productivity the interests of the nation as well as of the workers must suffer. The machinery and procedure relating to arbitration and adjudication of disputes should be so improved as to secure fair settlements, based on the principle of social justice and with the least expenditure of time and money. Legal technicalities, formalities and appeals should be reduced to the minimum.

17. Considerable improvement has been made in our railway services. The Chittaranjan Locomotives Works have been established as a state enterprise for the production of locomotives; the Hindustan Aircraft Ltd. are also producing

railway carriages. The objective is to move towards self-sufficiency; progress is being made in this direction, though it will necessarily take time. A continuous attempt has to made to bring about further improvements in administration and for the convenience of passengers, more especially those travelling in the lower classes.

18. In some States, transport services have been nationalised resulting in greater efficiency and convenience to the public. This policy should be continued.

19. The public services and methods of recruitment have to be conditioned and adapted for the purposes of the National Plan. Special training should be given, where necessary, for the purposes of the nationalised or public sector of our economy. It is essential that high moral standards should be maintained in our public work and while good work should receive commendation, bad work should be condemned. An effective machinery for this should be devised.

20. There has been frequent reference to corruption and there is little doubt that various forms of corruption exist as social evils to-day. Every effort must be made to put an end to this evil and some form of summary method must be devised to deal with such cases. At present the real difficulty in dealing with these matters is due to the dilatoriness of procedure in departmental inquiries and judicial proceedings in the law courts, and the standard of formal proof required, which often leads to the guilty escaping punishment.

21. The importance of education and public health is well recognised and yet no marked advance can be made in them so long as our resources are limited. At the same time, it is necessary to direct education in the right channels and remove many of the evils from which it suffers today. Education should be looked upon as something which trains the intellect and builds the character of the student, and not merely as a means for employment. What the next generation will be depends upon the education given now and the importance of this cannot, therefore, be exaggerated. Our system of education should not be divorced from the productive and other needs of the community, but should be related to them and be conducive to their fulfilment. The principles of basic education, i.e., learning

through a crat, should be utilised to the largest possible extent. Even in higher education, some form of manual work should form an essential part of the curriculum, without which degrees or diplomas should not be given. An essential part of education should be an appreciation of and devotion to Truth and Beauty in their various forms. Art and literature, music and drama, singing and dancing should be encouraged.

22. In regard to public health, considerable progress has been made in the control of epidemic diseases and provision of improved water supply and general sanitation. The control of malaria has been effective in certain areas and has resulted in freeing these areas for intensive cultivation. Both from the point of view of public health and of production, malaria control is important and should be encouraged. A significant indication of the improvement in public health is the considerable fall in the death rate and a higher expectation of life.

23. The Constitution has laid a special duty on government to bring about the economic and cultural advancement of Scheduled Castes and Scheduled Tribes and other backward classes. Both the Central and State Governments have given particular attention to this important matter. The Congress, under Gandhiji's lead, has always made this social uplift of these backward classes as one of its principal planks and has laboured to this end with considerable success. This work must continue until these classes enjoy the same economic and educational opportunities and advantages as others. In particular, the tribal people have to be helped to develop according to their own genius.

24. Owing to certain historical and administrative necessities of the moment, certain States in India were classified as Part B and Part C States. This classification was transitional and cannot be considered to be permanent. It has to be remembered that certain parts of India have developed differently during past years. Certain border areas, as well as certain areas inhabited by tribal people, require special treatment. The general policy in regard to Parts B and C States should be to speed up the removal of differential treatment as rapidly as possible. The chief difficulty in regard to these States has been the lack of a legislature in most of them. As soon as properly constituted

legislatures come into existence, the differences between them and Part A States will largely disappear. Where such legislatures come into existence, the differences between them and Part A States will largely disappear. Where such legislatures and Ministers exist, there is no longer any reason for any differentiation to continue, except to the extent that there are certain covenants which have to be honoured. In regard to some of the small Part C States, the question of merger into a large unit should be considered.

25. One of the major problems before us during the last four years, which has demanded and must continue to demand priority and full attention is that of the rehabilitation of the displaced persons from Pakistan. According to the figures of the last census, forty-nine lakhs came from Western Pakistan and about 26 lakhs from Eastern Pakistan. Of those coming from Western Pakistan, about 29 lakhs came from rural areas. Land-owners and cultivators from the West Punjab and displaced agriculturists from the rest of West Pakistan who were desirous to do cultivation here, have been settled on land except those who preferred urban occupation. The latter are estimated to number about 7 lakhs. Of the 27 lakhs urban people from West Pakistan, it is estimated that nearly 13 lakhs have been rehabilitated either by finding gainful employment in government or other services or by being given vocational or technical training. In addition, 9,63,000 persons (including dependents) have been provided with means of livelihood through grant of loans and maintenance allowances, allotment of shops and industrial concerns and admission to homes and training centres. Of the remaining nearly 4.5 lakh of urban displaced persons, the majority did not require or ask for governmental assistance.

The problem of displaced persons from Eastern Pakistan became serious early in 1950 and rehabilitation schemes were drawn up. The position was rather fluid as large numbers of migrants returned to their homes. Of the 26 lakhs that remained, nearly two-thirds have been rehabilitated or have received governmental assistance in rehabilitation. During the last few weeks a new problem has arisen in West Bengal, where a continuous stream of migrants from East Pakistan is flowing in. Every effort is being made to deal with this abnormal and disturbina situation.

By the end of the current financial year, the Central Government will have spent about Rs. 143 crores on relief and rehabilitation of displaced persons from Western and Eastern Pakistan. In addition, about 56 lakh acres of evacuee and other land have been given to them, and about 3,32,000 urban houses, shops and industrial premises have been provided. Of these 96,000 are new houses constructed by government. Further 52,000 developed plots have been alloted to D.P's of constructing houses. The question of properties left by displaced persons in Pakistan has remained unsettled in spite of repeated efforts of government. This is a vital matter affecting millions of people, which should be settled as early as possible.

In East Punjab, Delhi, West Bengal, Uttar Pradesh, Bombay and in some other parts of the country, many new townships and colonies for displaced persons have been built up. Some of these are models of their kind and are conducted on cooperative lines, and are engaged in productive activities which are very satisfactory. It may be said that the results obtained in our rehabilitation work for displaced persons are remarkable. During the last 20 years or so, the problem of displaced persons has been faced in various parts of Europe and Asia. The results we have obtained in our work compare very favourably with the results elsewhere. The fact remains, however, that a large number of displaced persons have to be provided for and more especially in West Bengal, where the problem at present is a growing one. High priority must necessarily continue to be given to this rehabilitation work for displaced persons both from Western and Eastern Pakistan.

26. As India is a secular State, every citizen has the same duties, rights, privileges and obligations as any other. He has full freedom to profess and practise his religion. It is the particular duty of the State to protect these rights of all minority communities in the country and to give them full opportunities for development, so that they might play their part in the economy and public life of the country. The Congress will make every effort to ensure proper representation for them in the legislatures and other public bodies.

27. The women of India in the past, and especially in the struggle for the country's freedom, have played a notable part and distinguished themselves in many ways. They suffer, however,

from a number of social and other disabilities. It is important that these disabilities should be removed so that they may take their full part in the economy and social progress of the country and make their special contribution to the life of the family and the community. In particular, they have to be intimately connected with all activities of social welfare and social education. Women are more responsible even than men for the next generation, and unless they are enabled to participate fully in all national activities, the progress of the nation suffers. The Congress is therefore of opinion that every effort should be made to open out opportunities of service for them in the legislatures and in social activities.

28. A demand for a re-distribution of provinces on a linguistic basic has been persistently made in the south and west of India. The Congress expressed itself in favour of linguistic provinces many years ago. A decision on this question ultimately depends upon the wishes of the people concerned. While linguistic reasons have undoubtedly a certain cultural and other importance, there are other factors also such as economic, administrative and financial, which have to be taken into consideration. Where such a demand represents the agreed views of the people concerned, the necessary steps prescribed by the Constitution, including the appointment of a Boundary Commission, should be taken.

29. In regard to foreign policy, India has pursued an independent line in her own national interest and in the interest of world peace, and has sought to maintain friendly relations with all countries. This has been a positive policy and, though sometimes criticised by others, has been vindicated by subsequent developments. This policy, which has borne some fruit already, will, no doubt, yield further results and should be pursued. Certain small foreign establishments continue in India. The Congress has declared that these must revert to India, and our policy must be so aimed as to bring this about by peaceful means.

    India's policy with our neighbour countries has been very friendly, and we have welcomed the recent developments in Nepal. Unfortunately, we cannot say this in regard to Pakistan, with which our relations have been full of difficulty. We have repeatedly endeavoured to find a solution of the many issues on which we are at variance but without success. The chief among these issues is that of Kashmir. In spite of aggression of Pakistan and the continuous provocative propaganda there, we have endeavoured to find a peaceful settlement in accordance with the wishes of the people of Jammu and Kashmir State. That policy holds and we cannot permit the Kashmir State to be disposed of in any other way. We owe a duty to the people of the State as well as ourselves and we have to discharge it fully.

30. The world is distraught and moves from one crisis to another. India is affected by these world crises and cannot escape their consequences. We live in dangerous times and a false step may well prove perilous to us. India can only play an effective part in the cause of peace in this tormented world by adhering to her ideals and building up her strength as a united nation. Separatist and fissiparous tendencies weaken the nation and make it ineffective and, at the same time, come in the way of all progress. These difficult and precarious times demand a large unity of purpose and endeavour and cooperation in achieving the objectives we have placed before ourselves.

Index

O

P

Q

R